T0309165

China's Economic Development Strategies

Transformation and Innovation

Series on Chinese Economics Research*

(ISSN: 2251-1644)

Series Editor: Fan Gang *(Peking University, China)*

Published:

Vol. 21: *China's Economic Development Strategies:*
Transformation and Innovation
by Liu Rui

Vol. 20: *China's Rural Labor Migration and Its Economic Development*
by Liu Xiaoguang

Vol. 19: *Environmental Economics Research and China's Green*
Development Strategy
by Zhang Youguo
translated by Xu Hao, Xie Linlin

Vol. 18: *The Transformation of China's Economic Development:*
Perspectives of Sino–US Economists
by Yang Wandong, Zhang Jianjun, Huang Shudong and Zhu Andong

Vol. 17: *Income Distribution and China's Economic "New Normal"*
by Wan Haiyuan and Li Shi

Vol. 16: *Research on Efficiency and Fairness of Resources Allocation by China's*
Governmental Administration
by Sheng Hong and Qian Pu

Vol. 15: *Industrial Overcapacity and Duplicate Construction in China:*
Reasons and Solutions
by Li Ping, Jiang Feitao and Cao Jianhai

Vol. 14: *Reforging the Central Bank: The Top-Level Design of the*
Chinese Financial System in the New Normal
by Deng Haiqing and Chen Xi

Vol. 13: *Social Integration of Rural-Urban Migrants in China:*
Current Status, Determinants and Consequences
by Yue Zhongshan, Li Shuzhuo and Marcus W Feldman

*For the complete list of volumes in this series, please visit
www.worldscientific.com/series/scer

Series on Chinese Economics Research – Vol. 21

China's Economic Development Strategies

Transformation and Innovation

LIU Rui

Renmin University of China, China

World Scientific

NEW JERSEY • LONDON • SINGAPORE • BEIJING • SHANGHAI • HONG KONG • TAIPEI • CHENNAI • TOKYO

Published by

World Scientific Publishing Co. Pte. Ltd.

5 Toh Tuck Link, Singapore 596224

USA office: 27 Warren Street, Suite 401-402, Hackensack, NJ 07601

UK office: 57 Shelton Street, Covent Garden, London WC2H 9HE

Library of Congress Cataloging-in-Publication Data
Names: Liu, Rui (College teacher), author.
Title: China's economic development strategies : transformation and innovation /
    Rui Liu (Renmin University of China, China).
Description: New Jersey : World Scientific, [2019] | Series: Series on
    Chinese economics research ; vol. 21
Identifiers: LCCN 2019019387 | ISBN 9789811205606
Subjects: LCSH: Economic development--China. | China--Economic policy--1949– |
    China--Economic conditions--1949–
Classification: LCC HC427.95 .L5856 2019 | DDC 338.951--dc23
LC record available at https://lccn.loc.gov/2019019387

British Library Cataloguing-in-Publication Data
A catalogue record for this book is available from the British Library.

This book is published with the financial support of Chinese Fund for the Humanities and Social Sciences.

《中国经济发展战略与规划的演变和创新》
Originally published in Chinese by China Renmin University Press
Copyright © China Renmin University Press 2016
Translators: Haifeng Li, Haiyan Zhu

For any available supplementary material, please visit
https://www.worldscientific.com/worldscibooks/10.1142/11423#t=suppl

Desk Editors: Vong Ser Kei/Ong Shi Min Nicole

Typeset by Stallion Press
Email: enquiries@stallionpress.com

Contents

About the Author

LIU Rui is a professor of the School of Applied Economics, Renmin University of China (RUC). He is also the president of the China Association for Macroeconomic Management Education (CAMEME). He received a doctorate degree in economics from RUC in 1996. Funded by the ISEF Project of the Korean Higher Education Foundation, he was engaged in a postdoctoral project at Seoul National University in 2001-02, and also conducted academic research on the Ministry of Social Welfare of the Government of the Netherlands in 1995 and the Taiwan Economic Research Institute of China in 2008. His research interests include development strategy and planning, industrial structure and policy. He has published *Research on the Macro Re-adjustment and Control System with Chinese Characteristics* (2015), *Road Map to the Capital Economic Structural Adjustment in the Context of Synergy Development for Beijing-Tianjin- Hebei* (2017), *Strategy and Planning for Socio-Economic Development: Theory, Practice, Cases* (2005) and others.

Chapter 1

The Paradigms and Schools of Economic Development Strategy

The rise and fall of an economy depend certainly in a great part on a spectrum of conditions, especially on its economic system, geographic location, natural endowments, and humanistic environment in a particular era. History also provides plenty of instances where a strategy became retardant for socioeconomic development (such as the mid-Qing China's adoption of the Canton system, which ultimately led to its decay and demise) or a catalyst for economic boom (such as the Communist Party of China design of the opening up and reform policy, which are propelling China toward prosperity). The research on national development strategy is, as it was, a key issue at the critical turning point of the current economic transformation. Over the past three decades, paramount priority has always been given to the formulation and implementation of an array of development strategies, ranging from the nationwide strategies of constructing a moderately affluent society, rejuvenating China through science and education, developing the Western provinces and autonomous regions, and "going out" to those small-scale strategies involving a specific region, industry, or enterprise. These strategies, after years of practices, have proved to be productive and originative. With the enrichment of strategic practices comes the theory of national strategic development, a very important disciplinary subject that has not received due attention in national economics to the extent that few findings in this domain are recommendable. This book addresses itself to delving into the theory of socioeconomic development strategy on the basis of a preparatory clarification of various schools of development theory.

1

1.1 UNDERSTANDING NATIONAL DEVELOPMENT STRATEGY

From antiquity to now, any strategy, be it rehabilitating economy by "corvée exemption and tax relief" for an agrarian nation, or expanding territory by armed invasion for a nomadic tribe, or colonizing overseas countries by military conquest for a maritime people, can be regarded as a development strategy. With the guidelines of these strategies came into existence an agrarian empire, which could last for thousands of years, or a trans-Eurasia nomadic empire that conquered many dynasties, or a transoceanic colonial empire on which the sun would never set.

The development of a nation, however, was prevented by some geographically small yet politically ambitious countries for possession of more *Lebensraum* and natural resources before WWII and thus the militarist strategy resorting to war for overseas expansion became a basic characteristic of national development for imperialist countries. Such a strategy on the basis of the law of jungle (survival for the fittest) brought about incessant wars and havoc around the globe, and therefore should be left in the ash heap of history. Despite the Cold War between 1947 and 1991 in the post-WWII global political order, the idea that a country is not supposed to develop by means of military expansion has been deeply rooted in the international community. Many colonies freed themselves from their suzerains, leaving behind an ugly history of enslavement and ushering in a new era of political and economic independence. Under such a circumstance, it is not only impossible for emerging countries to clone the imperialistic development model of overseas expansion but also for developed countries to obtain competitive advantages as how they did before by exploiting cheap natural resources and labor force. At present, peace and development are the epochal theme, and the militaristic strategy has been replaced by the peaceful socioeconomic development strategy. Still retaining the tint of military conception, the term "strategy" is widely loaned to business and relevant cases are introduced to the analytical frameworks of economic management, far beyond the militarily strategic and tactic concepts elucidated in *The Art of War* by Sun Tzu.[1]

In a nutshell, the contemporary national development strategy generally refers to an overall planning for future socioeconomic development of a country, initially conceived by the supreme decision makers and finally reached as a consensus of "strengthening a country and enriching its people." In light of this concept, a country seeks its national development orientation, path, and mode, and thus forms a comprehensive strategic blueprint covering strategic thinking, objectives, focuses, stages, layouts, and measures.

1.2 CLASSIFICATION OF NATIONAL DEVELOPMENT STRATEGIES

Of the various strategies since ancient times, some are deliberately conceived, others hastily decided. Only those strategies combining theory and practice deserve our attention. These strategies, despite their different historical origins and practical utilities, can be properly classified and abstracted in light of two basic categories: (dis)equilibrium in economics and paradigm in philosophy. Any strategy stressing the coordination of strategic essentials and appropriate proportion of relevant economic factors falls within the paradigm of equilibrium development strategy; any strategy stressing the importance of a particular strategic essential and disregarding the appropriate proportion of relevant economic factors finds its place with the paradigm of disequilibrium development strategy. Due to the rich connotations of strategies, this classification is somewhat indistinguishable, and some strategies have the duality of equilibrium and disequilibrium. Such being the case, it is advisable to have a brief review on each of them respectively.

1.2.1 The Paradigm of Equilibrium Development Strategy

The equilibrium development strategy emphasizes the coordination of the development process, i.e., achieving the goal of national all-around development by synchronizing the industrial, regional, and socioeconomic development with population growth, natural resource exploitation, and environmental protection. The representatives in this type of strategy include the schools of comprehensive equilibrium, sustainable development, and comparative advantage, each to be clarified briefly.

1.2.1.1 *The School of Comprehensive Equilibrium*

This school originated from the conception of Chen Yun, a renowned economist who, after the founding of the People's Republic of China, quickly terminated the hyperinflation left by the Kuomintang regime.[2] It came into being in a particular historical background against which China suffered the dearth of materials and capitals and later it was enhanced and refined in the course of socialist economic construction.

The theoretical source of the school of comprehensive equilibrium is the Marxist theory of social reproduction. As regards total social demand, this theory advocates the equilibrium between aggregate social product and aggregate purchasing power, between the value of material consumption and indemnity funds, and between consumptive and accumulative funds. As regards structural equilibrium, it also clarifies the three exchange relationships in the process of realizing aggregate social product: the inter-exchange between the means of production and the means of consumption; the intra-exchanges within means of production and within means of consumption. As an important outcome of sinicizing the Marxist theory of social reproduction (Wu and Chen, 2005), this school believes that a socialist country should maintain aggregate and structural equilibriums in economic development, especially attaching importance to the equilibriums in terms of finance, credit, materials, and foreign exchanges. It strictly adheres to the principle of adapting construction scale to national comprehensive strength, executes a fiscal policy with slight surplus, and takes into account national comprehensive strength in the increase of consumption and investment so as to coordinate the proportions of all factors in economic development. Judging from the contemporary perspective, some ideas of the equilibrium strategy are out of line with the notion of "fiscal deficit being harmless" in Keynesian economics against the background of excessive supply and insufficient effective demand, but its conception of coordinating socioeconomic development is still of value today.

1.2.1.2 *The School of Sustainable Development*

Sustainable development strategy is a typical vertical equilibrium as much as comprehensive equilibrium is a typical horizontal one. This strategy was proposed in 1987 by Gro Harlem Brundtland, Chairwoman of the World Commission on Environment and Development (WCED). Sustainable development is an action agenda that meets current increasing demands at social, economic, ecological, and environmental costs consistent with rising incomes without jeopardizing the survival and development of offspring over the indefinite future. It pays special attention to the rationality of all forms of economic activity, emphasizing the coordination and equilibrium of population growth, resource exploitation, and environmental protection. In the final analysis, this strategy applies itself to establishing a harmonious relationship between human and nature.

Sustainable development strategy has a profound impact on the conception of the current Scientific Outlook on Development (SOD). China, a developing country that is now believed to have hit a bottleneck in economic growth due to its large population and limited natural resources, is putting a premium on the coordination of the relation between economic development and social resources so as to shift the goal of blindly achieving the aggregate economic value without taking into consideration the increasingly deteriorating environment to the goal of comprehensively restructuring economic development, improving population quality, economizing natural resources, and protecting environment. In this sense, the ideals of the current Chinese national economic development can be traced to the same origin as those of sustainable development strategy.

1.2.1.3 *The School of Comparative Advantage*

This strategy, originating from the classic theory of comparative advantage in international trade, is another school of equilibrium development strategy although its ideas include some elements of disequilibrium development. In China, the advocate of this school is Justin Yifu Lin, former Senior Vice President of the World Bank. According to its ideals, any country should base its development strategy on its comparative advantages; otherwise, it engenders serious negative effects. This school holds that the reason the forging-ahead strategy motivated the nation to make remarkable progress is not because of its successful application to economic construction, but because of the distortion of domestic price levels and exchange rates, although it also stimulates the development of some industrial sectors (Lin, 2009a). It also insists that a later-development country can develop by leaps and bounds if it seizes the opportunity to take advantage of its factor endowments properly (Lin, 2009b). In addition, it argues that the forging ahead strategy cannot sustain long-term development simply because it will inevitably result in squandering natural resources to increase output value, especially for a country with a small population and scarce natural resources. According to this theory, a developing country should, on the basis of readjusting the structure of resource endowments, introduce technological innovations and optimize industrial structure, thus realizing a quick, stable, and sustained growth of national economy within a shorter period of time and ultimately overtaking advanced nations on the whole.

The strategy of comparative advantage assumes that each economy has its unique economic advantages that should be utilized to maximize its own interests through division of labor and international trade. This paradigm is a typical classic economic doctrine, and the economic world conceived by classic economics is none other than an equilibrium world. The comparative advantage of each economy can only be judged in an equilibrium world, without which comparative advantages are indistinguishable. It is worth mentioning that this strategy implies that an economy utilizes static comparative advantage to seek dynamic equilibrium development and thus evolves from the initial disequilibrium advantage to equilibrium advantage. Similar as it is to disequilibrium strategy to be discussed in the next section, it still falls under the category of equilibrium development strategy if judged from its overall strategic ideals. In the implementation of the comparative development strategy, German Democratic Republic (GDR, or East Germany, 1949–1991) provided a fine example. In the 1970s and 1980s, GDR proposed the strategy of "the unity of developing economy and improving people's living standards," actively advocating technological innovation and stimulating economic growth by all-round intensivism. According to the conception of this strategy, GDR utilized its advantage in technology, replaced oil with coal, fine-processed raw materials, and semifinished products, and exploited renewable raw materials. Oriented by the trend of the market, GDR attached great importance to product strategy, especially upgrading and updating products, improving product quality, and to investment rationalization strategy, especially strengthening infrastructure construction and renovating production facilities. GDR's economy grew stably at more than 4% annually, leading other Eastern European nations by a large margin although falling behind West Germany until communism collapsed in East Germany in 1989.

1.2.2 The Paradigms of Disequilibrium Development Strategy

Disequilibrium development strategy refers to a strategy whereby a country develops its core competitive factors according to its own unique yet actual situations by concentrating limited capital, technology, and resources on the development of those chosen top-priority industries and central or core regions so as to revive other relevant industries and peripheral regions and even the whole national economy. Specifically, disequilibrium development strategy can be subdivided into central–peripheral, forging ahead, and competitive advantage development strategies.

1.2.2.1 *Central–Peripheral Development Strategy*

Albert Otto Hirschman, a renowned development economist and advocate of unbalanced growth, emphasizes that disequilibria should be encouraged to stimulate the whole national economy and mobilize resources. Because the natural endowments and development levels across a country differ drastically, it is more realistic for this country to input its limited resources in economically efficient regions so as to boost economic growth than to equally distribute them in different regions. The rapid development of a core region can stimulate other regions through trickle-down effect. Hirschman also believes that disequilibrium strategy is also applicable to the development of industries, that is, the economic activities of a particular sector can exert an effect on the economic activities of other sectors through linkage effects. Industries with strong linkage effects are likely to engender forward, backward and side linkages, which then stimulate regional economic development through ripple effect that is caused by diffusion effect and gradient transfer. Only when the leading industries in a region have a broad yet close economic and technological relationship with other industries, can they stimulate the development of other industries and even the whole regional economy through the functions of agglomeration economy and multiplier effect. This strategy also holds that the equilibrium strategy of equally distributing investment in different sectors can never solve the problem of investment decision mechanism. Whatever strategy it is, the solution to this problem is the precondition for effective allocation of limited resources and robust economic growth (Ye, 2003). Those industries with strong linkage effects will motivate other industries and further realize the goal of equilibrium development once they have been developed fully. In the early years of reform and opening up, the top-priority export-oriented economic strategy exclusively set for eastern and southern coastal provinces and regions falls under this category of strategy. In the 1980s, the coastal provinces, boasting favorable oceanic transportation and abundant human resources, quickly established chains of industry clusters in Bohai Economic Rim, Yangtze River, and Pearl River Deltas, and gained advantage of high-tech personnel under some special policy arrangements and supports, while their demonstration effect and industry-pull effect motivated the development of relevant industries in the hinterland. After more than three decades of development, great changes have taken place in the economic and industrial structures, with the proportion of capital- and technology-intensive enterprises increasing and industrial clusters around high-tech industrial zones proliferating. Meanwhile, the industries in the inland and hinterland provinces accept capital, technology, and industrial advantage from the higher advancing or advanced coastal provinces or metropolitans, establishing their own unique and complete industrial system and forming an interactive development mode in the process of synthesizing and integrating internal and external resources, production factors, and product markets.

1.2.2.2 *Forging-Ahead Development Strategy*

The representative of the forging-ahead development strategy is Komiya Ryutaro. This strategy is implemented in a market economy regulated and controlled by governmental plans. Based on the market economy of an exploitation-type country and guided by forging-ahead-type policies and economic planning at different stages, this strategy aims at achieving rapid economic growth and actualizing rational allocation of resources by governmental intervention — a role that is by no means negligible — to make up for the market failure arising from imperfect market mechanism. At the end of the WWII, Japan's economy was seriously ravaged by war, so its government decisively adopted a forging-ahead development strategy, giving priority to the development of import substitution industries such as steel and coal, ensuring the supply of important means of production and resuming production. The Japanese government set the heavy chemical industry (an industry with big demand elasticity) as the flagship to pull the rapid growth of other industries and increase economic growth rate; meanwhile, it laid much emphasis on the development of knowledge-intensive industries to enhance its international competitiveness and economic strength. The strategy also produced a unique interpretation of the so-called flying geese paradigm.

1.2.2.3 *Competitive Advantage Development Strategy*

Michael Porter, the Bishop William Lawrence University Professor at Harvard Business School, elucidates national competitive advantage with his diamond model framework, a mutually reinforcing system composed of four core factors that determine national advantage (i.e., factor endowments; related and supporting industries; demand conditions; and firm strategy, structure, and rivalry) and two other invariables (i.e., government and opportunity). In this model, the market serves as the automatic equalizer of economic activities, and the government acts as a catalyst and challenger, encouraging, or even pushing companies to foster core competencies which, if successfully nurtured, will automatically help realize the overall equilibrium (Porter, 1990; Chen and Zhu, 2002). According to the theoretical interpretation by Zhang Jinchang (2001), the important source of national competitive advantage is the industry chain cluster — formed by relevant and supporting industries that are geographically adjacent, mutually supportive in technology and human resources and internationally competitive. Geographically relative concentration helps strengthen rivalry, shorten communicative channels, innovate ideas, and nurture professional and technical talents, thus eventually forming a self-reinforcing mechanism within the industry chain cluster. This international competitive advantage, formed by local complete upstream and downstream enterprises, is unlikely to be surpassed. The U.S. economic boom under the Clinton administration is a fine example. Shortly after Clinton took office, he and Vice President Gore issued a programmatic document titled "Technology for America's Economic Growth: A New Direction to Build Economic Strength," declaring that investment in technology is investing in America's future, and establishing the economic development strategy of building national competitive advantage by transforming Silicon Valley into a high-tech industry cluster. On the basis of the conception of this strategy, the Clinton administration set up National Science and Technology Council (NSTC), a Cabinet-level decision-making body chaired by the President and the Director of the Office of Science and Technology Policy, formally setting the advanced technology plan and the cooperation plan in the manufacturing sector as the national plan. The Cabinet formulated the Technology Reinvestment Project (TRP), designed to transfer military-oriented enterprises to civilian production and develop military–civil dual-purpose technology. During Clinton's tenure, universally regarded as a golden period of economic prosperity over the past three decades, this strategy proved to be effective and fruitful. With the formation of the system of national science and technology policy[4] and industry chains, America's gross domestic product (GDP) rose from $6.1 trillion in 1992 to $9.1 trillion in 1999, or from 23% to 28% of the global total and its economic aggregate nearly doubled, and the real economic growth rate (adjusted for inflation) was 4% annually. More importantly, the Clinton Cabinet reversed fiscal deficit from the record high $290 billion in 1992 to zero in 1997 and its fiscal surplus reached as an unprecedented high of $211 billion by 1999. More than 22 million new jobs were created in the Clinton era and the unemployment rate hit a record low.

1.3 OPTIONS OF STRATEGIC PARADIGMS IN DIFFERENT DEVELOPMENT STAGES

Different schools of strategies have their own characteristics and realistic implications. Whatever strategic paradigm is chosen, adequate consideration should be given to the national situations. Our surveys reveal that a country, if disregarding the ever-changing situations, doggedly pursuing a single development strategy is much less likely to make remarkable achievements than a country readjusting its strategy at different stages of development.

1.3.1 Initial Stage: Disequilibria Dominance

It is unrealistic for a country that is still at the initial stage of economic development to adopt equilibrium strategy and this country finds it hard to synchronize all industrial sectors due to its inefficient resource utilization, scientific and technological restraints, deficiency in capital investment, and a backward industrial base, to name just a few. In this sense, it is recommendable for such a country to concentrate on resources for the development of regions and industries that possess comparative advantages and pull the development of primary and intermediate industries and products by establishing core development zones and fostering end-use industries. Nevertheless, the adoption of disequilibrium strategy is obviously risky.

First, its success depends on the correct choice of top-priority core industries and regions. Without experience and ready economic development strategy suitable to its own conditions, a country at the initial stage is inclined to blindly follow the economic construction model adopted by advanced nations. If this country makes a blunder, particularly mistaking a region poor in natural endowments for the core region or setting an industry with weak linkages and potentials as the key industry, it will inevitably squander a lot of resources and funds and even bring about disastrous consequences. This is especially true for a country eager to develop its economy with its limited resources.

Second, under the influence of "polarization" and "trickle-down" effects, the ultimate goal of developing a core region and a key industry, that is, pulling the development of peripheral regions and related industries, does not necessarily ensure a step-by-step and mutually interactive development pattern but inadvertently dampens and discontinues interregional and interindustrial development, widens gap between the poor and rich, and intensifies social contradictions. Once the disequilibrium strategy is put into practice, the major problems arise as to how to pull the development of peripheral regions and how to use the linkage effect of top-priority industries to expedite competitive intermediate and primary industries.

In addition, cross-regional and cross-industrial imbalances will gradually unfold after the disequilibrium strategy helps a country effectuate its transition to the stage of economic takeoff. A country adopting a development model whereby low-end products are exchanged for high-tech and high value-added products finds no way to build its own competitive core industries and industry clusters and even loses its established core competency, thus reducing itself to an economic vassal to advanced nations. The former Soviet Union's development road provides a typical example in this regard. Its development strategy can be roughly divided into two periods: from the Lenin–Stalin era to the late 1960s and from 1970s to the collapse of communist regime. Before the October Revolution in 1917 in the first stage, Lenin had proposed the ideal of overtaking western European countries and it was carried through in the Stalin era. The core thought of this strategy was to bridge the gap between the Soviet Union and Western capitalist countries by speeding up technological progress to promote economic growth and forming a solid industrial foundation within a short period of time. After years of economic construction, it rose to the second largest industrial power, and many of its important industrial goods outnumbered those of the United States. In the second period, it attempted to reverse the unbalanced industrial structure and readjust economic development strategy and set the improvement of people's living standards as its objective. However, owing to its overdependence on heavy chemical industry, its economic transformation was not successful, far away from its ambitious goal of realizing a powerful economy.

1.3.2 Takeoff Stage: Transition from Disequilibrium to Equilibrium

Due to its preliminary completion of infrastructure construction and relatively favorable internal investment environment by the end of the initial stage, a country in the early takeoff stage can certainly continue to reinforce its competitive industries as well as remedies economic maladies through equilibrium development strategy. However, the disadvantages resulting from weak industrial base, low technological level, and impotent core competence will gradually emerge and it may even lose its cumulative advantages.

Furthermore, a developing country still in the early takeoff stage has many difficulties in turning its growth momentum into actual improvement due to its inability to create sufficient jobs for abundant or rather excessive workforce and bring potential sectoral advantages into full play.

Under such a circumstance, this country, by virtue of its strength in the comparative advantages it has accumulated in the initial stage of implementing disequilibrium strategy, can not only encourage early-development industries to pull later development industries and early-development regions to pull peripheral regions so as to create a balanced and reasonable development mode but also avoid the problems of the large-scale capital input and technology required of equilibrium development strategy. The success of the forging ahead strategy can be illustrated with the following two examples: the economic miracles that Japan and the Four Asian Dragons created in the early 1950s and 1960s and the strategic ideal that China proposed to prioritize the development of the coastal areas in the early years of reform and opening up. The disequilibrium strategic development in the takeoff stage is not static. The key to its success lies in timely and accurate readjustment according to specific conditions, the Japanese-type forging ahead strategy being most prominent in this regard. Prior to the 1970s, the Japanese government adopted an industrial rationalization policy designed to update equipment and innovate technology to stimulate the development of basic industries, and made a great success through special taxation measures, fiscal investment and loan, interest subsidy on maritime transportation, and foreign exchange quota. It surpassed major European economies in many industrial sectors such as steel, shipbuilding, machinery, and gradually became the second largest economy of the world. Nevertheless, Japan's forging ahead strategy was dynamic rather than static. Under the dual influence of the decrease of technology spill-over effect and diminishing marginal efficiency of capital in Western advanced nations, Japan adopted the competitive advantage strategy and proposed the guideline of "national strategy of technology," gradually shifting from resource-intensive industries to knowledge- and technology-intensive industries. It successfully developed advanced technology with proprietary intellectual property rights and fostered core competence, and thus got rid of its dependence on European countries and the United States and eventually commanded the technological vantage point.

South Korea followed the same process of shifting from disequilibrium to equilibrium strategy, undergoing the initial stage in the 1960s and the takeoff stage in the 1990s. Its high-speed economic growth brought about negative outcomes: the excessive concentration in the Capital Seoul Economic Circle and serious unbalanced layout of land resources. In view of the problems aforementioned, South Korean government took the initiative of adopting regional equilibrium strategy and actively realized strategic transformation. The three cores of South Korea's regional equilibrium strategy included the delegation of national central management function, the decentralization of executive and fiscal authority, and labor division of rational peripheral distribution of strategic industries. More than anything, South Korea's national equilibrium strategy was consistently executed in its frequent reshuffles of government cabinet.

Similarly, Singapore also went through the shift from disequilibrium development to equilibrium development. Confronting a series of problems such as a weak industrial base, and shortage of funds, technology and management personnel, Singapore focused on the attraction of FDI (foreign direct investment), equipment, production technology, and managerial skills to promote its industrial development. Its FDI once accounted for three-quarters of the total investment and was mainly concentrated in the major industrial sectors such as oil refining, electronic and electric products (EEPs), metal machinery, and shipbuilding. Meanwhile, Singapore readjusted its development strategy in a timely manner according to specific national conditions by introducing social development projects such as public housing, urban reconstruction, education and family planning, and finally succeeded in realizing a moderately balanced socioeconomic development.

In contrast, the former Soviet Union, though adopting the same forging ahead strategy oriented by heavy chemical industry as South Korea and Singapore, unknowingly thrust its national economy in the opposite direction toward the brink of bankruptcy as a result of its failure to readjust its industrial structure for one thing and of its increasing inclination toward heavy industry and military industry in the Soviet–U.S. arms and space races for another.

In the takeoff stage, it is necessary yet difficult to complete the transformation of development strategies in that few countries would willingly give up on a strategy that has proved to be successful in practice and instead adopt one that is orally alleged, without any solid evidence, to be necessary. No strategy is a silver bullet to cure social–economic ailments, and therefore it is difficult to alter the initial strategy if no other could function as a substitute.

1.3.3 Advanced Stage: Achieving Sustainability on the Basis of Equilibrium

Judging from the realistic perspective of unbalanced economic development worldwide, advanced nations are inevitably predominant in the manufacturing of some important products. It seems to be a logical choice for these early-development countries to adopt Porter's competitive advantage strategy so as to build national competitive advantages and thus gain advantages in the global industrial chain and obtain more profits in the global distribution of profits. But domestically, these advanced nations implement equilibrium development strategy. For instance, Japan implemented socioeconomic harmonious development strategy domestically as early as in the 1980s but failed to achieve a marked result. After it suffered stagnation in the 1990s, Japan resumed its economic growth as a result of brand-new industries. According to the latest edition of New Economic Growth Strategy of Japan compiled by the Ministry of Economy, Trade and Industry, Japan proposed the development strategy of juxtaposing and synchronizing the new economic growth strategy, the new energy strategy, and the global economic strategy, especially featuring international cooperation in new energy, energy emergency strategy, and development of high-sophisticated technology and brand building. South Korea, which also succeeded in implementing a disequilibrium development strategy, expressly announced that it shifted from disequilibrium stage to equilibrium stage in the era of economic globalization.

At present, the advanced economies have arrived at a consensus regarding equilibrium development. As a collective or generic expression of this equilibrium strategy, sustainable development strategy has become the top priority of developed countries. Interestingly, the desirable effect of this equilibrium strategy needs the cooperation of developing nations, which, however, find that only disequilibrium strategy is suitable to them because they are still in the inchoate or developing stage. Thus, an intricate situation comes into being due to the adoption of a different paradigm of strategy at a different developmental stage. At present, developed countries attempt to peddle their ideals of equilibrium strategy to developing nations and cajole them into altering the development strategy that is currently suitable to them. In this case, extra cost is necessary for win–win situation.

1.4 THE MIX OF CHINA'S DEVELOPMENT STRATEGY PARADIGMS

During the period from the founding of New China in 1949 to the early 20th century, China had constantly implemented the forging ahead strategy of the disequilibrium paradigm. On the whole, this strategy was successful. Nevertheless, the weak points of the disequilibrium strategy began to unfold after the achievement of rapid economic growth. A spectrum of problems increasingly worsened, such as environmental pollution, shortage of energy and resources, lack of core competencies for many enterprises, food safety, and widening gap between the rich and poor, and so on. Export-oriented development and the introduction of transferable technology under the guidance of disequilibrium strategy helped China establish its status as the "workshop of the world," but China made much less remarkable progress in fostering core competencies and technological innovation. As a result of this, since 2003, the widespread discussion on the transformation of development strategy paradigm triggered by SOD has become a hot issue of the theory of development strategy and the ideas of the equilibrium development strategy have once again attracted the attention of the intellectuals.

In the sense that China is still in the takeoff stage instead of the advanced stage, disequilibrium is a suitable option. China, an economy second only to the United States in terms of economic aggregate, cannot be counted as an advanced country if compared with geographically big advanced economies such as the United States, Canada and Australia or with geographically small countries such as western European countries like the United Kingdom, France, and Germany, to name just a few. Paradoxically, abandonment of disequilibrium development strategy too early is obviously unfavorable to China, but it indeed simultaneously induces an assortment of drawbacks which, under the pressure of the advantages of the equilibrium development paradigm, mismatch the world development pattern on the one hand and nibble away at the benefits from the adoption of the disequilibrium development strategy. Therefore, it is necessary to reassess the choice of a single paradigm.

A feasible and pragmatic development strategy should be a mixed type of the equilibrium and disequilibrium paradigms, the former designed to balance the tension between different factors, while the latter is designed to foster core competence that can rival with international advanced level. This implies that China will not simply abandon one and choose the other; instead, it should choose a set of development strategy paradigms to optimize its development pattern.

First comes with the adoption of equilibrium strategy for the development of domestic regions. After more than 30 years of development, the four regional economic plates of eastern coastal areas, western hinterland, northeastern old industrial base, and Central China have developed their own unique characteristics. Contrarily, the widening gap between regions has aggravated the imbalance of the national economy, causing serious negative consequences. Hence, it is unfit to continue the central–peripheral development strategy. Currently, it is extremely urgent to utilize equilibrium strategy to navigate the four economic plates to coordinate development in order that their own economic advantages can be brought into full play.

Second follows the adoption of disequilibrium strategy for the development of domestic industries. The irrational industrial structure caused by realistic conditions cannot be altered within a short period of time. In this case, there are realistic implications to continue the development of many strategic industries by means of disequilibrium strategy. It is still necessary to attach great importance to high-tech industries capable of earning foreign exchanges through export and emerging potential industries and cultivate the capability of autonomous innovation so as to be preemptive in high-tech field and international division of industry chains. Developing the seven strategic emerging industries (SEIs) and the "going out" strategy of large-sized state-run enterprises are in line with the strategic intention. As a matter of fact, the equilibrium conception of developing the sector of services conceived during the 11th Five-Year Plan (2006–2010) can be effectuated after the realization of industrialization. As far as industrial development is concerned, the implementation of competitive advantage strategy will not have serious negative impact on the imbalance of domestic industrial structure; on the contrary, it strengthens China's international competitiveness.

Third, export-oriented economic development is still a prudent choice. It is inadvisable to give up export-oriented strategy despite its drawbacks exposed by the past financial crises. It is still recommended for China to draw on the advantage of low-cost factor resources to attract advanced technology and capital from advanced economies, which in turn find it necessary to draw on this advantage. In order to address the drawbacks caused by solely relying on pulling the external demand, it is necessary to jumpstart domestic demand, though much less prospective.

Fourth, China should rationally and properly adopt the concept of equilibrium development. Many new ideals of development strategy in the 21st century are helpful in changing views about disequilibrium development. It is worth noting that some vanguard or pioneering ideas may also bring about negative consequences. For instance, the concept of "economic growth being of paramount importance" is certainly not absolutely right, but how can China, a developing country with per capita GDP of only several thousand dollars, realize its modernization by the mid-21st century if it fails to pursue the increase of economic aggregate? Paying no heed to social development ideals is certainly not right, but can social development be sustainable or stable if the economic foundation for development is weak? The concept of "human beings as the foundation of all values" is certainly right, but some advanced economies fell into a welfare trap between the 1960s and the 1980s because of their extravagant construction of livelihood projects.

Chen Yun, though arguing for comprehensive equilibrium development, warned that good economic measures should not go to extremes and suggested countermeasures should be adopted to ensure balance and coordination in the short run. At present, the starting point of equilibrium should be concentrated on shortcomings that severely constrain economic growth.

Fifth and finally, macroeconomic regulation should function as a short-term equalizer. Macroeconomic regulation is the most important experience that China gained in the process of economic transformation. It is not powerful enough as it is to readjust equilibrium in the long-term, yet it proves to be significantly efficient in tackling short-term imbalance. Adopting equilibrium development strategy requires macroeconomic regulation to discover and solve the onset resulting from economic imbalance and equalize the shortcomings resulting from local disequilibrium strategy.

REFERENCES

Chen, Weiping, and Zhu Shubin. "New Developments of Competitiveness Theory: Drawbacks of Porter's Diamond Model and Improvements." *International Economics and Trade Research*, 2002, 18 (3): 2–4. 陈卫平,朱述斌. 国外竞争力理论的新发展 — 迈克尔·波特 "钻石模型" 的缺陷与改进. 国际经贸探索, 2002 (3).

Chen, Yun. *Selected Works of Chen Yun* (Vol. 3). Beijing: People's Publishing House, 1995.

Lin, Justin Yifu. *Comparative Advantage and Development Strategy*. Beijing: Beijing University Press, 2009a. 林毅夫. 比较优势与发展战略. 北京: 北京大学出版社, 2009a.

Lin, Justin Yifu. *Development Strategy and Economic Development*. Beijing: Beijing University Press, 2009b. 林毅夫. 发展战略与经济发展. 北京: 北京大学出版社, 2009b.

Lu, Ming. "Market Economy with Chinese Characteristics: History, Reality and Future." In Youmei Li, Zhongzhen Xu, and Ming Lu (eds.), *Market, Society and Government: A Theoretical Interpretation of the PRC's Development Between 1949 and 2009*. Beijing: Encyclopedia of China Publishing House, 2009. 陆铭, "中国特

色的市场经济：历史、现实与未来". 李友梅, 徐中振, 陆铭编. 市场, 社会, 政府: 共和国 60 年发展理论解读. 北京: 中国大百科全书出版社, 2009.

Porter, Michael. E. *The Competitive Advantage of Nations*. New York: Free Press, 1990.

Wu, Yifeng. "Chen Yun's Comprehensive Equilibrium Theory and its Practical Values." *Studies on Marxism*, 2005 (3): 45–58. 吴易凤, "陈云的综合平衡理论及其现实意义", 《马克思主义研究》, 2005 (3): 45–58.

Ye, Jingyi. *Development Economics*. Beijing: Beijing University Press, 2003. 叶静怡, 发展经济学. 北京: 北京大学出版社, 2003.

Zhang, Jinchang. "A Theoretical Analysis of Porter's Theory of National Competitive Advantage." *China Industrial Economics*, 2001 (9): 53–58. 张金昌. "波特的国家竞争优势理论剖析". 中国工业经济, 2001 (9): 53–58.

NOTES

1. Jorge Alberto Souza De Vasconcellos e Sa cited some examples from military battles to illustrate offensive and defensive strategies that can be utilized to tackle business competitors in his book *Strategy Moves: 14 Complete Attack and Defense Strategies for Competitive Advantage*, published by Financial Times Press in 2005.

2. Translator's note: In the Third Civil War (1946–1949), the credit of the Kuomintang regime collapsed due to the devaluation of the *fabi* (legal tender) by hundreds of millions of times, with the largest face value of a paper note being 6 billion yuan, which could only buy 88 grains of rice. In a 1946 report to George Marshall, then mediator between Mao Zedong and Chiang Kai-shek, Ambassador Leighton Stuart complained of the stunning inflation in the Kuomintang-controlled area.

3. Translator's note: For instance, in 1958 the Central Committee of the CPC set the goal of catching up with Great Britain and then surpassing the United States within 15 and 50 years respectively, hoping to rapidly transforming China from an agrarian economy into a socialist society through rapid industrialization and collectivization. It is widely believed that this forging ahead strategy was blamed for the serious setbacks in the following years, but Lu Ming (2009) argued that this strategy was conducive to the establishment of a complete and independent industrial system that later benefited the opening-up and reform in the late 1970s and early 1980s.

4. The system of national science and technology policy roughly includes the following five aspects: creating a business environment favorable to private firms' innovation and competition; pushing forward the development, application, and diffusion of technology; supporting and promoting the construction of infrastructure relevant to the development of business; propelling the integration of military and civilian industrial bases; fostering first-rate workforce.

Chapter 2

Development Outlook and Development Strategy from A Global Perspective

2.1 DEVELOPMENT THEORY VERSUS CONVENTIONAL DEVELOPMENT STRATEGY

The post-World War II (WWII) movement of national independence swept across the world, with many Asian, African, and Latin American countries emancipating themselves from the fetters of colonialism. To consolidate their political independence, these new independent countries, with three-quarters of the world population and two-thirds of world land area, urged the international community to be concerned about their development and applied themselves to the pursuit of a development road suitable to their own economy. Meanwhile, Western advanced nations, under the influence of Keynesianism, maintained the momentum of economic growth by moderating governmental intervention and reduced, to some extent, the blindness of the free market. Thus, the world seemed to be in the grip of an "economic growth fever."

In this context, exploring the developing road, especially the research on the economic growth of some developing nations, has become a hot issue for economists. Prior to the 1940s, however, few economists used the phrase "economic development," which indicated that conventional economics made no special research in how underdeveloped nations gear up themselves. Advanced nations, for the sake of their own interest, placed a premium on their relationship with developing nations, hoping to yoke these developing nations into their development systems. Thus, development economics, a branch of economics that concerns itself with economic aspects of the development process of low-income countries, came into being as an independent disciplinary subject. In the 1950s and 1960s, a constellation of influential development economists proposed an assortment of development theories, bringing about a profound impact on the development of all countries.

In this period, the issue of the definition of "development" did not spark further discussion to the economists. Development was customarily equated with economic growth. For instance, Arndt (1997) asserted that the issue of economic development was, in essence, to raise the national income level and make everyone consume more by means of increasing the per capita output. He added that economic growth could be defined as persistent and constant improvement of material welfare, reflecting the increased flow of products and services.

It is obvious that the development economists of those times failed to distinguish economic growth from development. They simply boiled development down to the increment of gross national product (GNP) and focused only on economic growth, asserting that every other problem would be easily addressed so long as the cake of economic aggregate was indefinitely bigger. This conventional development concept prevailed in all countries and considered maximizing material wealth as the central goal. In the long course of history, it occupied a predominant position and had a significant impact on human socioeconomic activities.

2.1.1 The Schools of the Theory of Development and Their Major Views

Due to the lack of a systematic theory of development on the part of the developing nations, Western economists proposed the theory of development on the basis of established economic theories to interpret the backwardness of the developing nations and designed economic development strategies. Some of them doubted whether classic Western economic theory would be suitable for the developing nations. They argued that it could not be simply postulated that the price system has existed in developing nations. They also claimed that the full flow of factors in neoclassical economics and the assumption of market cleaning were not suitable for developing nations, and therefore it was necessary to introduce structuralism to analyze the problems of developing nations. This idea occupied a mainstream position. The influential schools included W. A. Lewis's dual-sector model, Paul Rosenstein-Rodan's theory of the big push and balanced growth theory, R. Nurkse's vicious circle of poverty, Rostovian takeoff model, and R. Prebisch's Latin American structuralism.

Structuralists hold the view that the market system in developing nations is not perfect, the price system is seriously distorted, socioeconomic structure lacks elasticity, and the economic activities of an individual person as a producer and a consumer are out of line with the logic of an "Economic Man." The particularity of the structure renders it impossible for the price system and market regulation to effectuate the equilibrium function. Disequilibria exist universally among developing nations, such as dual economy, excess of labor, disguised unemployment, structural inflation, all of which determine that developing economy is not only different from developed economy but also from the economy of the Western nations in the 18th and 19th centuries when their economy was on the development stage. It is necessary to explore the developing road of developing nations from the perspective of structural adjustment and reform.

The early development theorists noticed the different development backgrounds of developing and developed countries, but they still inherited the model of the developed nations in the analysis of choosing development objectives. That is, they still believed that economic growth was the sole yardstick of the level of development. Lewis (1955) expressed very clearly that economists' interest was in the analysis of growth rather than the analysis of distribution, that is, the analysis of the increment of per capita output.

In external economic relations, early development theory was generally not in favor of comparative cost theory and free trade policy. In order to pursue economic independence, developing nations must establish its national industrial system. Paradoxically, the comparative cost theory suggests that it is not recommendable for developing nations to develop finished goods, which do not have any comparative advantage. If a free trade policy is adopted, the weak national industry of developing nations cannot get a footing in the fierce international competition. Hence, the early development theory was in favor of protectionism. For instance, Lewis deduced from the unlimited supplies of labor that industrial sectors should be protected because marginal productivity would approximate to zero, and even a negative value due to unlimited supplies of labor in the countryside and the wages unavoidably high above the social opportunity cost were paid by modern industrial sectors. Prebisch (1950) argues, from the starting point of the central–peripheral system, that moderate and selective protectionism is favorable for peripheral (developing) nations to get rid of the control of the central (developed) nations in that the low-income elasticity of demand for primary products of peripheral nations and the high-income elasticity of demand for manufactured products of central nations can avoid allocating excessive production resources to primary products by means of import substitution, and thus offset the deterioration of the terms of trade of primary product–based economies.

The major viewpoints of the early development theory dominated by structuralism are:

(1) *Emphasizing the importance of structural changes (industrialization) on economic growth*

By combining the doctrines advocated by Adam Smith, David Ricardo, and Joseph Alois Schumpeter with the experience of developed countries to achieve industrialization, Western economists propose that the objective of the developing nations is to eliminate peasant economy and realize industrialization. Lewis's dual-sector model and Hollis B. Chenery's analysis of patterns of development, and multi-sectoral analysis are two representative examples in this field. They argue that industrialization and urbanization not only create considerable material wealth but also attract surplus labor in the countryside (a distinguishable characteristic of the developing country), and thus transform a traditional agriculture-based economy to a manufacturing-based economy and ultimately relieve developing nations out of poverty.

(2) *Highlighting the promotional function of capital accumulation on developing nations*

Economists represented by Harold and Rostow used a linear model to interpret the reason for the backwardness of developing nations. This model argues that the primary problem of developing nations is deficiency in capital and that sufficient capital can break the vicious circle of poverty. In the 1940s, the English economist R. Harrod and American economist Evsey David Domar proposed the first modern economic growth model (Harrod–Domar model) $G = S/V$, in which G stands for growth rate in real terms, S for average propensity to save, and V for acceleration coefficient, that is, the ratio of investment to output. The model assumes that V is invariable and that economic growth rate is determined by the only one variable savings ratio or rate of capital accumulation. Of the five stages in *The Stages of Economic Growth*, a frequently cited monograph by the American Economist Rostow, the takeoff stage is the preparatory and initial stage for developing nations to enter into the club of advanced nations. Three preconditions ensure the economic takeoff: rate of capital accumulation of 10% or above, one or more than one leading sector for economic takeoff, and a sociopolitical institution that guarantees takeoff, with the first one being of paramount importance.

(3) *Believing that planning is the most important channel to promote industrialization and capital accumulation*
Influenced by Keynesianism and demonstration effect of Soviet experiences, alongside with the Marshal Plan, officially known as the European Recovery Program (ERP), the development strategy underscored the functions of planning. Meanwhile, industrialization and capital accumulation call for intensifying government intervention, not merely depending on the spontaneous actions of private sectors. Rosenstein–Rodan's theory of the big push and Lewis's dual-sector model include, to some extent, planning and government intervention. Many developing nations formulated plans as a complement to "market failure," intending to set the development plan centering on considerable public investment and conscious industrialization as a universal policy tool. In 1951, a UN panel of experts suggested in a report that underdeveloped countries should establish a central planning office whose duty was to make economic surveys, formulate development plans with a focus on capital demand and domestic and foreign capital supply, and propose advice for planning and make regular reports (Rostow, 1959).

2.1.2 Conventional Development Strategy and Practice

The early development theory was based on the lack of a perfect market system in the developed countries, and therefore it emphasized the governmental role in resource allocation. Under the influence of Keynesianism, the developed countries universally attached importance to government intervention in the market. Under such circumstance, the development theory should be closely integrated with the development strategy, helping decision makers in developing nations develop national strategy, and make prudent choices on those important issues. In the literature on development economics in the 1950s and 1960s, there are numerous cases where development theory and development strategy are combined. Lewis combined an analysis of the historical experience of developed nations with the central ideas of the classical economists to produce a broad picture of the development process. Hirschman (1958) used the term "the strategy of economic development" for the first time and underwent research on the problems of economic development of developing nations.

Accompanying early development theory is the conventional development strategy prevailing in developing nations in the 1950s and 1960s. They share the following common characteristics: (1) as regards the strategic guiding ideals and objectives, striving for overtaking advanced economies and setting the growth rate of GNP as the sole measure of economic growth; (2) as regards the choice of strategic priorities, pushing economic growth by industrialization and prioritizing heavy industries; (3) as regards the strategic solutions, pushing capital accumulation, protecting national industry, and creating basic preparations for industrialization by means of government development plan and protectionism.

The conventional development strategy was fully demonstrated in the "First UN Development Decade (1960–1970)" for developing nations. This development strategy set an increase of GNP by 5% per annum as the goal of economic development and recommended large-scale industrial construction and capital accumulation to developing nations as an indispensable means to achieve economic growth. During this period, developing nations tried every conceivable means and adopted the following conventional development strategies.

(1) *Export strategy for primary products*
This strategy is usually implemented in some developing nations abundantly in a particular natural resource and with single economic structures, such as Kuwait, Iraq, Burundi, Ethiopia, and Jamaica, and so on. With the strength of abundant natural resources, these countries concentrate on the production of primary products for export, foreign exchange, and capital accumulation for the development of national economy. As a result, these countries heavily depend on their single product economy and have never altered it.

(2) *Import substitution industrialization (ISI)*
Essentially, this strategy aims at realizing industrialization by mass-producing industrial products that could replace imports to meet the demands of the domestic market. Some Latin American nations that have won independence in the 19th century such as Argentina, Chile, and Uruguay implemented ISI in the early 1930s. Raúl Prebisch, an Argentine economist known for his contributions to structuralist economics, proposed in his influential study *The Economic Development of Latin America and Its Principal Problems* suggestions for Latin American countries and laid a good theoretical foundation for this strategy. In the 1950s, ISI was promoted to some East Asian countries such as South Korea and Philippine. This strategy was also introduced to African countries such as Ghana, Zambia, Kenya, and Nigeria in the 20th century.

(3) *Strategy prioritizing heavy industry*
This is a strategy that leverages the preferential policy toward the industrial sectors of production means to promote industrialization and overtake developed nations. The conception of this strategy, otherwise known as Feldman–Stalin model, was reflected as early as 1928 in the development plan formulated by Grigorii A. Feldman for the Soviet Planning Committee and in the principle of "prioritizing the development of the production sectors of production means." Socialist nations represented by the Soviet Union and some other nations such as India, Brazil, Egypt, and Mexico adopted this strategy before the 1970s.

(4) *Strategy prioritizing light industry*

This strategy, focusing on the development of light industry responsible for the production of consumer goods, allows full play to the advantages of labor resources and accumulates funds for industrialization. Singapore and South Korea, while implementing the strategy of ISI, prioritize the development of labor-intensive light industry such as textiles, garments, and foodstuffs, and gradually accelerate the development of heavy industry, which establishes a relatively complete national economic system.

The implementation of the conventional development strategy centered on economic growth accelerated economic growth in some developing nations in the 1950s and 1960s, with an average annual growth rate of 4.8% from 1950 to 1960 exceeding the average annual growth rate of the developed nations in the same takeoff stage and that of the developed countries in the same period. However, it also brought about some unexpected ramifications.

First, one-sided emphasis on industrialization caused a serious imbalance in economic structure. The negligence of agricultural production led to the shortage of foodstuff. For example, from 1948 to 1960, the average annual growth rate of per capita grain production in developing nations was only 0.6%, which was far below the population growth rate in the same period. Stagnant agriculture triggered a series of problems such as the increase of rural poor people, the urban–rural cleavage, deteriorating uneven distribution of income. Furthermore, the dual structure was not eliminated, but instead resulted in secondary differentiation. As the rural surplus labor force was beyond the absorption capacity of the industrial sectors, an excess of labor force flowed into cities or remained in the rural areas, thus leading to a quaternary structure or double dual structure.

Second, economic growth formed a striking contrast with the deterioration of social problems. Economic growth failed to give everyone equal rights to share its fruits, but instead led to a widening class gap and social dichotomy. Social wealth was in the grip of a small number of people, and the life of most urban and rural residents did not improve but deteriorated. Concomitant with economic growth came a spectrum of social problems such as population explosion, worsening unemployment, environmental pollution, ecological imbalance, and so on, bringing heavy burden and pressure on economic growth.

Third, a variety of drawbacks were exposed under the centralized planning management system, with enterprises invigorated and inefficient and the allocation of resources difficult to be optimized. After the Second World War, many countries failed to realize their expected or even the most conservative objective of economic growth, except for some sporadic years. What worried some social observers was that the situation has not improved but deteriorated.

Fourth, ISI had adverse consequences. In the primary stage of ISI, the substitutes for imports were usually low-added value, nondurable consumer goods that could easily occupy the domestic market. However, in the advanced stage of ISI, the substitutes for imports were durable goods and capital goods whose production required imported technology, equipment, and funds; this would undoubtedly exert great pressure on the feeble international payment. In addition, protectionism is initially designed for expanding the range of import substitution-distorted price signal, resulting in low-efficient allocation. These problems have posed a formidable challenge to industrialization. It is no wonder that the First UN Decade for developing nations was humorously dubbed as the "Ten Year Frustration." The conventional development strategy engendered a situation where developing nations got stuck in an impasse of economic growth without development.

2.2 THE TRANSFORMATION OF DEVELOPMENT THEORY AND ALTERNATIVE DEVELOPMENT STRATEGY

2.2.1 Evolution of the Development Concept: Socioeconomic-Coordinated Development

In the late 1960s, as a result of the problems exposed in the implementation of the development strategy, people were conscious of the different implications of "growth" and "development" when they have a retrospection on growth-centered development concept. While growth is a prerequisite for development, it is not the case that growth can solve all development problems. Thus, a new development concept — socioeconomic development concept (otherwise known as alternative development strategy) — began to replace the growth-centered development concept. This development concept lays much emphasis on the "socialization of development goals," explores the profound implications of development from the perspective of coordinating socioeconomic development, and enriches the ideals of development. The alternative development strategy reflects the evolution of the development concept in the following aspects.

First, it distinguishes economic growth from economic development. Kindleberger (1958), an American economic historian, who discovered the linkages and differences between economic growth and development, argued that economic growth denoted more output, while economic development implied both more output and the improvement of technological and institutional arrangements on which the manufacturing and distribution of products depends. Simon Smith Kuznets, a Nobel Prize Laureate for his contribution to development economics and other relevant disciplinary subjects such as statistics and demography, interpreted the term economic growth in a broad sense: Economic growth of a nation can be defined as a long-term growth of the ability to provide its countrymen with increasingly diverse economic goods. Now the economic community has arrived at a consensus that economic growth is by no means equated with economic development.

Second, the concept of alternative development strategy sets human basic needs as the objective of development, insisting that the government should improve income distribution in the process of stimulating economic growth, bettering social public welfare, reducing or abolishing poverty, and mobilizing the role of the overwhelming number of people in the process of development.

Finally, the concept of the alternative development strategy puts a premium on the investment and development of human capital, shifting its focus solely on the function of physical capital. In his speech delivered at the Nobel Prize Award Ceremony, Theodore W. Schultz (1980) pointed out that the decisive factors of production that enhance the welfare of the poor are not space, energy, and arable land, but the quality of population. Economic development requires a qualitative measurement and that is what the economic growth depending only on widening process lacks. The improvement of labor (i.e., the formation of human capital) will engender a qualitative change and thus achieve real development.

2.2.2 Revival of Neoclassical Development Theory

The realistic predicament of development pushes forward the evolution of human outlook on development, while the intellectuals reflect on the early development theory dominated by structuralism. Since the mid-1960s, the momentum of developing nations has clearly diverged. Those countries continuing to strictly follow the "recipe" prescribed in the 1950s, that is, those adopting ISI, especially some Latin American nations, confronted a series of problems, such as international payments balance gushing in red, worsening domestic inflation, the limitation of the import substitution of durable goods and capital goods by foreign exchange bottleneck and domestic manufacturing, underwent economic recession in succession. On the contrary, those countries and regions shifting to export-oriented strategies, such as the Four Asian Dragons, made great economic achievements. This divergence ultimately resulted in a considerable shift from structuralism to neoclassicism in the development theory. Myint, a Burma-born development economist, used the phrase "revival of neoclassicism" when demonstrating the historical transition of development theory. The neoclassical development theory is represented by D. K. Lal, H. Myint, G. Haberler, and so on.

The neoclassical development theory first corrects the pro-industry and anti-agriculture idea, an idea of "prioritizing industry over agriculture." Schultz, a critic of Lewis's "economic development with unlimited supplies of labor," argued that the basic assumption in the Lewis model (the dual-sector model) that there existed labor whose marginal productivity was zero in the agricultural sector in developing nations was disqualified. He tried to remove a universal misconception about agriculture, insisting that traditional agriculture in developing nations, though backward, was still efficient, and peasants could respond reasonably to economic incentives. He also proposed that supplying traditional agriculture with new production factors, that is, investment in human capital in agriculture was one of the important channels to transform traditional agriculture (Schultz, 1964). In this period, development economists, enlightened by Schultz's doctrine, had a new understanding of the status of agriculture and realized its contribution to economic development on the aspects such as product, market, factors, and foreign exchange. Therefore, due importance should be attached to the development of agriculture and its modernization.

The revival of Neoclassicism has promoted reinterpretation of the market mechanism. Since the end of the 1960s, the practice of economic development has been far from the expected objective of economic planning. An increasing number of economists disapprove of too much government intervention and planning, and hold that market mechanism plays a greater role in economic development. The advantages of Neoclassicism are reflected in the following aspects: making allocation of resources more effective and spurring economic growth; achieving policy objectives and avoiding low efficiency and corruption that may otherwise occur under direct control as an effective management tool; providing a wide range of information at a low cost. As for the relationship between planning and market, neoclassical development theory is more inclined to emphasize the role of the market mechanism and take it as a desirable tool for economic development.

Neoclassical development theory embraces trade liberalization and financial liberalization. In contrast to the early development theory, neoclassicism resolutely maintains the comparative cost theory, believing that international trade can achieve the optimal allocation of international resources through complementary effects, and free trade is beneficial to all countries. Lal and Haberler, proponents of free trade, thoroughly criticize ISI and protectionism, believing that protectionism aggravates the distortions in domestic prices and renders the domestic market dislocated and disintegrated from the world market. They add that protectionism frees domestic manufacturing from international competition to the extent that there is no pressure and impetus for domestic producers to reduce production cost and that protectionism allows the industrial sector to expand production capacity irrespective of the actual costs of resources, resulting in resources being increasingly concentrated on capital-intensive industries, a mismatch with the actual situation of labor resources in developing nations. Furthermore, they have discovered that import licensing contributes to corruption (Lal, 1985). Besides, supporters of financial liberalization argue that the inward ISI distorts prices, enervates economic efficiency, and slows down economic growth. Arbitrarily twisted and marked down, the capital and local currency prices stall economic growth and engender financial restraint. Therefore, they argue for replacing financial restraint with financial liberalization, replacing financial shallowing with financial deepening, that is, restoring, through liberalization of financial markets, the interest rate to the level that can truly reflect the degree of scarcity of capital resources and the foreign exchange rate to a reasonable level.

To conclude, neoclassical development theory advocates freedom from planning and a more liberal and vigorous market economy. As regards the development road, neoclassicism emphasizes the contribution of agriculture, outward development, and market mechanism, reversing the orientation of conventional development strategy. However, with the ideals of neoclassicism permeating in the field of development research, development economics, a subject concerning itself with the development of developing nations, receives formidable challenges and declines to obscurity or even to death.

2.2.3 Alternative Development Strategy

Under the influence of the alternative development concept and neoclassical development theory, many developing nations turned to the alternative development strategy, that is, coordinated socioeconomic development strategy after the 1970s. Compared with the conventional development strategy, this strategy is characterized by the following aspects. First, in the strategic approach, it recognizes the importance of coordinated and harmonious development of society, economy, and people and emphasizes the promotional role of institution and social structure reform in development instead of depending on large-scale capital accumulation to spur the economy. Second, in the choice of strategic objectives, it attaches great importance to the harmonious socioeconomic development, gives priority to satisfying the public's "basic needs" and takes into account poverty relief, employment, income distribution, and education in its development blueprint. Third, in strategic priorities, it highlights the basic position of agriculture and deems science and technology, education, and human resources as a major driving force of development. Fourth, in strategic countermeasures, it addresses itself to teasing apart the relationship between the government and the market so as to allow full play to the role of market mechanisms, improving the vitality and efficiency of economy through economic liberalization, and expanding international economic exchange. As it is put in the UN document "International Development Strategy for the Second United Nations Development Decade":

> As the ultimate purpose of development is to provide increasing opportunities to all people for a better life, it is essential to bring about a more equitable distribution of income and wealth for promoting both social justice and efficiency of production, to raise substantially the level of employment, to achieve a greater degree of income security, to expand and improve facilities for education, health, nutrition, housing and social welfare, and to safeguard the environment. Thus, qualitative and structural changes in the society must go hand in hand with rapid economic growth, and existing disparities-regional, sectoral and social-should be substantially reduced. These objectives are both determining factors and end-results of development; they should therefore be viewed as integrated parts of the same dynamic process and would require a unified approach.[1]

This strategy also proposes other social development goals and objectives, reflecting a pragmatic and down-to-earth exploration of the development strategy inclusive of all forms of social objectives. Developing nations and some international organizations have adopted one of the following alternative development strategies to varying degrees.

(1) *Export substitution industrialization (ESI)*
Export substitution was first put forward by Gustav Ranis, a leading development economist and the Frank Altschul Professor of International Economics at Yale University. According to this strategy, developing nations replace agricultural exports with industrial exports to promote the industrialization process and enhance their international competitiveness. South Korea, Singapore, Chinese Hong Kong, and Chinese Taiwan (a popular generic term for them is the Asian Four Dragons) have succeeded in implementing this strategy.

(2) *Basic-needs strategy (meeting basic human needs)*
The representative of this strategy is Mahbub ul Haq, chief economist of Pakistan Planning Commission. At the World Employment Conference in 1976, the International Labor Organization (ILO) advocated that top

priority should be given to creating new jobs and satisfying basic human needs. The chairman of the Conference defined basic human needs as follows:

> First, it includes a basic minimum requirement for a family on personal consumption, such as adequate food, shelter, clothing, home facilities and services. Secondly, it includes basic services provided by the community and in turn benefiting the community, such as safe drinking water, sanitation, public transport, health and education facilities.

In addition to needs for materials, he added the needs for human rights, employment, and participation in decision making that is associated with people. In the late 1970s, this strategy began to influence advanced nations' assistance and relief policies. Thanks to the initiative that its government carried forward the basic-needs strategy, Sri Lanka, a small island country in the Indian Ocean, overtook some middle-income countries in many social indices.

(3) *Redistribution with growth*
In the 1970s, the World Bank made a research on the income distribution of some developing nations. A research report from the World Bank Development Research Center, chaired by Hollis B. Chenery, strongly supported the strategy of redistribution with growth. The basic idea of this strategy is that the government, through policy regulation, enables economic growth to create more income-generating opportunities for low-income people and to provide resources for the utilization of these opportunities so as to change the living conditions of the poor.

(4) *Strategy of developing agriculture*
This strategy directed at pro-agricultural sector investment, relying on the advantages of agriculture to speed up the industrialization process and thus promote the national economic development. This was a nonmainstream school in the development strategies of developing nations after the Second World War. In 1945, Zhang Peigang, a Chinese intellectual, analyzed the interdependence between industry and agriculture in his doctoral thesis *Agriculture and Industrialization* and proposed that backward

nations realized industrialization through agricultural development. Unfortunately, against the social background of "prioritizing industry over agriculture," no slight attention was paid to Zhang's proposal. It was not until in the 1960s when agriculture remained stagnant for long and grain crises frequently harassed the world population and the governments began to attach great importance to agricultural development. In 1964, Schultz's *Transforming Traditional Agriculture* critically examined the economic logic underlying concept of traditional agriculture and had a profound impact on the community of economics. Thailand, Malaysia, and other countries, navigated by the ideals of this strategy, altered a single structure and laid a good foundation for industrialization. India, Sri Lanka, and the Philippines promoted agricultural development by introducing modern agricultural technology and "green revolution."

The alternative development strategy reflects a retrospection on the social, economic, and even political problems arising from the practicing conventional ideals of development strategy. So far as the developing nations are concerned, it is an attempt to get rid of the Western development model and to explore a development strategy suitable to their own specific and unique conditions. However, in its evolutionary course it obviously had the characteristic of "being transitional" for the following reasons.

First, alternative development strategy did not establish its solid theoretic foundation and meanwhile it was challenged by the neoclassical theory. It is generally accepted that in developing nations, poverty relief and satisfaction of basic needs, as well as the combination of economic growth and the readjustment of distribution structure can be effectuated through government intervention, social welfare programs, or distribution policies. In contrast, the core of neoclassical development theory objects to government intervention, which is believed by neoclassical theorists to cause new perverse distortions and twists and thus greater costs. Moreover, neoclassical development theory lavishes an enviable emphasis on the "pure" economic problems such as utility, income, and wealth, but disregards the effects of noneconomic factors such as society, culture, politics, and institutional arrangements on development, rendering the research on development once again bounded to a limited domain. More seriously, neoclassicism ignores the reality of the imperfect market economic system in developing nations, examines the problems of developing nations with the standards of developed countries, and the roadmap and guideline are designed for developing nations fails to grasp the essence of the problems. Moreover, the research aiming at the optimal allocation of resources within a short term is far from the requirement of coordinating socioeconomic development.

Second, the alternative development strategy remained more at an ideal level than concerned with the reality of the developing nations. Although the comprehensive development concept arrived at a consensus as to the coordinated socioeconomic development, there was no definite answer as to how to deal with the relationship between economic and social development particularly in the case of addressing the problems of developing nations. In the social context of the widening gap between developing nations and developed countries and the rigid social structure of the latter, it is obviously very difficult to implement the comprehensive development strategy, and its successful implementation relies, to a large extent, heavily on the aid from developed nations. Therefore, it is not a rare case that strategic efforts which seem to be good and cater to the public will fizzle out due to obstructions in the process of implementing them.

The two oil crises in the 1970s diverted the attention of the developed nations to domestic macroeconomic stability, contributed to the reduction of their assistance to developing nations, and undermined the basic-needs strategy in terms of economic support. Nonetheless, the alternative development strategy has left its own traces in the history of strategic evolution and laid a new theoretical foundation for development strategy.

2.3 THE NEW TREND OF DEVELOPMENT THEORY AND INNOVATION ON DEVELOPMENT STRATEGY

2.3.1 New Studies of Development

The concept of coordinated socioeconomic development followed a series of problems arising from the practice of conventional development concept. It is a revision of the concept merely concerned about economic growth, reflecting a strong desire for human progress. However, this development concept is still confined to the human's own economic and social activities. With further development of industrial civilization, the humans face new challenges, which are mainly from the following two aspects.

First, humans are constantly engaging in development. With the improvement of productivity, the goal of human development will be accordingly uplifted: apart from satisfying the basic needs of the people, the government should take into consideration material, spiritual, and cultural aspects to enhance the welfare of the people. The humans will be centered on the development strategy. After having studied comprehensively the nature of human development, Dennis Goulett (1999) argued that development comprised the core ideals of subsistence, self-esteem, and freedom. Subsistence, roughly equated with basic needs, involves food, shelter, health, and protection. Self-esteem, a sense of one's own dignity and worth, has the implication that a social being desires to be respected instead of being employed like a tool. Freedom implies that the enlargement of the choices a society and its members may make or the contraction of limitations.

Second follows the harmony between human activities and natural systems. In the process of human civilization of industrialization, disastrous events, particularly environmental pollution and ecological destruction have sounded the alarm that the human beings are in jeopardy. The development model of "development preceding governance" among the developed nations in the first half of the 20th century brought about a lot of serious consequences.[2] Since the 1960s, some intellectuals have been calling for environment protection. In 1962, the American biologist Rachel Louise Carson's *Silent Spring* sounded the alarm of the process of human civilization, arousing people's concern over destructive regression of the environment due to the abuse of chemical pesticides. Later, various views and doctrines about the relationship between human beings and environment welled up, one of the most influential views being Kenneth Ewert Boulding's spaceship economy in the mid-1960s. Bouilding believes that the greatest ecosystem humanity lives by is Earth, a planet that is nothing but a small spaceship in the boundless universe. By the time the growth of population and economy eventually exhausts, the limited resources in the small spaceship and the wastes produced by production and consumption completely contaminate the whole small space; the whole society will collapse. In the early 1970s, "Club of Roman," a global think tank dealing with a variety of international issues such as population, resources, environment, and the future of humanity, released a report entitled *The Limits to Growth,* which studies the relationship between population, industrial development, pollution, grain production, and resource consumption. The report, by establishing a system dynamics model, concluded that the growths of these five factors, including population, are exponential. Once hitting their limits, they will be forced to stop. Although the above points of view are pessimistic, they reveal the urgency and reality of solving these problems and arouse a worldwide concern over environment and development.

2.3.2 A Giant Leap of the Concept of Development: People-Centered Sustainable Development

2.3.2.1 *The People-Centered Concept of Development*

In the 1980s, the people-centered concept of development, driven by international organizations headed by the United Nations, became popular. Francois Peroux, a French economist who used the concept of growth pole for the first time in 1949, argued that development is aimed at satisfying human needs, including both material needs and social, cultural, and spiritual needs.

The conventional concept of development sets economic growth as the fundamental purpose, while the new concept of development holds that development is holistic, integrative, and endogenous and that economic growth is only the means through which development is achieved. From a hierarchical point of view, development is supposed to be a deep, comprehensive, and systematic development, rather than a superficial development only related to economic growth, finance, and currencies. Moreover, economy is a phenomenon not purely confined to its own small domains, but is instead dependent on cultural values.

Peroux's "new development concept" embodies the value orientation centered on satisfying the human need for economic prosperity, political democracy, moral perfection, cultural enhancement, and ecological balance. It is a more comprehensive development concept centered on the all-round development of human beings.

The people-centered development concept began to gain recognition in 1990 when the United Nations Development Program (UNDP) used the term "human development" for the first time. Since then, the Program releases a Human Development Report every year, assesses the situations of human development of every country and region, and plays a significant role in directing the governments toward the formulation of people-centered action plan. The 1995 Copenhagen summit meeting released two documents, *Copenhagen Declaration on Social Development* and *Program of Action of the World Summit for Social Development,* arrived at a consensus, which included the following[3]:

(1) Social development is central to the needs and aspirations of people throughout the world and to the responsibilities of governments and all sectors of civil society.
(2) Social development should be the top priority of the 21st century.
(3) The ultimate goal of social development is to improve and enhance the quality of life of all people. It requires democratic institutions, respect for all human rights, and fundamental freedoms.
(4) Social development is inseparable from the cultural, ecological, economic, political, and spiritual environment in which it takes place.

Amartya Sen, Nobel Prize Laureate for economics in 1998 and enthusiastic advocate of the people-centered concept of development, believes that the highest standard of value centered on humans is freedom. His unique research approach to the nature of development from the perspective of freedom has a great influence on economics, including development economics and welfare economics. The important idea that runs through Sen's theoretical system is to view development as an effort to advance the real freedoms that individuals enjoy, rather than simply focusing on metrics such as gross domestic product (GDP) or income-per-capita and that the advancement of real freedoms is the paramount purpose and a major means of development (Sen, 1999). In Sen's view, freedom plays a constitutive role in development. It is a value metric and an indispensable constituent of development, central to the improvement of life quality. Furthermore, freedom also plays an "instrumental" role. He outlines five specific types of freedoms, namely political freedoms, economic facilities, social opportunities, transparency guarantees, and protective security.

2.3.2.2 *Proposal of the Concept of Sustainable Development*

The Declaration of the United Nations Conference on the Human Environment, or *Stockholm Declaration*, the first document in international environmental law adopted by the UN Conference on Human Environment (UNCHE) in Stockholm in 1972, is a milestone in the history of human understanding of the environment and development. It proclaims: "The protection and improvement of the human environment is a major issue which affects the well-being of peoples and economic development throughout the world; it is the urgent desire of the peoples of the whole world and the duty of all Governments."[4] This meeting aroused worldwide concern for the environment and development. In 1980, the International Union for Conservation of Nature (IUCN), for the first time, explicitly formulated the concept of sustainable development and its prospects and approaches in *The World Conservation Strategy*, laying a solid cornerstone of thinking for sustainable development.

The World Commission on Environment and Development (WCED, otherwise known as Brundtland Commission), established in 1983 and chaired by former Norwegian Prime Minister Gro Harlem Brundtland, submitted to the United Nations in 1987 a report "Our Common Future." This report makes a comprehensive and systematic evaluation of the problems existing in human development and environmental protection, and clearly defines and formulates the implications of sustainable development, asserting that "sustainable development is the development that meets the needs of the present without compromising the ability of future generations to meet their own needs. It contains within it two key concepts: the concept of **needs**, in particular the essential needs of the world's poor, to which overriding priority should be given; and the idea of **limitations** imposed by the state of technology and social organization on the environment's ability to meet present and future needs."[5] This definition properly describes the characteristics and ideals of sustainable development, and reflects, to a large extent, human consensus on this strategic objective, providing a basis of a coordinated action exploring the future development and progress of the humanity.

The Earth Summit in Rio de Janeiro in 1992, unprecedented for a UN conference in terms of both its size and the scope of its concerns, adopted a series of documents on sustainable development, such as Rio Declaration on Environment and Development and Agenda 21 and important legally binding agreements, proclaiming, "To achieve sustainable development and a higher quality of life for all people, States should reduce and eliminate unsustainable patterns of production and consumption and promote appropriate demographic policies."[6] The Rio Earth Summit marked the beginning of a world coordinated action of sustainable development.

The World Summit, hosted by Johannesburg, South Africa, in 2002, reviewed the implementation of *Agenda 21*, achievements and existing problems since the Rio Earth Summit, adopted the *Johannesburg Declaration on Sustainable Development* and laid out the *Johannesburg Plan of Implementation* as an action plan. The concept of sustainable development has become the guiding theme of a series of seminars on the issue of development and the dominant thinking of the current development strategy.

2.3.2.3 *Implications of the Concept of Sustainable Development*

The implications of the concept of sustainable development are embodied in its various definitions, all of which derive from the definition given in "Our Common Future." Since the 1990s, research about it has been continuously made and some influential definitions from a large amount of literature are listed as follows:

> the improvement of life quality to the extent that subsistence is within the assimilative capacity of the ecosystem *Care for the Earth-A Strategy for Sustainable Living* by International Union for Conservation of Nature and Natural Resources (IUCN), United Nations Environment Programme (UNEP) and World Wildlife Fund (WWF) in 1991.

Human beings are at the centre of concerns for sustainable development. They are entitled to a healthy and productive life in harmony with nature.
The Rio Declaration on Environment and Development 1992.

To address the growing challenge of human security, a new development paradigm is needed that puts people at the centre of development, regards economic growth as a means and not an end, protects the life opportunities of future generations as well as the present generations and respects the natural systems on which all life depends.
UNDP, Human Development Report 1994.

To sum up, sustainable development is a fair development road considering the benefits of both the current and future generations, targeted at fulfilling the all-round development of human and social progress and coordinating the relationship between human individuals and that between human and nature by sustaining the ecological system.

2.3.2.4 *Sustainable Development: A New Progressive Development*

The concept of sustainable development is a completely new one, a giant leap in the evolution of the human development concept for the following reasons:

First, it is a denial of the conventional development concept that one-sidedly pursues economic growth. It enlightens human beings to reexamine economic growth and development in a new perspective and abandon the idea of "growth without development." It draws human attention to the importance of coordinating economic, social, and environmental development while maintaining robust and healthy economic growth.

Second, the concept of sustainable development is superior to the alternative development concept, which emphasizes the coordination of socioeconomic growth. It broadens its horizon of development, pursuing coordinated development of all factors such as population, resources, environment, and economy in a macro-system that integrates economy, human, and nature rather than focusing on socioeconomic activities only. More importantly, it positions its goal as satisfying the needs of the current generation while creating a condition for offspring to sustain a high standard of life instead of jeopardizing their subsistence.

Third, the concept of sustainable development is the advancement and promotion of people-centered concept of development. Between the two concepts are some similarities in terms of emphasizing the human's central and dominant position and the human overall development, which testifies to their progressiveness. However, the people-centered concept of development is prone to be one-sided in that it focuses on human development without sparing any attention to the human–nature harmony. In contrast, sustainable development is environmentally friendly, pursues a moderate and sound development within the carrying capacity of the ecosystem, satisfies the need for human overall development in a context of human–nature harmony and finally realizes the alternation of human generations.

2.3.3 Latest Developments of Development Concept

The "neoclassical revival" in the 1970s laid the theoretical foundation for some developing nations to rectify their conventional development strategy and put their policies back in gear for a more liberal and resilient economy. However, when the neoclassical economics prevailed, the research on the development theory increasingly confined itself to the "pure" domains of economics, such as utility, income, and wealth, but ignores the noneconomic factors such as history, society, culture, politics, and institutional systems. More seriously, neoclassicism examines the problems of developing nations using standards tailored to developed ones, irrespective of the reality of the imperfect market economy system in developing nations. Its prescriptions for economic malaise were prone to be palliative not curative. Moreover, the research aiming at the optimal allocation of resources within a short term was a far cry from the requirement of coordinating socioeconomic development. Since the mid-1980s, a series of research approaches, perspectives, and trends have been introduced in development economics with the application of revolutionary technological means in production activities, the deepening of economic globalization, the increasingly rich and complicated development practice in different nations around the globe.

(1) *Development theory of neo-institutionalism*
Neoclassical development theory, abstracting the institutional factors, exclusively highlights the role of market mechanism but regards various institutional factors as established and exogenous, and thus finds it difficult to give a convincing explanation to the economic growth of some developing nations, especially those with complicated institutional backgrounds. Why are some countries with similar natural endowments and development stages successful in economic growth, while others get stuck on the development road? Why are some strategies successfully carried out in some countries but stalled in others? Since the late 1980s, the neo-institutional economics represented by Ronald H. Coase has gained its recognition as a powerful means to tackle economic issues and quickly found itself extensively applicable to the domain of development economics. Neo-institutional economists argue that the gap in terms of per capita income between developing nations is only the representation of economic backwardness and that institutional imperfection is the real root. They believe that economic growth can be promoted by rectifying institutions. Douglass C. North (1991) argued that "Institutions provide the incentive structure of an economy; as that structure evolves, it shapes the direction of economic change towards growth, stagnation, or decline." Williamson (1994) took a bottom-up, microanalytical approach to economic development and reform and argued that institutional reform, a necessary choice for economic growth, could better the micromanagement mechanism of enterprises and the market and further boost economic growth. Neo-institutional development theory sets institutional factors as a key endogenous variable of economic activity and explores, by neoclassical supply and demand analysis, institutional barriers thwarting developing nations in their economic construction and every institutional option to overcome these barriers; it hence provides new theoretical evidence for institutional innovation and reform of these nations.[7]

(2) *Development theory of neoclassical political economics*
Because neoclassical economics failed to provide a reasonable explanation of the real source of development in developing nations due to its confinement of research domains to the "pure" economic factors, the classical economic system in the era of Adam Smith reignites the interest

of those economic intellectuals who address themselves to the issues of economic development from a broader perspective. At that time, the writings of classical economics generally labeled themselves as "political economy," with the research scope involving politics, ethics, population, law, history and culture, and so on. In the fever of the studies of the "Revival of Adam Smith" since the late 1970s, the scope of developmental research has been expanded to noneconomic factors, restoring the classic–economic traditional approach to economic studies from a more comprehensive angle including social, political, and cultural systems. This period of time is known as "neoclassical political economy" stage, following the stages of "structuralism" and "neoclassical revival" (Tan, 1999). While grasping the fundamental goal of overall human development, economic intellectuals are concerned about the research on every aspect of development, and establish a new framework with the help of the research approach of the school of neo-institutional economics.

(3) *Development theory of globalization*
Against the background of globalization characterized by advances in information technology sweeping across the world, the increasingly close linkage between developed and developing nations, and the cross-national cooperation and rivalry in economy since 1980s, the research on the development road of the developing nations could not be simply conducted from the perspective of regionalism but from the perspective of totality. World system theory in the late-1970s argued that development took place not in any isolated country or nation, but in a particular world system, which is the basic unit of development. The development theory of globalization analyzes the law of development by taking the world as a unified whole and bring insights into nature of the national development of some countries. The financial crises that broke out in South Eastern Asia, Korea, and Latin America and the United States had a global impact since 1990s remind people that the global economy is an inseparable entity. However, in the tide of globalization, the development imbalance is worsening and the income gap between developed and developing nations is widening. As a result, in view of the fact that development of any country is associated with the world, it is necessary to abandon the stereotypical idea that development is single and linear westernization on the one hand and refute the notion that

development is an internal affair of a country or a nation on the other. In the era of globalization, national development is successful if and only if this nation integrates itself with the whole world and explores a path suitable to its own specific conditions.

(4) *Sustainable development theory*
Since the 1990s, sustainable development theory has gradually shifted from formulation of concept and theory to action. As an integral part of development theory, it has brought vitality into the field in the following aspects:

First, sustainable development advocates a new development model, distinct from "zero growth" and "traditional growth," that is, neither to stop the development for environment protection nor to rely on large-scale resource consumption for economic growth. It encourages moderate and sound development without doing any harm to the ecosystem. It is necessary to explore a path to realize a fair, reasonable, and effective distribution of sources by means of technological improvement, structural reform, and institutional innovation.

Second, sustainable development emphasizes the fairness of development. It pursues three kinds of fairness: intragenerational fairness with the aim at meeting the basic needs of all the people of the same generation, and at giving them equal opportunities to pursue a better life; intergenerational or cross-generational fairness ensuring the enhancement of the current generation without compromising the welfare of future generations; the fairness to utilize limited resources, that is, the equal right to exploit resources. This gives development theory more space to explore theories. For example, neoclassicism emphasizes the role of the market mechanism. However, market mechanism is navigated by current maximization of economic interests and its adjustment is not oriented toward a long-term consideration, much less of moral implications. This is obviously not in line with the requirements of sustainable development. The principle of fairness makes it necessary to reexamine the role of government and deal with the relationship between government and the market in sustainable development.

Third, the research on sustainable development combines theory and practice closely. It requires the real integration of population, resources, environment, economy, society, institutions, and other factors into one whole to study, from a perspective of systematic, dynamic coordination, their intrinsic relationship. This is indeed a challenging job. Granted, the previous development theory emphasizes that development is a dynamic evolution process, but in the analysis, it often separates different factors from each other. Sustainable development introduces a new approach into the development theory.

REFERENCES

Arndt, Heinz W. *Economic Development: The History of an Idea*. Chicago: University of Chicago Press, 1987.

Goulett, D. "The cruel choice: A new concept in the theory of development". *Political Science Quarterly*, 1999, 88 (1): 116-117.

Hirschman, Alberto O. *The Strategy of Economic Development*. New Haven: Yale University Press, 1958.

Kindleberger, C. P. *Economic Development*. New York: McGraw-Hill, 1958.

Lal, Deepak. *Poverty of "Development Economics."* Cambridge, MA: Harvard University Press, 1985.

Lewis, Arthur W. *The Theory of Economic Growth*. London: George Allen & Unwin, 1950.

North, Douglas C. "Institutions," *Journal of Economic Perspective*, 1991, 5 (1): 97–112.

Prebisch, Raúl. *The Economic Development of Latin America and Its Principal Problems*. New York: United Nations, 1950.

Rostow, W. "The Stages of Economic Growth." *The Economic History Review, New Series*, 1959, 12 (1): 1–16.

Schultz, T. W., "Nobel Lecture: The Economics of Being Poor," *Journal of Political Economy*, August, 1980, 88 (4): 640.

Schultz, T. W. *Transforming Traditional Agriculture*. New Haven: Yale University Press, 1964.

Sen, Amartya. *Development as Freedom*. New York: Oxford University Press, 1999.

Tan, Chongtai. *New Developments in Development Economics*. Wuhan: Wuhan University Press, 1999.

UNDP. *Human Development Report 1994*. New York: Oxford University Press, 1994.

NOTES

1. Translator's note: See "Resolution adopted by the General Assembly 2626 (XXV). International Development Strategy for the Second United Nations Development Decade," approved by the UNGA on October 24, 1970. http://www.un-documents.net/a25r2626.htm (accessed October 6, 2017).

2. From the 1930s to the 1970s, eight notorious public hazards broke out in succession in advanced nations: the Belgian Smog Incident in Meuse Valley in December 1930, the Photochemical Smog Incident in Los Angeles in 1943, Donora Smog Incident in Pennsylvania, London Smog Incident in 1952, the Minamata Disease Incident in Kumamoto Prefecture, Japan in 1953–1968, Asthma Incident in Yokkaichi, Japan in 1961, Yusho Disease Incident in Aichi-ken, Japan, in 1968 and the Itai-itai Disease Incident in Fuji Mountain Region, Japan. For more, see Li, Huiming. *Environment and Sustainable Development*, p. 9. Tianjin: Tianjin People's Publishing House, 1998. 李慧明. 环境与可持续发展. 第 9 页. 天津: 天津人民出版社, 1998.

3. Translator's note: See *Copenhagen Declaration for Social Development. http://www.un-documents. net/poa-wssd.htm.* (accessed October 7, 2017) and *Program of Action of the World Summit for Social Development,* http://www. un-documents.net/cope-dec.htm (accessed October 7, 2017).

4. Translator's note: See *Declaration of the United Nations Conference on the Human Environment,* http://www.un-documents.net/unchedec.htm (accessed October 7, 2017).

5. Translator's note: See *Our Common Future, From One Earth to One World.* http://www.un-documents. net/ocf-ov.htm (accessed October 7, 2017).

6. Translator's note: See The Rio Declaration on Environment and Development (1992). [PDF] https://wenku. baidu.com/view/140948d549649b6648d74797. html (accessed October 7, 2017).

7. See Williamson, O., "The Institutions and Governance of Economic Development and Reform," *Proceedings of the World Bank Annual Conference on Development Economics*, 1994.

Chapter 3

China's National Development Concept and Economic Development Strategy

The formation of development concept is influenced by various factors such as ideology, the incipient socioeconomic conditions, domestic and international economic and political environment, and scientific (natural and social sciences) development. So to speak, development concept is the outcome of the interaction of internal and external contradictions. In view of this, a reliable survey of the development concept must be based on an understanding of the historical background against which it is formed or to which it is suitable or not. Regardless of development concept, those who are lagging behind the times are not recommendable, and those who surpass the realistic condition are prone to incur negative effects.

Since a development concept is the outcome of a specific historical environment, it is very likely that a new development concept may advance or deny the schools of development concept preceding it. If such a development concept is counted as a theory, then this theory has its own "hardcore" and "protective belt," both of which can be termed as "constituents" of the development concept. Some of the constituents may derive from an "old" development concept, some have been revised under the constraints of real conditions, and others have revolutionized.

As an idea, a development concept is embodied as a development strategy and a guideline or a policy in practice. A development strategy, or a guideline or a policy is more likely to be readjusted as compared with the development concept under the influence of the external environment. The development concept can remain relatively stable as long as the changes in the external environment have not yet accumulated to the extent that it may trigger its "hardcore." The impact of the development concept on reality varies according to the different stages and phases of the course of practice. Therefore, as a realistic embodiment of the development concept, the development strategy, or guideline or policy accordingly differ in different stages and phases. There are many paradigms of internationally popular development concepts. Within a particular period of time, the fact that a country chooses a paradigm does not necessarily mean that it has abandoned others (or some factors of other paradigms) in practice because, as mentioned above, the choice of development concept is conditioned by the external environment, the variability, and the complexity of which is far more than the hypothetical premises of the paradigm, which could be taken into consideration. In this case, the development concept in practice is more likely to be one in which the constituents of many paradigms interact. It is nevertheless the case that some of the constituents address major contradictions, while others address secondary ones. From the perspective of the government's behavior, the initial development concept is *ex ante,* and not necessarily the most appropriate. This development concept needs to be constantly tested in practice, and the government should adjust its constituents. What interests an economic observer is this *ex post* development concept restrained by objective conditions.

In terms of core guiding ideology, since the founding of the People's Republic of China (PRC), it has undergone two stages: from 1953 to 1965 and from 1977 to 1994. Although both are centered on economic growth, the development paths of the two stages are greatly different. The former adhered to the planning economy, attaching great importance to industry, especially heavy industry and emphasizing self-reliance, while the latter reduced the regulation and control of planning economy of the national economy, establishing decentralization, a commodity economy, and opening up as most important means of economic development. After attending the United Nations Conference on Environment and Development in 1992, the Chinese government and academia gradually realized the significance of harmonious development and intergenerational fairness. Meanwhile, the socioeconomic asynchronism has objectively contributed to the formation of the "people-centered, comprehensive, coordinated, sustainable" development concept in the 21st century.

3.1 DEVELOPMENT CONCEPTS BEFORE THE REFORM AND OPENING UP

From 1949 to 1977, the development of China's development concept was directed toward either or both of the following ideals: the growth-centered development concept formed in the long-term practice of economic construction and some ideas that were implemented in sporadic years or never under practice, but may affect some economic intellectuals and decision-makers. These ideas, to some extent, reflect the spirit of "people-centered." Some of them have not established their own complete and scientific system, but attempted to explore socioeconomic equilibrium development, thus becoming an important source of thought for the Scientific Outlook on Development.

3.1.1 The Thought of Equilibrium in the Development Concept in Early New China (1949–1953)

From the concept to practice, the concept of development at the beginning of the founding of the PRC is single, mainly embodied in the neo-democratic doctrine that included the guidelines for economic and social development. The doctrine was targeted at rehabilitating the economy in a down-to-earth manner, without any overtaking objectives, to avoid social upheavals caused by socioeconomic revolution, so as to achieve a smooth transition.

3.1.1.1 *The Ideals of Equilibrium Development in Neo-democratic Treatises by Communist Leaders*

Before the founding of the Communist Party of China (CPC), from early 1947 to the Second Plenary Session of the Seventh CPC Central Committee in March 1949, the communist leaders, through scientifically analyzing productivity and realistically assessing economic factors, conceived a clear blueprint: first, transforming China from an agricultural economy into an industrial economy under the guidance of neo-democratic ideology, and then under the guidance of socialist ideology (Lin, 1993: 31), transforming it from a neo-democratic economy to socialist economy. As a matter of fact, in January 1940, Mao Zedong, in his *On New Democracy*, put forward the policies and guidelines for the establishment of a neo-democratic China[1]:

> Enterprises, such as banks, railways and airlines, whether Chinese-owned or foreign-owned, ... , shall be operated and administered by the state, so that private capital cannot dominate the livelihood of the people: this is the main principle of the regulation of capital.
>
> ... In the new-democratic republic under the leadership of the proletariat, the state enterprises will be of a socialist character and will constitute the leading force in the whole national economy, but the republic will neither confiscate capitalist private property in general nor forbid the development of such capitalist production as does not "dominate the livelihood of the people," for China's economy is still very backward.
>
> ...
>
> China's economy must develop along the path of the "regulation of capital" and the "equalization of landownership," and must never be "privately owned by the few"; we must never permit the few capitalists and landlords to "dominate the livelihood of the people ..."

Before the founding of the People's Republic of China (PRC), the Communist regime adhered to the blueprinted roadmap in *On New Democracy* in Communist-controlled regions and then it was spread to the whole country after the CPC seized power. At the Chinese People's Political Consultative Conference in September 1949, Liu Shaoqi, one of the founders of the PRC, specifically pointed out: "It is in the far future that China can take serious socialist steps. If socialist steps are prescribed in *The Common Programme*, they will be easily confused with the pragmatic steps we should take today."[2]

The CPC consistently adhered to this principle until June 1953. In March 1951, Liu Shaoqi pointed out in the report of the First National Conference on Organizational Work: "The ultimate goal of the Chinese Communist Party is to realize the communist system in China. It is now struggling for the consolidation of the new democratic system, in the future for the shift toward socialism and eventually for socialism."[3]

3.1.1.2 *Practice and Effect of Equilibrium Development Concept*

Consistent with the idea of consolidating the neo-democratic system, the policies were protective toward neo-democratic elements (Dong, 1999: 120, 136, 137).

(1) Between 1950 and 1952, the Central Bureau and the Military and Political Commissions of the Six Grand Districts[4] issued documents, allowing liberal land purchase, sale and tenancy, liberal employment, liberal loan, and liberal trade in the rural areas.
(2) In March 1953, the Central Committee of the CPC made an unequivocal criticism against the attempt to abolish the above-mentioned "liberals" in the rural areas in the "Instructions on the Spring Production to the Party Committees at All Levels."
(3) In December 1952, the Financial and Economic Commission affiliated to the Government Administration Council (the Predecessor of the State Council) issued the "Circular on Several Amendments to Tax System and Execution Date," abolishing preferential tax rates on the state-operated and cooperative economies in accordance with the principle of equal taxation and putting state-operated, cooperative, and private industrial and commercial economies under the same treatment.

After the implementation of these policies, the national economy quickly recovered, with industrial and agricultural production reaching a record high. In 1952, grain production amounted to 163.92 million tons, and cotton production to 130.4 million tons, both surpassing the highest level in history. In 1952, the gross industrial output value exceeded the pre-Anti-Japanese-War record high, 23% higher than that in 1936. The rapid growth of industrial and agricultural output value laid a solid foundation for the rapid improvement of the state financial status. In 1950, the tax revenue from nonstate industrial and commercial sectors hit 2.36 billion yuan, tax revenue from agriculture 1.91 billion yuan, and two years later, the former two figures increased to 6.15 billion yuan and 2.70 billion yuan, respectively.

The ideas of new democracy embody the idea of equilibrium development. In the blueprint of new democracy, all classes of the society harmoniously develop and jointly propel social progress. The government did not intervene in economic activities; instead, it was mainly responsible for straightening out and coordinating the interests of all parties and clearing the obstacles for economic and social development. In this period, the adoption of this development mode was totally conditioned by domestic situations. On the one hand, against the background of formidably low productive forces caused by years of civil wars and national independent wars against foreign invasions, a radical readjustment of economic structure would inevitably bring about an immeasurable impact on the whole society. The option of the new democratic road to developing productive forces was viable and recommendable in that the industrial structure inherited from Old China of the Kuomintang regime was far behind those of modern industrialized countries by a large margin. Moreover, for a country with a large population of China, foreign aid, especially aid from the former Soviet Union, could never alter its socioeconomic backwardness in the short run; therefore, reliance on the consolidation of regime to drive society and develop productivity step by step was also a good choice. However, the conception of new democracy had not been realized yet. The superstructure that surpasses the development stage of economic base would inevitably call for an adaptable adjustment of the economic base. In 1953, Mao Zedong criticized the formulation of the new democracy, marking the end of its practice.

3.1.2 Growth-Centered Development Concept (1953–1965, 1976–1978)

3.1.2.1 *Basic Features*

The period from 1953 to 1978, with the interruption by the "Great Cultural Revolution" from 1966 to 1976, was obviously characterized by economic growth as the center.

(1) *Economic growth guided by overambitious yet unrealistic targets and centered on quantity*

This was particularly reflected in the "Great Leap Forward" (1958–1960), with the basic idea of equilibrium development being put behind and one-sidedly pursuing high yields. For example, in August 1958, the Enlarged Session of the CPC Central Committee Political Bureau at Beidaihe proposed the following targets: the 1962 gross industrial and agricultural output value would increase by 5–5.7 times over 1957, or with an average annual growth rate of 43%–46.4%; the average annual output value of agricultural and sideline products would increase by 28.5%–30.7%; investment in infrastructure construction would amount to 385–430 billion yuan, or 6.8–7.7 times over the First Five-Year Plan. This was also reflected in the general line of socialism proposed in 1958: "Go all out, aiming high and achieve greater, faster, better and more economic results in building socialism".

Likewise, the 1977 "Foreign Leap Forward" set overambitious and unrealistic targets. The National Planning Work Conference held in November 1977 proposed that by the end of the 20th century, China's major industrial products should be close to, catch up with, and exceed the most developed capitalist countries and all economic indicators would be close to, catch up with, and exceed the world's advanced level. The Fifth National People's Congress held in March 1978 reverted to the slogan of "surpassing the UK and US." These plans and indicators were far beyond what China's economy and technology could afford.

(2) *Emphasis on industrialization*
The general line of the transitional period proposed in 1953 was a general line of industrialization. In the first session of the National People's Congress in 1954, Zhou Enlai first proposed to achieve the four modern tasks. In 1956, the Eighth CPC National Congress pointed out that the main task of the people of the whole country was to concentrate on developing social productive forces, realizing national industrialization, and gradually meeting the growing material and cultural needs of the people.

(3) *Imbalance in socioeconomic development*
As a result of overemphasizing industrialization and deliberately marking down the prices of agricultural surpluses to support industrial development, the class gaps between urban and rural areas and between workers and peasants were increasingly widened in 1953–1978. Blind expansion

of capital construction led to a serious imbalance in the proportion of accumulated consumption. The investment in capital construction was 36.744 billion yuan in 1976, 38.237 billion yuan in 1977, and 50.99 billion yuan in 1978, an increase of 31% over the previous year, and the accumulation rate in 1978 was as high as 36.5%.

The preparatory period for the "Great Leap Forward" spanned from the end of 1952–1956. By the end of 1952, national economy was rehabilitated and thus laid a good foundation for further development. In addition, the Central Committee of the CPC did a lot of propaganda work. For example, at the end of 1952, the Central Committee announced the general line of *yihuasangai*, that is, industrialization and transformation of agriculture, handicraft industry and capitalist industry, and commerce in 1953. The economic policy in the preparatory period was to readjust production relations and stabilize the macroeconomy, rather than pursue economic growth. However, the policy was obviously intended to lay a foundation in terms of productivity and production relation for future "forging ahead" strategy because the Central Committee had proposed the objective of realizing industrialization within 15 years. Admittedly, the preparatory work was accomplished exceedingly well. If China had boosted their economy from this starting point in a systematic and methodical manner, it should have achieved satisfactory results during the "Great Leap Forward" from 1956 to 1960; however, due to unrealistic objectives such as "surpassing the UK and the US", China's national economy regressed. The readjustment period started from August and September 1960, when the slogan "readjustment, consolidation, enrichment, improvement" was put forward to cure the economic trauma caused by "Great Leap Forward" and it ended in 1965, when the Third Five-Year Plan was outlined.

The "Foreign Leap Forward" experienced a similar but relatively shorter course. Basically, it was the replica of the "Great Leap Forward," a slight difference being the realization of industrialization as soon as possible by purchasing foreign advanced technology and equipment.

From December 1976 onward, oriented by the slogans "grasping the key link and stabilizing the country" and "boosting national economy," China was in the grip of a series of meetings, such as agricultural meetings to learn from Dazhai, industrial work meetings to learn Daqing, and other scientific and planning work meetings. The convention of these meetings, on the one hand, met people's needs for economic growth and the improvement of living standards, but it sparked radical and aggressive audacity on the other hand. In 1977, when revising the "Ten-Year Plan (Draft)" formulated in 1975, the Central Committee once again came up with some unrealistic slogans and objectives for the "Fifth Five-Year Plan" and the "Sixth Five-Year Plan." Many problems were exposed in the implementation of the 1976, 1978, and 1979 annual plans formulated under the guidance of the 1975 "Ten-Year Plan (Draft)," slowing down economic growth and unbalancing the economic structure.

3.1.2.2 *Realistic Reasons for Growth-Centered Development Concept*

Despite a spectrum of problems arising from the implementation of the growth-centered development concept, there was a historical logic for China to opt for this concept in such a historical period (1953–1978) in its course of socialist construction.

To begin with, this is a manifestation of China's trend of thought in its economy. Due to its poverty and backwardness since the Opium War (1839–1842) onward, many thinkers and politicians chose "rejuvenating China" as their responsibility. The Self-Strengthening Movement (1861–1895) and the industrial plan in Sun Yat-sen's *The International Development of China*[5] reflected the trend of thought to rejuvenate China within a short period of time, which inevitably brought about influence on the decision makers of the Communist China. Second, in the first years after the birth of the New China, modern industry accounted for only about 10% of the national economy and heavy industry was even weaker, with only 26.4% of total industrial output value in 1949 (Zhao, 1988). The Mao-led generation of leadership realized that only by vigorously developing China's industry, especially heavy industrial sectors navigated for national defense because of the Cold War, could it reverse its backwardness. Third, China was encouraged and enlightened by the success of the Soviet paradigm. The former Soviet Union's successful transformation from an agricultural country to an industrial power within only one five-year plan set an exemplary model for the Chinese government. For nations that implement a planning economy, quantity-centered growth is the inevitable outcome of the path that is dependent on the planned allocation of resources. Finally, growth-centered development was the outcome of the ideological influence on top leaders, who believed that the achievement of a much quicker economic growth could testify to the governance ability of the ruling party and the superiority of socialism.

Seen from the development model, growth-centered development concept in this stage is also characterized by radicalism, specifically reflected in the following two aspects.

First, few international economic exchanges, especially isolation from Western major industrial nations over a long period of time, objectively helped China get rid of its economic dependence on capitalist countries. Aided by the Soviet Union, China began to establish its own relatively complete national economic system.

Second, domestically, through confiscation of bureaucratic and imperialist capitals, the state-owned economy controlled the major economic lifeline of the country. In 1949, the state-owned industrial output value accounted for as much as 40% of the total value of its large industry, power generation capacity being 58% of the total, coal production 68%, pig iron 92%, and steel production 97%. In addition, it controlled the whole railway system and a large part of modern transportation, banking, and international trade (Zhong, 2000). Policy makers readjusted the public–private and employer–employee (labor) relations and brought them into national control. By doing so, the Chinese government drew on the factors beneficial to national livelihood and restricted the negative factors for the ultimate purpose of removing the capitalistic influence on its economy.

3.1.3 War-Preparing Concept in Peace Time (1965–1976)

China's economic activities in this period mainly focused on war preparation. In a strict sense, by no means can it be counted as a strategy for economic development, but this national policy had a profound impact on its distribution of industrial activities and structures in the long run. Therefore, it is necessary to make a brief review of the strategy.

3.1.3.1 *Historical Background*

The U.S. involvement in the Vietnam War (1964) and the Sino–U.S. ideological confrontation (cold war) and the U.S. strategic encirclement of China posed a war threat on Chinese decision makers.

The Sino-Soviet split in the early 1960s escalated into border conflict, culminating in the Zhenbao (Damansky) Island Incident in 1969. Even until 1977, the *Press Communiqué of the Eleventh National Congress of the Communist Party of China* remarked "the United States and the Soviet Union are the sources of a new world war, especially with the latter a greater risk … The National Congress expresses, … we must … continue striding forward, advancing from victory to victory, carrying on revolution, promoting production and war preparation."[6]

Heavy industry was concentrated in the eastern coastal areas, vulnerable to attack in case of war.

In view of the above considerations, the CPC Central Committee issued "Instructions on Strengthening War Preparation" in April 1969. Later in that month, Mao Zedong repeatedly stressed the need to prepare for war at the Ninth CPC National Congress and at its First Plenary Session. In the subsequent arrangement of the national economy, Mao stressed "War Preparation as the Key," incorporating economic construction into war preparation. The situation continued throughout the Great Cultural Revolution and late 1977s.

3.1.3.2 *Characteristics of Socioeconomic Development of the War-Preparing Concept*

In this period, the guideline of socioeconomic developments can be summarized as "preparing against war and famine and for the people," specifically, prioritizing national defense industry over everything else and speeding up the "sanxian"[7] (third line) program so as to reshape industrial layout; boosting agricultural production and light industry to improve people's living standards; allowing full play to the production potentials in coastal areas and central provinces; and sparing no efforts to develop new technology to surpass the world's advanced level. This is a war preparation plan centered on national defense and third line program.

The third line program, if viewed from the angle of economy, is somewhat of an equilibrium paradigm. To ensure strategic needs, the capital construction and industrial production in this period were readjusted for higher speed and larger quantities, paradoxically to a certain degree alike to the growth-centered development concept.

Perversely, the third line program failed to achieve comprehensive equilibrium due to the desire for quicker success, overemphasis on war preparation, large-scale relocation of industrial plants, and prevailing political campaign frenzies. Nevertheless, it inadvertently improved productivity layout, coordinated interregional socioeconomic development, and balanced the economic growth rate in the coastal provinces and hinterland. Not focused as it was on the betterment of economic efficiency, war preparation arbitrarily allocated strategic resources to central and west provinces where inefficient allocation of resources formed a striking contrast to higher efficiency in the coastal provinces. Obviously, war preparation brought a relatively limited benefit due to its high opportunity cost.

3.1.4 Legacy of the Development Concept Before Reform and Opening Up

An *ex ante* development concept is generally conditioned by historical contexts, so decision makers tend to reconsider and readjust some of its constituent elements. Reflections on the growth-centered development concept are as follows.

3.1.4.1 *The Equilibrium Development Concept Embodied in "On the Ten Major Relationships"*

Challenging the "Old Brother" Soviet Union's paradigm of economic development, Chairman Mao Zedong delivered at an enlarged meeting of the Politic Bureau of the Central Committee on April 25, 1956 a speech *On the Ten Major Relationships*, which expressed a thought of coordinated and comprehensive development. He affirmed, "The emphasis in our country's construction is on heavy industry. The manufacturing of the means of production must be given priority that's settled." He stressed "… to adjust properly the ratio between investment in heavy industry on the one hand and in agriculture and light industry on the other in order to bring about a greater development of the latter." He also added, "... to develop agriculture and light industry more. In the long run, ... lead to a greater and faster development of heavy industry." In addition, Mao also mentioned the relationships between industry in the coastal regions and hinterland; between economic construction and national defense; between the state, production units, and individual producers; between central and local authorities; and between China and other countries. As it was, Mao's speech summed up the pre-1956 development concept which should have, in the years to come, put China's economy in gear. But contrariwise, domestic political climate and the supreme leader's disposition derailed economy from the growth-centered development track.

3.1.4.2 *The People-Centered and Equilibrium Development Concepts Reflected in the "Third Five-Year Plan"*

In 1965, the State Planning Commission proposed *The Preliminary Formulation of the Third Five-Year Plan* (1966–1970), which set out the following basic tasks:

(1) To spare no efforts to develop agriculture, solve problems concerning people's food, clothing, and other basic needs.
(2) To moderately strengthen national defense and make great endeavors to create breakthroughs in sophisticated technology.
(3) To enhance infrastructure, and continue improving production quality, increasing production variety and quantity, to build an economy of self-reliance, and to develop transportation, commerce, culture, education, and scientific research so as to support agriculture and national defense.
(4) To prioritize the basic components of economy and avoid one-sided and speed-overstressing development.

The plan revised the growth-centered development concept and shifted to people-centered development concept: putting people's basic needs above everything else. Though not implemented as it was scribed in black and white due to preparation against war risks and especially against nuclear blackmails from the former Soviet Union, this plan reflected the decision-maker's redirection of development concept, indicating that the decision-maker adapted his subjective development concept to real conditions, which had a restriction on ex ante development concept.

3.1.4.3 *Scientific Approach Embodied in Chen Yun's Comprehensive Equilibrium*

Chen Yun's comprehensive equilibrium is not equated with the "Four Technical Equilibria" of finance, credit, foreign exchange, and material. As a matter of fact, it was inherently consistent with the "Five Overall Arrangements" formulated by President Hu Jintao in Scientific Outlook on Development. This can be illustrated from the following aspects.

(1) *Improving the Urban–Rural Relation and Peasants' Welfare Through Coordination of Industrial and Agricultural Development*

To begin with, Chen Yun stressed that due proportion should be given to agriculture and industry. In 1950, he observed that emphasis was lavished on industry but no regard was paid to agriculture, which accounted for 90% of the national economy. When compiling the Second Five-Year Plan, he remarked, "The proportion of investment on heavy industry, light industry, and agriculture should be planned in accordance with the guideline by Chairman Mao in his *On the Ten Major Relationships*. The investment on heavy industry will still predominate over other sectors. There must be an increase on the proportion of investment on light industry and agriculture. The absolute figure of investment on heavy industry should also be increased in that it serves light industry and agriculture. This arrangement seems to slow down industrial development, but on the contrary, this will speed up it." In 1979, when the "Foreign Leap Forward" was prevailing, Chen tartly pointed out, "The key problem is the disproportion of agriculture and industry ... The arrangement and priority of agriculture, light industry and heavy industry is the combination of Marxism and the Chinese revolutionary practice." In addition, he believed that mutual exchange between rural and urban areas could facilitate economic coordination. As early as in the beginning years of the Communist China when large quantities of industrial products were overstocked, he improved peasants' purchasing power by purchasing farm produces and hence speeded up the sales of industrial products. In 1951, when the problem of food was solved, he demanded that coordination of agriculture and industry be realized through urban–rural exchange.

(2) *Coordinating Population Growth with Economic Development*
In 1957, when the demographer and economist Ma Yinchu's *New Population Theory* came for much criticism, Chen also advocated birth control and family planning. At the Third Plenary Session of the Eighth CPC Central Committee, Chen observed: "The Second Five-Year Plan failed to increase per capita supply. On the contrary, it is on a downward trend. One of the major reasons is the population growth … One of the basic preconditions for the improvement of living standards is to decrease the number of new babies." Later on, he repeatedly urged birth control so as to acclimatize it to economic growth.

(3) *Domestic and International Coordination*
Chen Yun attached great importance to the overall arrangement and coordination of imports and exports. He viewed international trade as a means to readjust surplus and shortfalls and more importantly he incorporated imports into his comprehensive equilibrium. Furthermore, he warned China of the negative effect in the process of drawing on foreign experiences and capitals.

In addition to the above three aspects, Chen's approach to all-round regional development is very much similar to the Scientific Outlook on Development. He strongly demanded to abolish the barriers of local self-departmentalism and also laid emphasis on rational layout of regional industries.

3.2 THE EVOLUTION OF DEVELOPMENT CONCEPTS SINCE OPENING UP AND REFORM

Since 1978, China has made conspicuous achievements in social and economic development and the interaction between the guideline (outlook on development) and socioeconomic development is obvious. Over the past four decades, the understanding of outlook on development underwent three phases: spontaneous adoption of growth-centered development concept; continuation of growth-centered development concept and conscious self-reflection; and the formulation of Scientific Outlook on Development.

3.2.1 The Growth-Centered Development Concept (1978–1990)

In 1978, the CPC's central committee resolutely terminated the use of the slogan "taking the class struggle as the key link," reorienting its emphasis on the right track of socialist construction. Indeed, this resolution has dramatically reshaped the socioeconomic landscape characterized with robust economic growth and drastic improvement on people's welfare.

Viewed from the value orientation, the 1978–1990 development concept had much to do with the one between 1949 and 1965 in the sense that both are growth-centered. On the whole, this development concept was suitable for the actual conditions at that time for the following reasons. First came the urgent need to rehabilitate the tumbledown economy heavily hit by the 10-year tumultuous Great Cultural Revolution and to improve the extremely low living standards. Associated with this urgent need was the pressure exerted by the widened gap between China and advanced nations and by the improved social welfare in neighboring emerging countries. Third, China's wholehearted devotion to economic construction also benefited from its own prudent judgment that peace and development were to be an irresistible onrush around the globe. Fourth, at the initial stage of development, there seemed no need to take environment and rational collocation of resources into consideration and therefore the benefits from economic growth far above the cost incurred by environment and resources. Fifth and finally, the benefits accruing in the inchoate stage of opening up and reform won popularity because they could be trickled down to the grassroots.

However, due to lack of theoretical awareness, the development concept in this period equated development with economic growth and interpreted "solving the problems cropping up on our way forward through development" as "removing social contradictions through economic growth." The principle of "giving priority to efficiency with due consideration to fairness" was sometimes distorted as "giving priority to efficiency and disregarding fairness," thus causing such problems as irrational economic structure and incompatible socioeconomic development.

The development of a theory entails practice. However, much of the pre-reform era was not expended on down-to-earth attitude toward growth-centered development concept, but frequently suspended by frenzies of political campaigns. Such being the case, the decision makers failed to have a comprehensive view of it but only noticed its rationality.

Noticeably, this development concept assumed some new characteristics, which provided new evidence for its evolution. For instance, in 1987, the Chinese government put forward the three-step strategy, an overtaking strategy, which qualified its objective as "improving people's living conditions and increasing their livelihood." Using such concrete expressions as "simply having adequate food and clothing," "moderately well-off," and "affluent" to describe the objective of its modernization reflected the implications of people-centered development concept. As a matter of fact, the three-step strategy originated from past conceptions: the awareness of the importance of coordinating development in Mao's *On the Ten Major Relationships* in 1956, the roadmap conceived for the Third-Five Year Plan, despite abortion due to war preparation, and the concern for people's livelihood in Chen Yun's doctrine of economy.

3.2.2 Conscious Self-Reflection and Exploration of Development Concept

Overemphasis on the role of economic growth in development resulted in myriads of negative effects, such as stalled social development decoupled with high-speed economic growth, widening interregional gap, worsening rural–urban cleavage, and insufficient momentum for sustainable development due to economic structural contradiction. Besides, ecological environment was seriously damaged and pressures resulting from insufficient natural resources gradually emerged. All of these perverse effects prompted reconsideration of growth-centered development concept.

The evolution of development concept around the world in the 1990s expedited China's reconsideration. Two years after its participation in the

1992 Rio Earth Summit on environment and development, the Chinese government issued *China's Agenda 21*, a document that showed people-centered development concept had a profound realistic impact on the Chinese decision makers and marked the beginning of the strategy of sustainable development.

The internal demand for sustainable development and the introduction of new concepts from foreign countries helped China rethink its own development concept. In designing the guideline for the 10th Five-Year Plan in 2001, just two years before the Scientific Outlook on Development was proposed, China identified structural adjustment as the principle line and resolved to combine structural adjustment in industry with that in ownerships, regions, and urban–rural areas. It also stressed attaching great importance to population, resources, ecological environment, solving the problems of strategic materials such as foodstuff, water, and crude oil and raising the implementation of sustainable development to a higher level.

Having realized how significant sustainable development could be to a country with such a large population, the Chinese government made great endeavors in institutional construction, publicity, and financial investment. As mentioned above, the Chinese government issued *China's Agenda 21,* reinforcing the governmental function of overseeing environment protection and resource conservation. Later in 1998, the government availed itself of the opportunity of the "Development of West China" to put a premium on "returning farmland to grassland." Undeniably, a spectrum of problems such as social security and environment destruction continued to exist because the growth-centered development concept instigated the majority of local executive heads (provincial governors, magistrates, etc.) to speed up economy without paying due regard to environment and resource utilization so that they could be promoted to a higher executive position.

Thus, for a development concept to be carried out, it must acclimatize itself to the current situation. Generally, only limited attention is paid to intergenerational equity before the problem of subsistence and development could be solved; large quantities of resources could hardly be utilized for sustainable development if there is no institutional guarantee in the early stage of economic development. At any rate, the socioeconomic situation at the turn of the 20th and 21st centuries signaled a new development concept.

3.2.3 The Formation of the Scientific Outlook on Development (Since Early 21st Century)

At the beginning of the 21st century, China's economic and social development came to a critical point where remarkable economic achievements formed a striking contrast with its social problems such as ever-widening interregional disparities and urban–rural gaps, declining ranks of per capita investment in public health and education, deteriorating ecological environment, growing shortfalls in resources, and coexistence of overcapacity and insufficient domestic demand, to name just a few. These problems, if not resolved, would stall economic development.

A decade of theoretical exploration allowed the Chinese political and intellectual circles to view the issue of development in a dialectical way. Therefore, the principle of "adhering to the people-centered principle, establishing a comprehensive, coordinated and sustainable development concept" put forward by the Third Plenary Session of the 16th CPC Central Committee came into existence and gained popularity soon. Since then, the theory of the Scientific Outlook on Development has been continuously enriched and consolidated, forming a theoretical system of a concept with people-centeredness as the core and comprehensive, coordinated and sustainable development as the basic requirements. This theoretical system is complementary to the objective of building a harmonious society and become an important theoretical foundation for ensuring the successful completion of socialist modernization in China.

From the realistic background, the Scientific Outlook on Development was not under any circumstance a fortuitous or accidental outcome, but a product of the interactive forces between internal and external environmental conditions at a higher stage of China's economic and social development.

First, sufficient financial resources amassed in the previous two decades of reform and opening up ensured the solution to the problems mentioned above.

Second, increasing economic aggregate was no longer an urgent need for China. The contradiction between growth quality and social effects gradually escalated from a minor one into a major one. During the new stage of building a moderately affluent society, a historical period featuring economic transition and social transformation, how to balance various interests of different social groups and how to properly solve the major social issues determines largely the orientation of socioeconomic development. Naturally, the issue of coordinated development was put on the agenda in such a historical context.

Theoretically, the Scientific Outlook on Development inherits and carries forward the people-centered development concept.

To begin with, the word "all-inclusive" repeatedly stressed in formulating Scientific Outlook on Development originates from the report of the 16th CPC National Congress: turning a low-level, noncomprehensive, and unevenly developed country into a well-off country where economy prospers, democracy advances, science and education progresses, culture booms, society harmonizes, and people's livelihood becomes better. In other words, it intends to achieve common or collective affluence instead of "allowing some regions and some people to get rich first."

Second, the thought of "being comprehensive and coordinated," that is focusing on the solution to interregional and urban–rural cleavages can also be traced back to the 15th Five-Year Plan.

Third and finally, sustainable development emphasized by the Scientific Outlook on Development corresponds to one of the major tasks of the 16th CPC National Congress: steadily enhancing sustainable development, improving ecological environment, significantly increasing efficiency of resource utilization, enhancing harmony between human and nature, pushing the whole society onto a path to civilized development featuring the growth of production, an affluent life and a sound ecosystem.

To sum up, theoretical preparations and realistic demand jointly contributed to the birth of the Scientific Outlook on Development.

3.3 A HISTORICAL REVIEW OF CHINA NATIONAL DEVELOPMENT STRATEGIES

3.3.1 Development Strategies (1949–1978)

After the founding of the People's Republic of China in 1949, the formidable task confronting the first generation of leadership was to cast off the impoverished situation left by the old regime. At that time, there was a heated discussion about the path of socialist industrialization among top officials and the intellectuals. Although not any concept of "development strategy" was put forward as it is today, it was set forth in Five-Year Plans in the form of either general guideline or general policy.

Initially, the Communist Party of China conceived of building neo-democratic economy first and then made a transition to socialist economy when conditions were mature. Based on this conception, China issued some policies to protect neo-democratic economic elements and quickly rehabilitate economy.

With the revival of national economy, Mao Zedong announced in the summer of 1953 that the general line of the Transition Period (1949–1956) was to "accomplish a socialist transformation of agriculture, handicraft industry, capitalistic industry and commerce within a fairly long period of time." Navigated by the general line, China made remarkable achievements in the First Five-Year Plan and its comprehensive strength improved a lot. However, waves of "leftist" political campaigns derailed the choice of national strategy from economic construction and thwarted the implementation of the general line.

In the late 1950s, inspired by the domestic successful completion of the First Five-Year Plan in advance and threatened by the Cold War between the United States and the former Soviet Union, China put forward the development strategy of "surpassing the UK and the US" and "Great Leap Forward," which were reflected in the general line of "going all out to strive for socialism in a quicker and more economical way." Hoping to realize industrialization through massive political campaigns, China concentrated human, financial, and material resources on the development of heavy industry, particularly on the increase of steel production. As a result of the desire for quicker success and serious departure from reality, it proved to be "Great Leap Backward." Such being the case, China had to make a three-year readjustment, which, however, was only an interim slight change of the disproportionate elements of the national economy without thorough reflection on the strategic guiding ideology.

In December 1964, China put forward the strategic goal of "four modernizations" and the two-step strategy of modernization: to establish an independent and relatively complete industrial system and national economy within three Five-Year Plans; to strive to realize the modernization of industry, agriculture, national defense, and science and technology in a relatively short historical period and bring its national economy at the forefront of the world. However, 18 months later, the "Great Cultural Revolution" that would last 10 years dashed these great expectations into bubbles.

After the crackdown of the "Gang of Four" (a political faction that controlled the Party power organs) in 1976, the primary task confronting the new supreme leaders was to promptly reverse the economic slippage and political disturbance. However, due to the failure to thoroughly clean up the residual influence of long-standing "leftist" measures and unrealistically propose a new target of "foreign leap forward" and "catching up" the world's advanced level, the national economy once again came to a standstill.

On the whole, the national development strategy in this period falls under the traditional development strategy and has the following characteristics:

(1) Its guiding ideology attempted to allow full play to the superiority of the socialist system and quickly catch up with the developed capitalistic countries led by the United States and the United Kingdom.
(2) It aimed to boost national economy at a high speed.
(3) It concentrated on heavy industry, trying to rely on itself to use its own capital goods to equip agriculture, light industry, and other industrial sectors and then gradually establish its own independent and complete industrial and economic system.
(4) It was driven by centrally planning economy characterized with mobilizing all social resources and investing large quantities of labor, capital, and means of production in economic construction.

The formation of the above development strategy was related not only to the domestic economic situation and political guiding ideology but also to the international political and economic pattern. Due to the Western countries' imposition of blockade and embargoes on the newly established Communist China, China had no choice but to develop relations with the Soviet Union-led socialist camp and follow its model. Besides, its national economy was seriously retarded by outmoded industrial system, especially by the extremely backward heavy industry. This national situation also contributed to China's emulation of the Soviet Union development model that centered on heavy industry.

3.3.2 Disequilibrium Overtaking Strategy Focusing on Economic Construction (1978–1990)

3.3.2.1 *From "Four Modernizations" to "Three Steps"*

The third Plenary Session of the 11th CPC Central Committee marked China's entry into a new era of reform and opening up. As the objective situation changed and the focus of work shifted, its development strategy underwent fundamental changes. Taking into account the national situation that China is a developing country with a large population, weak industrial foundation, and unbalanced development, Deng Xiaoping reconsidered the strategic objective of "four modernizations" and gradually formed the strategic thought of the "three steps."

The 12th CPC National Congress held in 1982 correctly estimated the potential of China's economic development and put forward the task of "gradually realizing the modernization of industry, agriculture, national defense and science and technology and building our country [China] into a highly civilized and highly democratic socialist country" and meanwhile resolved to build China into a well-off society by the end of the 20th century. It established a two-step strategy for the last 20 years of the 20th century: laying a solid foundation, accumulating strength, and creating favorable opportunities in the first half and reviving economy in the second. The 13th CPC National Congress revised the two "highlys" in the previously set goal and morphed it into "building China into a prosperous, democratic and civilized socialist country" and for the first time established a complete three-step strategic design: to double the 1980 GNP and ensure that the people have enough food and clothing; to quadruple the 1980 GNP (gross national product) by the end of the 20th century so that China entered into a well-off society; and to increase the per-capita GNP to the level of the medium-developed countries by the mid-21st century so that people will be affluent and modernization will be basically realized. Compared with the strategy of "four modernizations," the three-step strategy is much richer in connotations. It considers both economic modernization and national development from political, cultural, and social perspectives. Moreover, the three steps are more reasonable, realistic, and pragmatic, modernization will be by no means achieved at one go, and setting the realization of a well-off society as a transitional period is also in line with the general law of development.

This development strategy has been embodied in the Sixth Five-Year (1981–1986) and the Seventh Five-Year (1986–1990) plans. The Sixth Five-Year Plan, following the principle of "readjustment, reform, rectification and improvement," endeavored to solve the problems left from the economic development over the past years and finally explored a sound path whereby economic efficiency bettered and more benefits became accessible to the people. The Seventh Five-Year Plan established the basic guiding ideology of the three-step strategy, laying a solid foundation for the revitalization of the economy in the 1990s. As for the planned targets, the "Seventh Five-Year Plan" proposes to change gross social production value into the gross national product so as to match the strategic goal better.

3.3.2.2 *The Development Path of Disequilibrium*

In order to achieve quicker economic growth and move toward a moderately prosperous society, China chose the disequilibrium strategy, which was reflected in the following aspects.

(1) *Focusing on key sectors*
In response to backward agriculture, infrastructure, education, and science, the 12th CPC National Congress specified that the focus of work in the following 20 years was on agriculture, energy, transportation, science, and education.

(2) *Coastal areas: bellwether of economic development*
In order to allow full play to the relatively regional advantage and improve the efficiency of investment, China attached greater importance to coastal areas. The Sixth Five-Year Plan proposed that coastal areas should draw on their advantage in economic base to attract foreign investment and then radiate economic potentials to the hinterland, which, in turn, would support the coastal areas with its natural resources, raw materials, agricultural products so as to improve the overall economic efficiency. The Seventh

Five-Year Plan further reflected the principle of "giving priority to efficiency" and "disequilibrium" and for the first time set different goals for eastern, middle, and western regions according to the economic–geographic division of China, thus forming the gradients of industrial and technological development from east to west, from coastal areas to hinterland.

(3) *Encouraging some people to get richer than others first and eventually realizing common prosperity*

The slogan of "allowing some people to get richer" at that time authentically qualify the features of the realistic situation. In terms of income distribution, the proportions of the state, collectives, and the individuals drastically changed, with the former one decreasing and the latter two increasing. The distribution of personal income mainly tilted toward rural residents from 1979 to 1984. With the implementation of the contract responsibility system and the substantial increase in the purchase price of agricultural and sideline products, the farmers' income increased rapidly. The income ratio between urban and rural residents fell from 2.52 to 1 in 1978 to 1.84 to 1 in 1984. Between 1985 and 1991, personal income distribution slanted to urban residents. With the reform of the urban economic system came various kinds of economic ownership and the significant increase in income sources. The income ratio between urban and rural residents increased from 1.86 to 1 in 1985 to 2.40 to 1 in 1991. Among the urban residents, the income of the residents in the eastern area increased fastest, and the employees of foreign-funded enterprises and private businesses earned much more than those in the state-owned and collective enterprises.

3.3.2.3 *Completion of the First Step Ahead of Schedule*

The implementation of the Sixth and Seventh Five Year Plans substantially improved people's livelihood and strengthened agriculture, infrastructure, education science. If comparing the planned target and actual outcome of the two five-year plans from the perspectives of economic growth, agriculture, industry, infrastructure, and income of urban and rural residents, we could easily find that the actual growth rates were much higher than planned (see Table 3.1), with the Sixth Five-Year Plan in particular. In 1987, China's GNP reached 1195.45 billion *yuan* (current price), 2.1 times that of 1980 in comparable price, three years ahead of the

Table 3.1   Socioeconomic Development in Sixth and Seventh Five-Year Plans

Five-Year Plans		AAGR (%)	AAGR of GIOV (%)	AAGR of GAOV (%)	Scale of Construction (billion)	AAGR of Total Salary Income of Employees (%)	AAGR of Peasants' per Capita Net Income (%)
Sixth Five-Year Plan (1981–1985)	Planned	4 (GNP)	4–5	4	360	4.9	6
	Actual	9.7 (GNP)	11.3	8.1	799.76	8.6	13.7
Seventh Five-Year Plan (1986–1990)	Planned	7.5 (GDP)	7.5	4	1296	4	7.6
	Actual	13.2 (GDP)	13.2	4.8	1974.4	4.1	4.2

AAGR: annual average growth rate; GIOV: gross industrial output value; GAOV: gross agricultural output value.

Source: Yao (2003), Guo (1993), and Liu (2006).

schedule. However, attendant with the achievements were overoptimism and overconfidence that resulted in violent and irrational fluctuations in macro-economy, especially in the outbreak of severe inflation in 1988. Later, China had to undergo three years of readjustment and rectification, which relieved the contradictions between supply and demand on the one hand but led to weak market and imbalanced structure on the other.

3.3.3 Systematic Strategy Pursuing Comprehensiveness and Coordination (1990s)

3.3.3.1 *From "Moderate Prosperity" to "Three Steps"*

Since the 1990s, the Jiang-led third generation of leadership geared up for a new development strategy while aiming at the goal of the second step of the three-step strategy.

The tremendous change of the world political and economic situation in the late 1980s and the early 1990s, such as the disintegration of the former Soviet Union, the upheaval of the Eastern European socialist countries, and the end of the Cold War heralded a trend of multi-polarization. In addition, a new technological revolution represented by information technology greatly promoted the development of productive forces and accelerated economic globalization. Domestically, a dozen years of rapid economic development solved the problem of food and clothing, but some new problems and challenges such as the quality and efficiency of economic growth, the relationship between economic growth and increasingly serious resource and environmental constraints, and the social contradictions arising from widening income gap were far beyond the mere economic means, necessitating a broader vision to review the national development strategy.

Against this background, the Seventh Plenary Session of the 13th CPC Central Committee ratified a proposal on a 10-year program of national economy and social development and the Eighth Five-Year Plan, proclaiming that the major task was to drive for the second step of the development strategy. The proposal raised the overall quality of national economy to a new level and gave a detailed description of the "moderately prosperous" society. In 1995, the Fifth Plenary Session of the 14th CPC

Central Committee ratified a proposal for the Ninth Five-Year Plan and the Long-Range Objective by 2010, issuing clear guidelines on how to successfully realize the second step and how to advance toward the third step. Among the guidelines, promoting "the two fundamental changes of the overall significance" — transitioning from a planned to socialist market economic system and from an extensive to intensive mode of economic growth — became the key of the objectives in the 15 years to come.

With the passage of time, the development guideline for the first half of the 21st century has been gradually clarified. In 1997, the 15th CPC National Congress further specified the third-step goal that was expected to achieve in 50 years: doubling the GNP of the year 2000 by 2010; further developing national economy and bettering all systems and institutions by the 100th anniversary of the founding of the Communist Party of China (2021); basically achieving modernization and building China into a prosperous, democratic, and civilized country by the 100th anniversary of the founding of the People's Republic of China (2049). The 15th CPC National Congress also demanded to advance comprehensive development in political system, culture, and humanities and handle the relationship between human and nature.

3.3.3.2 *Rejuvenating China by Science and Technology and Transforming the Mode of Economic Growth*

The Jiang-led third generation of leadership also made a great contribution to development mode and strategic approaches. The strategy of rejuvenating China through science and education, first proposed in "The Resolution on Accelerating Science and Technology" by the Central Committee and the State Council in 1995, was a key plank to shore up the "three-step" strategy. It quickly won popularity. The Ninth Five-Year Plan made it clear that the successful transformation of mode of economic growth must be based on scientific progress, the enhancement of the quality of labor force, and an increase of scientific content in economic growth. The 15th CPC National Congress reiterated this strategy and regarded it as a strategic decision. Thus, this strategy was no longer confined to the development of science and education alone, but significantly promoted the transformation of the mode of economic growth.

3.3.3.3 *Sustainable Development and Regional Coordinated Development*

In the 1990s, the national development strategy shifted from disequilibrium to coordination, sustainable development and regional coordinated development were the reflections of this development path in the spatial and temporal dimensions.

Sustainable development, as a new development concept of pursuing equity between human and nature, between contemporary people, and between future generations, has evolved into a worldwide new development mode and strategy in the 1990s. As mentioned above, the State Council issued *China's Agenda 21*, building the framework of sustainable development. Together with the strategy of rejuvenating China through science and education, it was officially incorporated into the Ninth Five-Year Plan and became a basic national policy in 1995. Since then, governments at all levels have actively promoted this strategy in designing plans, issuing laws and regulations, publicizing policies, and calling for public participation. The departments and bureaus affiliated to the State Council respectively made plans of actions accordingly in education, science, and culture.

During the Eighth Five-Year Plan, in order to reverse the widening interregional differences caused by disequilibrium development, the state began to consider an adjustment of relevant policies and hence in the Ninth Five-Year Plan coordinating regional development and shortening interregional gap came to be the new guideline of socioeconomic development. Navigated by the new guideline, much attention was paid to the relatively underdeveloped western part of this country. In 1999, President Jiang Zemin stressed the need to seize the historical opportunities and speed up the opening up at a forum on the reform of the state-owned enterprises in the five provinces and autonomous regions (Sinkiang, Qinghai, Gansu, Ningxia, and Shaanxi) of Northwest China. By the 10th Five-Year Plan, the central government further proposed "Great Western Development Strategy" (GWDS) to facilitate coordinated development between regions. Accordingly, a series of fiscal and investment policies were issued to support this ambitious and challenging strategy.

3.3.3.4 *The Realization of the Goal of the Second Step and Existing Problems*

With the implementation of the Eighth and Ninth Five-Year Plans, China's national economy was in high gear. Particularly after Deng Xiaoping delivered his talk during his tour to Shenzhen and other major cities in South China in 1992, economic growth further accelerated and all indicators exceeded the planned targets (see Table 3.2). In 1995, China's gross domestic product (GDP) reached 5,847.8 billion yuan (current price), 4.3 times that of 1980 in comparable price, realizing goal of doubling GNP five years ahead of the schedule. By the end of 2000, China's GDP reached 8,822.8 billion yuan (current price), with per-capita being 7,084 yuan, 4.9 times that of 1980 in comparable price. In the meanwhile, people's livelihood had a leap forward from "adequate food and clothing" to "moderate prosperity." The China National Bureau of Statistics and other institutions used 16 indicators and their critical values in the five aspects of economic development, material life, population quality, spiritual life, and living environment to evaluate the real conditions of China's "moderately prosperous society": by the end of the 20th century, the overall average living standard of the Chinese people stepped into the initial stage of a moderately prosperous life. About 75% of them crossed the threshold of it, but 13% were in the vicinity of it and 12% had a long way to go (Xie and Wen, 2000: 42). The Fifth Plenary Session of the 15th CPC Central Committee in October 2000 officially proclaimed that China had already achieved the first two goals of modernization and that people's lives had by and large reached a well-to-do level.

However, the implementation of the development strategy was far from being satisfactory. For instance, during the Eighth Five-Year Plan, inflation with the retail price increasing at an annual rate of 11.4% seriously affected the improvement of people's living standards. Meanwhile, a spectrum of problems emerged such as irrational industrial structure, relatively backward agriculture, uncoordinated regional development, widening income gap, weak technological innovation capability, deficiency in resources like fresh water and crude oil, and deterioration of ecological environment.

Table 3.2   Socioeconomic Development in Eighth and Ninth Five-Year Plans

Five-Year Plans		AAGR (%)	AAGR of GIOV (%)	AAGR of GAOV (%)	Scale of Construction (billion)	AAGR of Total Salary Income of Employees (%)	AAGR of Peasants' per Capita Net Income (%)
Eighth Five-Year Plan (1991–1995)	Planned	6 (GNP)	6.5	3.5	2600	–	3.5
	Actual	12 (GNP)	17.8	4.1	4300	7.7	4.5
Ninth Five-Year Plan (1996–2000)	Planned	8 (GDP)	7.5	4	13,000	5	4
	Actual	8.6 (GDP)	10.2 (IVA)	3.5(AVA)	13,900	5.7	4.7

AAGR: annual average growth rate; GIOV: gross industrial output value; IVA: industrial value-added; AVA: agricultural value added.

Source: Yao (2003), Guo (1993) and Liu (2006).

3.3.4 The National Strategy Guided by the Scientific Outlook on Development (Since 2000)

3.3.4.1 *The Scientific Outlook on Development and the Strategic Goal of Building a Well-Off Society Comprehensively*

Since the 21st century, economic globalization has intensified, and a new wave of technological revolution has sparked further industrial adjustment around the world. Against such a backdrop, China ushered in a new era of building a well-off society in an all-round way. On the basis of the new "three-step" strategy, the 16th CPC National Congress in 2002 conceived of the strategic goal of the first half of the 21st century, especially that of the first two decades: "… to concentrate on building a well-off society of a higher standard in an all-round way to the benefit of well over one billion people in this period. … further develop the economy, improve democracy, advance science and education, enrich culture, foster social harmony and upgrade the texture of life for the people." It is thus evident that building a well-off society is a goal of public sharing of fruits of economic construction and of promoting all-round social progress.

After the 16th CPC National Congress, the Hu Jintao-led leadership thought over the relationships between nature, economy, and society and gradually formed a more farsighted and more comprehensive and systematic development concept. The Third Plenary Session of the 16th CPC Central Committee put forward a people-centered, comprehensive, sustainable Scientific Outlook on Development required of the coordination between urban and rural areas, between different regions, between social and economic development, between human and nature and between domestic development, and opening up to the outside world. The Fourth Plenary Session of the 16th CPC Central Committee put forward the idea of constructing a harmonious socialist society, viewing "harmony" as an essential attribute of socialism with Chinese characteristics. The proposal of the Scientific Outlook on Development and harmonious society broadens the connotations of development strategy and enriches approaches to development, providing a scientific guide for building a well-off society in an all-round way. Under the guidance of Scientific Outlook on Development, the 17th CPC National Congress put forward new requirements for building a well-off society in an all-round way: to quadruple the per capita GDP of 2000 by 2020 on the basis of optimizing structure, improving efficiency, reducing energy consumption, and protecting environment. It also put forward higher requirements in the aspects of socialist democracy, cultural construction, social undertakings and development of social undertakings, and ecological civilization.

The 10th and 11th Five-Year plans reflected the actual implementation of the Scientific Outlook on Development. The 10th Five-Year Plan centered on the betterment of people's livelihood, structural development, technological innovation, and coordinated development. The 11th Five-Year Plan focused on people-centered scientific development, stressing the innovation on development pattern and improvement of development quality. It also emphasized the construction of rural areas, interregional coordinated development, resource conservation, and environment protection high on the agenda and concerned itself with such livelihood issues as employment, education, and social security.

3.3.4.2 *Characteristics of the National Development Strategy Toward Maturity*

In the process of theoretical exploration and practical efforts over the past nearly four decades, China has gradually formed a new national development strategy navigated by the Scientific Outlook on Development. It has the following characteristics.

(1) *Comprehensiveness of Development Objectives*
The national development strategy not merely stresses economic growth, but also put social and human development high on the agenda. This increasingly mature strategy incorporates political institutions, cultural construction, and ecological civilization in its broader scope of objectives.

(2) *Coordination of Development Paths*
After years of incessant exploration on development strategy and summing up the experiences and drawbacks, China shifted from disequilibrium development to coordinated development and successfully solved the relations between regions, between countryside and cities, between

development speed and quality, and between economic growth and environment carrying capacity, advancing along the correct road of development.

(3) *Sureness of Each Step*

The national development strategy subdivided the ambitious objective into three steps, each of which is by no means an extravagant fancy, which can be demonstrated by the realization of the previous objectives ahead of schedule. With the passage of time, the central government substantiates and concretizes each strategic step by formulating 5-year plans and 10-year programs, thus providing a clear direction for each development stage.

3.3.4.3 *Effects of Implementing the National Development Strategy Since 21st Century*

The rapid development since the 21st century has attracted worldwide attention. The GDP maintained a relatively rapid yet stable growth rate and the income of both urban and rural residents increased significantly (see Table 3.3). Nevertheless, many problems remain unsolved. (1) Extensive economic growth mode has not changed fundamentally. Economic growth still depends to a large extent on high investment, high energy consumption, and high pollution, so quality and efficiency of growth have not improved significantly. (2) The contradiction between economic growth and utilization of resources and environment protection is still apparent. For instance, many of the economic and social indicators in the 10th Five-Year Plan have been successfully achieved ahead of schedule, but energy conservation and emission reduction missed the target. (3) The growth of peasants' income is slower than that of urban residents and binary urban–rural structure is obvious. The income ratio between urban and rural residents increased from 2.97:1 in 2000 to 3.22:1 in 2005 and 3.28:1 in 2006.[8] (4) The interregional gap continues to widen. Although West China and Northeast China achieved a quicker growth rate with the implementation of the GWDS and the strategy of revitalizing the old industrial bases, interregional gaps are still obvious. For instance, compared with 2000, the proportion of GDP in the 11 coastal provinces and municipalities increased from 57.7% to 65.4%, while the proportion of GD in Central China and West China declined accordingly.[9] (5) Social

Table 3.3 Socioeconomic Development in the 10th and 11th Five-Year Plans

Five-Year Plans			AAGR of GDP (%)	Ratio of R&D Inputs to GDP (%)	Changes of Emissions of Major Pollutants	AAGR of per Capita Income of Urban Residents (%)	AAGR of per Capita Income of Rural Residents (%)
Tenth Five-Year Plan (2001–2005)	Planned		6	1.5 (2005)	–10%	5	5
	Actual		9.5	1.3 (2005)	<–10%	9.6	5.3
Ninth Five-Year Plan (1996–2000)	Planned		7.3	2 (2010)	–10%	5	5
	Actual	2006	10.7	1.4	Increase	10.4	7.4
		2007	11.4	1.5	Slight decrease	12.2	9.5

development lags behind economic growth. For instance, in addition to deficiency in supplying public services and products such as education, medical and health, the management of public safety, transportation, and environment is relatively backward, and the pressure of employment is on the increase.

The contrast between the reality of development and the strategic objectives suggests that a sound strategy entails viable implementation. The key to the process from designing to practicing a concept lies in the match between operational institutions and policy system. For a country with more than one billion people to make a giant leap in living standards, it is inevitable to consume large amounts of natural resources and have an impact on environment. Besides, various institutional and policy problems have also emerged in the transition from planning economy to market economy. The negative effects of the market mechanism on the comprehensiveness, coordination, and sustainability of socioeconomic development are particularly worth a more insightful thinking.

REFERENCES

Dong, Fureng. *An Economic History of the People's Republic of China* (Vol. 1). Beijing: Economic Science Press, 1999. 董辅礽. 中华人民共和国经济史 (上卷). 北京: 经济科学出版社, 1999.

Guo, Zicheng. *A History of the PRC's Planning*. Shijiazhuang: Hebei People's Publishing House, 1993. 郭子诚. 中华人民共和国计划史,石家庄,河北人民出版社, 1993.

Lin, Yunhui. *The 40-Year Strategic Evolution of the New China: Successes and Failures*. Shenzhen: Haitian Publishing House, 1993. 林蕴辉. 新中国四十年发展战略的演变———风雨兼程. 深圳: 海天出版社, 1993.

Liu, Rui. *Socio-Economic Development Strategy and Planning: Theories, Practices and Cases*. Beijing: China Renmin University Press. 刘瑞:《社会经济发展战略与规划:理论、实践、案例》,北京,中国人民大学出版社, 2006.

Xie, Mingguang, and Jianwu Wen. *The Road to a Moderately Prosperous Society*. Beijing: China Statistics Press, 2000. 谢鸣光. 文兼武. 中国小康之路. 北京: 中国统计出版社, 2000.

Yao, Kaijian. *The Ten Five-Year Plans Reshaping China*. Beijing: China Economics Publishing House, 2003. 姚开建. 改变中国的十个"五年计划". 北京: 中国经济出版社, 2003.

NOTES

1. Translator's note: *On New Democracy* was written by Mao in January 1940 and later revised by Mao himself in 1952. It was first published in the first number of *Chinese Culture,* a magazine founded in January 1940 in Yen'an.

2. Translator's note: See *The Selected Works of Liu Shaoqi* (Vol. 1, p. 435), compiled by the Editorial Committee of the Party Literature. *The Common Programme*, approved and adopted by the first Plenary Session of Chinese People's Political Consultative Conference (CPPCC) in September 1949, was a *de facto* provisional constitution until it was replaced by the first Constitution of the PRC in 1954.

3. Ibid.

4. After liberation in 1949, the Communist China had Six Grand Districts, each of which geographically overlapped with what is now North East China, North China, North West China, South East China, East China, Central–South China.

5. Translator's note: See Sun Yatsen's *The International Development of China* (《建国方略》, *Jianguo Fanglue* in Chinese *pinyin*), New York and London: The Knickerboker Press in 1922.

6. See "The Press Communiqué of the Eleventh National Congress of the Communist Party of China," *People's Daily*, August 21, 1977.

7. Translator's note: With the deterioration of Sino–Soviet relations and a series of surveillance activities by United States unmanned scouts in the early 1960s, the central government launched a "third line" (*sanxian*) program of relocating industrial bases to hinterland from coastal areas (the first line) and central provinces (the second line) vulnerable to attack by missiles from the Soviet Union or the United States. This "third line" program, which guided the national capital investment and industrial development for more than a decade and finally ended in the late 1970s, resulted in the relocation of a large number of factories, workers, and their families into mountainous area in the hinterland.

8. These figures are calculated according to *China Economic Yearbooks* (2001–2010) and *The Statistical Bulletin of National Economy and Social Development (2006)*.

9. This figure is calculated according to *China Economic Yearbooks* (2006–2010).

Chapter 4

The National Economic Development Strategy in Xi's Era

China's quick rise from a small economy to a big one over the past four decades attracted the attention of the world. A good understanding of the process of the formulation and implementation of its national strategy development will discount such astonishment not only because it has been repeatedly demonstrated by the history of economic development that a rational and effective strategy, if other conditions are satisfied, can navigate its economy but also because China is resourceful in strategic designing. Kissinger (2011: 23), a sinologist who knows a few things about the Chinese wisdom remarked, "What was most remarkable about the Chinese approach to international affairs was less its monumental formal pretensions than its underlying strategic acumen and longevity." He made an impressive contrast between the Western and Chinese strategic thinking by using the strategies in chess and China's most enduring game *wei qi*, the former being about "decisive battle" and "total victory achieved by attrition or more rarely, a dramatic, skillful maneuver … a draw, meaning the abandonment of the hope for victory by both parties," while the latter about a "protracted campaign" with the objective of accumulating relative advantage by the "art of strategic encirclement." Kissinger's judgment was basically accurate and hence his thoughts are justified.

4.1 DENG'S THREE-STEP STRATEGY AND ITS PRESCRIPTION ON THE 100-YEAR DEVELOPMENT PATH

However, strategic thinking and wisdom are far from being enough, and what is more important is a rational strategy applicable to national development. Over the past four decades, China has basically followed the pragmatic three-step strategy designed by Deng Xiaoping, who had ever presided over the central government and attempted to push forward the four modernizations (of industry, agriculture, national defense, and science and technology) initiated by Zhou Enlai in 1964. Deng's strategic longevity transcended "four modernizations" that he had put forward during his meeting with a Japanese delegate, a strategy that was to be known as the "three-step" strategy in 1980, when the objective of economic reform had not yet been clearly formulated. Later, after research, supplementation, revision, and improvement by the think tank and academic circles, the "three-step" strategy, decomposed in accordance with the basic components of a national strategy, became clearer and more pragmatic. Its strategic guiding ideology was growth-centered economic construction and adherence to reforming and opening up to the "Four Basic Principles." According to its strategic goal, the per-capita gross national product (GNP) would reach US $800 and the economic aggregate would be quadrupled by the end of the 20th century. It also had set a "modernization" goal to build China into a moderately developed country. Its strategic focus was on energy, transportation, education, science, and technology. Its strategic steps were divided as follows: to double the GNP in the first and second 10 years in 1980 and 2000, respectively; by the middle of the 21st century, modernization would be by and large realized. Its strategic layout started with the coastal provinces and municipalities to allow some regions and some people get rich first and then help others get rich and finally achieve common prosperity. The strategic major measures were institutional reform, attraction of foreign investment, and the establishment of special economic zones. The "three-step" strategy endeavored to catch up with economically developed countries, so it was an overtaking disequilibrium strategy.

Deng's "three-step" strategy was a product of his astute evaluation of domestic economic situations and external strategic trends. On the basis of his judgment that China's economy would be in the primary stage of socialism for at least 100 years, the development strategy was designed into steps, each of which would be completed within at least 20 years. In addition, on the basis of his assertion that peace and development would be the two major irresistible historic trends and that U.S.–USSR hegemony and arms race would not lead to an all-out war, he resolutely made a bold decision to disarm one million troops in 1984, thus guaranteeing human resources and workforce for economic development.

To be fair, the historical opportunities for the "three-step" strategy were not favorable for China for the following two reasons: the great onset of the upheaval in eastern European socialist countries due to their failure in reform at the end of 1980s and early 1990s and the financial wobbles in neighboring countries such as South Korea and Thailand. Both political disturbances and financial crises slowed down the realization of the "three-step" strategy; however, the leadership never vacillated, but instead actively took measures to turn crises into opportunities and allowed full play to its own strengths and avoided weaknesses. More importantly, the "three-step" strategy specified a strategic guideline of "centering on economic construction" except for the condition that there was a foreign invasion. Though the policy makers did not use the formative Strengths, Weaknesses, Opportunities, and Threats (SWOT) method to analyze strategic situations when formulating this strategy, history showed that their initial judgment of external and internal situations was pertinent and accurate. The Chinese leadership was keenly aware that advanced nations, for saturated market and excessive funds, were willing to cooperate with such an emerging economy as China and that China also had its comparative cost advantage in international division of labor.

The objectives of the first two steps of the "three-step" strategy have been achieved by 2000. However, according to the changes of realistic situations, it was complemented by the Great Western Development Strategy (GWDS) and "going out" strategy for enterprises in Jiang's era. The GWDS was viewed as a bugle for the third step in that this continuity of the first two steps aimed to improve the livelihood of the people in the relatively backward Western provinces after the eastern coastal provinces made remarkable economic achievements. The strategic direction for the "three-step" strategy was to use external resources and attract foreign direct investment to promote China's economic strength. However, since the 1997 Asian financial crisis, China's economy had a turnabout from social overall shortage to surplus. Up to now, overcapacity remains to be a stubborn problem. The "going out" strategy was designed to find overseas markets for homemade household appliances and sought overseas energy and resource markets so as to maintain its domestic high-energy-consuming economic growth mode with a ready and steady source of supply. Perhaps the "going global" strategy was beyond the policy makers' expectation when they initially designed the "three-step" strategy. In this sense, it was innovative and originative. It was put forward at the turning point of the domestic economic operation, presaging the proposal of what is to be known as the Silk Road Economic Belt.

4.2 THE COMPONENTS OF PRESIDENT XI'S ECONOMIC DEVELOPMENT STRATEGY

In view of the characteristics of the Chinese political and economic systems, especially of the generations of its leadership, the strategy in each new generation is a continuity and further development of the predecessors. The "Great Western Development" and "Going-out" strategies in Jiang's era were followed by the Hu's Scientific Outlook on Development (SOD) strategy and Xi's economic development strategy.

The formation of Xi's economic strategy underwent a progressive process. Shortly after he was elected as president, Xi put forward the "Chinese Dream" to rejuvenate the Chinese nation. As he puts it, "The essence of Chinese dream is the prosperity of the country, rejuvenation of the Chinese nation and felicity of the Chinese people." It inherits Deng's strategy of realizing four forms of modernization and stresses the well-being of the country fellows; therefore, it considers the country, the nation, and each individual, making the goal of the "three-step" strategy more popular. As for the prosperity of the country, Xi urged to build China into a moderately prosperous country by the 100th anniversary of the founding of the Communist Party of China (2021) and build China into a modernized country by the 100th anniversary of the founding of the

People's Republic of China (2049). Obviously, the above two goals are more concrete and observable when compared with the "Chinese Dream."

The economic strategy crafted by President Xi can be dichotomized into domestic and foreign constituents. Domestically, new-type urbanization was inaugurated with the official publication of its overall plan in June 2014, followed up by the strategies of the Yangtze River Economic Belt and Beijing–Tianjin–Hebei Regional Synergetic Development (BTHRSD). The launch of the new-type urbanization is, to a large extent, to fill the vacancy of urbanization over the past three score years when too much emphasis was lavished on industrialization. Meanwhile, it is also conducive to jumpstarting a new round of economic upturn, and thus protecting China's economy from plunging into recession that has plagued the globe since 2008. The new-type urbanization proposes an all-round conception and a brand-new road map for the urbanization with Chinese characteristics, involving so wide a scope of undertakings that golden opportunities and formidable challenges coexist. Hence, for all the overall planning declared to the public in June 2014, no sign could be seen of the comprehensive implementation of this strategy even after half a year passed; instead, 64 cities and towns have been selected as pilots. It is evident that the strategy should be pushed forward in the logical order of overall planning, prudent promotion, and integrated support measures. As it is, the new-type urbanization not merely affords opportunities but also poses a myriad of challenges in utilization and conservation of land resources, construction, and supply of urban housing and the reform of household registration system as well as urban improvement in the aspects of environment protection, pollution abatement, infrastructure construction such as urban transportation, creation of jobs, industrial development, public facilities, construction investment, and cost-sharing of new city dwellers, to name just a few. Supposing urbanization is slated to increase urban population by an annual rate of 1%, that is, increasing, within the three decades to come, the current urbanization rate of 53% to the target of 75%, that is, the current level of advanced nations, this strategy is destined to be an engine for sustained and stable economic growth. As a systematic and dynamic project, this comprehensive, endogenous, and positive process of socioeconomic transition, evolution, and development will naturally sustain China's economic growth in the long run even if no other strategy is blueprinted for its prospects. This is why the Chinese leadership is optimistic about the prospects of its economic growth.

Both the Yangtze River Economic Belt and BTHRSD fall within regional development strategy. China had earlier created two developed regions, the Pearl (Zhu) River and the Yangtze River deltas. The subsequent Great Western Development and revitalization of northeastern old industrial bases greatly facilitated regional economic development. However, the Beijing–Tianjin–Hebei region is left far behind the Pearl River and the Yangtze River deltas due to its failure to form a relative regional advantage resulting from the cleavage of administrative and executive systems. Xi's speech on February 26, 2014, pushed the consensus on BTHRSD and expedited the overall planning, which is likely to become a new spotlight of China's regional economy. The Yangtze River Economic Belt strategy is a continuity and expansion of its Shanghai-centered delta economic circle (including Suzhou, Wuxi, and Hangzhou), radiating upstream along the world's third longest river (6300 km) to the China's hinterland and forming a regional economic belt, which combines the industry and value chains of the 11 provinces and municipalities in the Yangtze Valley.

Internationally, Xi's "Belt and Road" — the Silk Road Economic Belt and the 21st-Century Maritime Silk Road — is more innovative and originative than his domestic strategy. In September 2013, when addressing a speech at Nazarbayev University in Kazakhstan, Xi proposed a strategic initiative on the international connectivity of policy, infrastructure, trade flow, finance, and people. In October 2013, at a speech delivered to the Indonesian Congress, Xi proposed the concept of "the 21st-Century Maritime Silk Road," expressing China's willingness to strengthen maritime cooperation and develop partnership with ASEAN countries. At the Third Plenary Session of the 18th CPC Central Committee in November 2013, the Belt and Road was officially incorporated into "The Decision of the CCCPC on Some Major Issues Concerning Comprehensively Deepening Reform," which set the objective of "creating an all-round new pattern by establishing an open financial institution, speeding up the interconnection and construction of infrastructure with neighboring countries and regions, and promoting the construction of the Belt and Road." The implication of this strategy is to achieve the Chinese Dream through expanding commerce and heightening friendship and partnership with countries along with the ancient land and sea silk roads based on the principle of complementary advantages and win–win cooperation. Major steps have been taken for this strategy, such as the founding of the Asian Infrastructure Investment Bank (AIIB), the Silk Road Fund, the establishment of the free trade area with countries (regions) along the road and belt, and the promotion of RMB (*renminbi*) clearing.

The "Belt and Road," which cannot be simply viewed as an export-oriented strategy, contains far more strategic implications than Xi's trio of domestic strategy and will have a profound impact on world economy for its following strategic intentions.

First, it takes into consideration domestic and foreign economic development. Before 2000, China gave importance to domestic economic construction above everything else and its national development strategy was mainly concentrated on attracting foreign direct investment and technology, which is the reason why China's robust economic growth seemed to be aloof from such economic fluctuations as the Asian financial wobbles in 1997. However, after its entry into the World Trade Organization (WTO) in 2002, it could not be immune from global economic disturbances as it had before; what's more, its heavy reliance on world economy — mainly reflected in excessive manufacturing capacity, ever-increasing foreign exchange reserve, large quantities of imports of energy resources and industrial raw materials — spotlighted the issue of dealing with the relationships between domestic and foreign markets and between commerce and economy in its strategy designing. It was the economic globalization that necessitated the "going out" strategy for the Chinese enterprises, and its economic growth depends largely on joint development and utilization of the global markets. As early as in 2000, the "Going-out" strategy was first introduced, but it paled in comparison with the "Belt and Road."

Most countries along the belt and road are developing nations, many of which, especially Central Asian countries are abundant in energy and mineral resources. For instance, the workable reserves of Tengiz Oil Field in Kazakhstan rank Top 10 of the world; its demonstrated reserves amount to 4 billion tons, more than China's 3.2 billion tons. According to *A Guide to Investment in the Five Central Asian Countries* compiled by the Commerce Department of Shaanxi Province, the Central Asian nations Kazakhstan,

Uzbekistan, Turkmenistan, Kyrgyzstan, and Tajikistan are willing to make joint efforts with China to develop their abundant natural resources. These bonanzas bring large fortune for these countries and raise their country-men's income, thus forming an increasing demand for China-made com-modities. This complementary relation can stimulate the consumption level of Central Asian nations on the one hand and help solve China" manufacturing overcapacity and shortage of energy and natural resources on the other hand. Meanwhile, commercial and economic cooperation also helps renminbi clearing in this district.

Second, the Belt and Road realigns the countries or regions which ever had good relations in cultural and economic exchanges with China in history. The ancient Silk Road extended from Xi'an, China in the east to Turkey in the west and the ancient Maritime Silk Road from Fujian and Guangdong to many island countries and coastal regions of the Pacific and the Indian oceans, including Japan, Korea, and African east-ern coastal areas. It is obvious that China intends to incorporate the countries along the belt and road into a broader scope of cooperation. More than half of provinces, autonomous regions and municipalities from Sinkiang in the northwest to Guangdong in the southeast, from Heilongjiang in the northeast to Hubei in central China benefit from this strategy.

Historically, a community of interest formed between China and its neighboring countries or regions, but later it disintegrated with the collapse of the Chinese feudalist dynasties. Now, the rejuvenation of China brings an opportunity for the realignment of this community, a bloc involving not merely economic mutual progress but also cultural exchange and friend-ship enhancement. This strategic friendship is by no means an appeal for economic interest or an alignment of ideology, nor a relationship of tribute or protectorate, but one of mutual aid and complementation on the basis of equality and mutual benefit.

Finally, the Belt and Road is the first foreign-oriented choice made by China on its own initiative to adapt to its revival. For decades, China has been applying itself to its own internal affairs to raise its people's living standards, and even the "going out" strategy in the early 21st century was also centered on domestic demand rather than on overseas expansion as its name suggests. At the historical turn when early national strategies elevated China into the second largest economy of the world, would it continue to mind its own business or take the advantage of the opportunity to undertake the international responsibilities commensurate with its economic strength?

On the other hand, the United States, the only superpower that dominates the world, is showing its uneasiness about the revival of China. During his two terms in office, the former U.S. President Barack Obama declared a high-profile pivot to Asia and designed in succession the strategies of "Return to Asia-Pacific Region" and "Asia-Pacific Rebalance." The United States is pushing forward three "encirclements" to counter China. First comes strengthening its diplomatic ties with its "old allies" such as Japan, South Korea, Philippines, Singapore, Malaysia, and Thailand and establishing new ties with Vietnam and Burma. Second follows the introduction of regional economic and commercial cooperation zone, such as Trans-Pacific Partnership (TPP, sometimes vaunted by media as Economic North Atlantic Treaty Organization [NATO]).[1] Third, to the east of China, the United States has completed its military deployment and dominance on the First and Second Island Chains and decided to station 2500 marines in Australia, as President Obama puts it: "… stepping up its commitment to the entire Asia-Pacific."[2] To the west of China, the U.S. force has already penetrated into new spheres of influence such as Afghanistan and Pakistan in the name of counterterrorism and in October 2011 U.S. Secretary of State Hillary Clinton rolled out a new plan called "New Silk Road Initiative" in Central Asia. Nevertheless, the U.S. influence on South Asia and Central Asia is comparatively less significant than on the Asia-Pacific, West Asia, and Europe because it is constrained by Russia and some regional big powers like Iran and India. If China introduces its "rejuvenation" strategy in their spheres of influence, its strategic intent is likely to be thwarted, but there are legitimacy and justification for China to reestablish strategic cooperative relations with those countries that have had traditional interests in China throughout the history. China's westward and southward expansion will not spark a violent backlash from the United States and have more win–win opportunities with Russia and India. Obviously, it is prudent for China to choose the "Belt and Road" strategy to push forward its peaceful rejuvenation.

Xi's economic strategy is becoming more mature and sophisticated. Its basic contents can be summed up as follows:

(1) Guiding ideology: national prosperity, rejuvenation, and people's felicity in addition to the basic principles advocated in Deng's era.
(2) Strategic objectives: implementing the "moderate prosperity" program in a well-rounded way by the 100th anniversary of the founding of the Communist Party of China; and building China into a modernized socialist country by the 100th anniversary of the founding of the People's Republic of China.
(3) Strategic focuses: new-type urbanization and renewal of strategically new industries in Hu's era.
(4) Strategic layout: the Yangtze River Economic Belt; BTHRSD; the "Belt and Road."
(5) Strategic measures and means: deepening all-round reform; establishing pilot-free trade zones, AIIB, and the Silk Road Fund.

In accordance with the traditional classification of strategic paradigms and types, Xi's economic strategy is an overtaking one, but now it is much closer to equilibrium (Liu & Yu, 2011: 18–22). In its fundamental sense, an overtaking strategy is a "new normal" before the realization of the China Dream.

4.3 A SITUATIONAL ANALYSIS OF XI'S ECONOMIC STRATEGY: A NEW NORMAL

The designing of a judicious strategy must be preceded by a discreet situational analysis. The common analysis method uses a SWOT matrix combined with sequential analysis which reveals the internal and external factors — including SWOT — of the strategic object that is being studied. In general, a strategic type is thus accordingly determined by a four-dimensional sketch. However, a sagacious strategy is not under any circumstance a sketchy operation but an outcome of cool nerves, long-term observations, and expertise, including the wisdom of strategists and experts.

Xi's unique analysis and articulation in his speeches and works about the Chinese strategic situation are assigned a new term "new normal," currently a subject of intense curiosity in the economic community. Much has been discussed about its origin, but what is more important is the new strategic situational perspective it entails. Xi had earlier judged that China was to face three challenges of slowdown in economic growth, throes in structural adjustment, and cushion of previous radical stimulus packages, but this judgment has not been mentioned any more since his assertion of the "new normal."

The Central Economic Work Conference from December 9–11, 2014 held that China's economic development has the following new characteristics:

(1) In terms of consumption demand, "wave of emulative consumption" pattern (bandwagon consumption behavior) seems to have ended. Personalized and diversified consumption has gradually become the mainstream. More emphasis is laid on product quality and innovation.

(2) From the perspective of investment demand, after 30 years of high-intensity and large-scale development and construction, the traditional industries are relatively saturated. However, the infrastructure interconnection and exchange opportunities and investment opportunities in new technologies, products, industries, and business models will emerge.

(3) From the point of view of exports and the balance of payments, prior the 2008 financial crisis, China's international market expanded quickly and export became a chief engine for robust economic growth. Now the global total demand is insipid, but China's comparative advantage of low costs is changing and its export advantage remains. High-level importing and large-scale exporting occur simultaneously.

(4) In the aspect of production capacity and industrial organization, China used to be plagued by insufficiency of supply for so long, but now the supply capacity of traditional industries exceeds demand. Industrial structural optimization, merger and acquisition, relative concentration of production are inevitable. Emerging industries and services, and small and miniature firms are playing a more important role. Production miniaturization, intelligentization, and specialization will be more prominent.

(5)   From the relative advantages of factors of production, the advantage in low labor cost in the past could quickly transform imported know-how into productivity, but now the changes in the population and labor structure such as aging population, decrease in surplus agricultural labor, and in scale-driven force of factors shifted economic growth model to the improvement of capital quality and technological innovation.

(6)   The market competition has shifted from quantity and price competition to quality- and differentiation-based competition. A uniform national market and the improvement of resource allocation are endogenous requirements for economic development.

(7)   Environment has reached or is nearing the upper limit of its carrying capacity. A green, low-carbon, and sustainable environment should be created.

(8)   A variety of hidden risks gradually release along with economic slowdown. Risks can be managed on the whole, but it will take a long time to eradicate highly leveraged and bubbled risks.

(9)   Considering the resources allocation mode and macro-adjustment method, the marginal efficiency of overall stimulant policies is decreasing. China should address the problem of production overcapacity and explore the future direction of industries through the market mechanism.

The above trends indicate that China has entered a "new normal," a higher-level economic situation with more complicated division of labor and more reasonable structure: (1) the deceleration of economic growth from double-digit levels to medium–high rates; (2) the replacement of extensive growth based on the expansion of quantity of inputs by intensive growth based on quality and efficiency; (3) the shift of economic structural readjustment from incremental expansion to optimization; and (4) the shift of economic growth momentum from traditional to new sources of growth. Naturally, the next logical step of its economic growth is understanding and leading the new normal and adapting to the new normal.

The citations from the Central Economic Work Conference laconically express the analyses of the economic strategic trends by the Xi-led generation of leadership. These analyses include observable trends and evaluation of value based on assumptions. Basically, the division of an economy's developmental stage, which should follow strict scientific criteria and *ex post* data analyses, is within the province of an economic historian's expertise. History shows that an outstanding strategist must make a prompt yet resolute strategic decision because waiting means losing a good opportunity. Therefore, in the case of asymmetric and inadequate information, the current strategic situation analysis is to some extent subjective and risky.

What enchants economists is that China's regional economy differs so great that there will be a coexistence of local and national markets, a differentiated pattern that can be used by judicious market subjects to gain a comparative advantage. Economic risks exist in all periods and can be reduced only when they are perceived and prevented. In reality, real risks break out unknowingly and without precaution. When the U.S. subprime mortgage crisis broke out in 2008, few of the economics professors and Nobel Prize winners in economics could issue a warning against this disastrous economic event that was no less serious than the Great Depression in 1929–1933. What are the economic risks in current China and how serious will they be if any? These questions require further discussion and verification.

Another two points must be stressed here about China's current economic situation. First, an attempt to prove that China would follow the tracks of Japan and South Korea and end its high-speed growth disregards the dissimilarities between the countries. As a matter of fact, both Japan and South Korea revived their economy after the end of the mid-1970s oil crisis, but did not continue for long. Japan's fall into a prolonged economic slump should be attributed to the outbreak of the internal structural crisis as a result of the failure of the governmental interventional policy in the early 1990s, while the subsequent remedial actions seemed to be of little avail. The application of filtering method and production function to forecasting China's potential economic growth rate revealed that annual rate would still be as high as 8%–10% on the condition that bloated production of traditional industries could be dissolved. Second, individualization and diversification of consumption, as well as the specialization, miniaturization, and intelligentization of production, have not yet become popular in the developed economies. According to Marsh (2012), manufacturing has entered the fifth stage, that is, "mass personalization," which roughly started in 2000 from Paris-based Essilor, the world's biggest maker of spectacle lenses. Marsh declared, "When 3D printing techniques become an everyday part of manufacturing, mass personalization will truly have come of age." Just as agricultural, industrial, and information economies coexist for long in China, so do standardized mass production and mass personalization in manufacturing. The triad structure or pluralistic structure of China's economy is perhaps the real "new normal."

A dynamic rather than static judgment should be made about the strategic situation that China's economy will face in the future. As mentioned earlier, the judgment is unavoidably a synthesis of objective observations and subjective assumptions due to information asymmetry and inadequacy. Chen Yun, an exceptional economic advisor directly involved in the details of planning and construction of the national strategy adopted by Deng, warned that a strategist was not supposed to deify book knowledge and authoritative ideas as unchallengeable dogmas but act in accordance with the reality.[3] It is more difficult yet more influential to make a judicious judgment about strategic situation than to introduce and formulate a strategic move, and therefore repeated observations, analyses, and refinements are required. The more incisive an understanding and analysis of a strategy is, the more feasible and pragmatic program can be formulated.

So far in the Chinese intellectual circles, much more has been discussed about the opportunities than about threats; but on the contrary, tremendous difficulties are always beyond expectation. Take the "Belt and Road" as an example.

First, among the countries and regions along the belt and road, some are friendly but others are alert to China. The U.S. allies along the belt and road have internalized China's advocacy of win–win cooperation, but acted very passively under the influence of the United States. For instance, South Korea had ever had much interest in the AIIB, but eventually did not participate in the founding of it under the pressure from the United States.

Second, both ISIS (Islamic States of Iraq and alShams) terrorists and Somali pirates are rampant along the land and marine routes of the belt and road, which will inevitably increase the cost of strategic promotion and even temporarily delay its process.

Third, political instability, civil disturbance, and frequent reshuffles of governments or cabinets stirred by color revolution in some countries or regions increase the uncertainty of the implementation of strategic agreements.

Fourth, never-ceasing conflicts between different religious sects, especially among Muslims in the countries and regions along the land routes that run through Central Asia, Middle East to Turkey make it more difficult to deal with the religious relations with them and to win understanding of support for the strategy.

Fifth, remote distance is also one of the unfavorable factors. A contemporary economic strategy requires all-round cooperation and economic globalization intensifies butterfly effect.

Sixth, the "Belt and Road" is posterior to the U.S. "New Silk Road" and some countries have been incorporated into its sphere of influence. How to avoid conflict with the United States is a key and sensitive issue.

Besides overall economic planning, diplomatic, and military strategies should also be complemented to guarantee the smooth promotion of the "Belt and Road" abroad. For China, diplomatic means should always be preferable over military actions. Economic prosperity mainly buttressed by peaceful diplomatic means and supplemented by military instruments should be the basic principle of the promotion of the "Belt and Road" strategy.

REFERENCES

Dong, Fureng. *An Economic History of the People's Republic of China* (Vol. 1). Beijing: Economic Science Press, 1999. 董辅礽. 中华人民共和国经济史 (上卷). 北京: 经济科学出版社, 1999.

Kissinger, Henry. *On China*. New York: The Penguin Press, 2011.

Marsh, Peter. *The New Industrial Revolution: Consumers, Globalization and the End of Mass Production*. New Haven and London: Yale University Press, 2012.

Yerkin, Daniel. *The Quest: Energy, Security and the Remaking of the Modern World*. New York: Penguin Press, 2011.

NOTES

1. Translator's note: On January 4, the U.S. President Donald Trump declared formal withdrawal from TPP. And soon the Office of the U.S. Trade Representative (USTR) issued a letter to signatories of the TPP Agreement, emphasizing the commitment of the United States to free and fair trade, and encourages future discussions on "measures designed to promote more efficient markets and higher levels of economic growth." See https://ustr.gov/trade-agreements/free-trade-agreements/trans-pacific-partnership (accessed February 6, 2018.)
2. "Obama: More US Troops to Be Stationed in Australia," *BBC News*, November 6, 2011. http://www.bbc.com/news/av/world-asia-15755253/obama-more-us-troops-to-be-stationed-in-australia (accessed February 6, 2018).
3. Translator's note: See "News of the Communist Party of China." http://cpc.people.com.cn/GB/34136/2543702.html (accessed February 10, 2018).

Chapter 5

A Historical Review of National Planning Management

It is much easier to question or doubt a historical event retroactively. However, it is impossible to have *a priori* design for the road map of national planning management; the process of China's economic transformation was much alike to what Deng Xiaoping puts it as "wading across a river by feeling the pebbles at its bottom." Therefore, the national plan over the past decades is the outcome of the interaction between theory and practice. In other words, the incidental drawbacks in the practice of the planning management prompt doubts and revisions and improvements of the planning theory. The reform of China's planned management can be divided into two phases: the exploration phase from 1978 to 1991 and the maturity phase from 1992 up to now.

5.1 THE FIRST PHASE: FROM MANDATORY PLANS TO GUIDING PLANS

Since the establishment of the basic line of "one central task and two basic points" by the Third Plenary Session of the 11th CPC Central Committee in 1978, China has entered a stage of large-scale economic construction. However, as to the question of what kind of management system should be determined as the cornerstone to promote economic construction, most intellectuals still theoretically insisted on restoring planned management for the following two reasons. One was the stereotypical idea deeply influenced by dogmatic Soviet economic theory that planning economy was the basic characteristics of socialist economy and the other was the restoration of seriously damaged planning economy, a most important part of the political campaign of "bringing order out of chaos" shortly after the end of the Great Cultural Revolution. At that time, adhering to and improving the planning economy was theoretically correct as well as practically necessary.

Nevertheless, the ideological emancipation upsurge in the early period of reform and opening up freed the theoretical community from this rigid idea. They have come to a consensus that China's socialist economy is still in its primary state where the overriding task is to develop its commodity economy that at any rate requires the establishment and development of exchange relationships, which, alongside with places, constitute a generic term — market. Since then, the central government has heightened the legitimacy of commodity economy and market while keeping and improving planning economy.

5.1.1 Unity of Planning and Commodity

The pre-reform academic theorists agreed that socialist economy was a planning economy on the basis of public ownership, but they had different opinions about the issue of commodity: Is commodity economy only an attribute to socialist economy or is it equated with socialist economy? (Jinglian, 1993).

The Third Plenary Session of the 12th CPC Central Committee in 1984 issued the first milestone document of China's economic transformation, "The Decision of the Central Committee of the CPC on Economic Restructuring," asserting: "On the whole, China is implementing a planning economy, i.e., a planned commodity economy rather than a market economy that is completely regulated by the market." A consensus of the unity of planning and commodity gradually came into being: commodity production and exchange continue to exist under socialist system; a socialist economy is a planning economy with commodity relations, or a planning economy with market mechanism; a socialist economy is a unity of planning economy and commodity economy (Hong, 1990). The theoretic cognizance at that time failed to realize that market economy should also be regarded as something of socialism.

The consensus directly led to a theoretical "by-product," an idea that planning should be emancipated from institutional attributes and that planning is only a form of management (Guoguang, 1990). The decoupling of planning and institutional attributes activated the theoretical community to view planning as they do with technical means and management methods without being ideologically shackled.

5.1.2 Combination Forms of Planning and Market

The theoretical community, whatever their attitude toward socialist planning and commodity, almost unanimously agreed that the two regulation methods should be coupled to serve for socialist economy. Nevertheless, as to the question of how the two are coupled, economists held different opinions such as plate-type, penetrative, colloidal, and macro–micro combinations as well as second regulation and primary–secondary function.

Proponents of plate-type combination proposed that national economy be divided into different sectors or products, some of which were regulated by plans and the others by the market. For instance, some products vital to the national well-being and people's livelihood were regulated by the plan (in other words, production, price, and allocation of these products were unitarily planned by the nation) but other products by the market. A dissimilar view is that plate-type combination was only a rudimentary form since plan and market were inseparably interpenetrative and jointly contributive to the economic process. This view was based on the understanding that the plan could not be readjusted without drawing on the law of value of the market, and the direction of market regulation could not be ensured without a plan (Wang *et al.*, 1991). This is otherwise called a penetrative combination.

Advocates of colloidal combination argued that once the two mechanisms were glued as a whole, national economy could no longer be divided into market and plan, and the unity played its role as a market mechanism under the guidance of the unified national plan (Guoguang, 1986).

From the angle of the regulation mechanism of socialist economy, some theorists, while stressing that planning economy is one of the characteristics of socialist economy at the institutional level, argued that plan and market were both equally functional and effective means of allocation of resources at the operational level and that whichever was preferred over the other as a major regulation mechanism depending on the changes of economic conditions. Adherents of the macro–micro combination theory believed that the most ideal economic model in the primary stage of socialism was dual: improving macro-control through the national plan and invigorating micro-economy through market regulation. In other words, plan played a role mainly in the domains of macro-control, total quantity control, structural adjustment, and economic layout, but market played a role mainly in the microeconomic field, daily production, and management activities (Liqun *et al.*, 1994). A similar view is the second regulation theory, which argued that economic activities should be freely regulated by the market without any slightest government intervention, which proved to be necessary if and only the market regulation failed to meet the expected goals. The government intervention, if any, was called second regulation, an *ex ante* or *ex post* regulation. Market and plan should be both viewed as two levels of regulation, the latter being higher than the former (Li, 1993).

Advocates of the primary–secondary function theory, another main-stream of thought, held three different opinions as to the question which, of market and plan, played a primary role in socialist economy. The first view believed that plan played a primary role while market a secondary role. This view, derivative from planned economic theory, maintained that China's economic base determined plan-focused economic operation just as capitalist countries' economic base determined the market-oriented economic operation (Guoguang *et al.*, 1991). The second view argued that market and plan were equally important in regulating economy from the perspective that plan regulation was motivated by market mechanism, while market regulation was guided by plans (Tao, 1991). The third view argued that whatever role market or plan plays, primary or secondary, were not always invariable because it changed with the changes of space, time, and other conditions (Hong, 1990).

The improvement in theoretical understanding encouraged bold explorations of the practice of national planning management, such as "replacing governmental appropriations by loans" in the capital construction project, shifting from mandatory plans to guiding plans, and specially designing central cities and large state-owned enterprises in the national economic plan. The "Provisional Regulations on the Improvement of the Planned

System" approved by the State Council on October 4, 1984, was of monumental significance because in accordance with this document, China's national plan management system was divided into mandatory plans and guiding plans for the first time.

For a long time, the state planning agencies adopted administrative measures to allocate resources among departments; localities; and enterprises, and mandatory plans almost covered all aspects of the national economy. Vertically, from the top central planning agency, through intermediate departmental and local planning offices down to the bottom enterprises, what, how much, and for whom does an enterprise produces had been determined by mandatory plans. Horizontally, mandatory plans directed nearly all activities such as production, distribution, circulation, and consumption, severely limiting the regulatory role of the market. The national economic plan in that historical period had the following defining characteristics: mandatory, physical management centered, hard-and-fast, and inclusive of all.

However, the practice over the past three decades has proved that it is one-sided to interpret planning economy as merely mandatory. As a matter of fact, it was impossible and unnecessary to manage all economic activities through mandatory plans. In addition to mandatory plans vital to the national well-being and people's livelihood, it was preferable that guiding plans be used for a large number of general economic activities. For this sake, the "Provisional Regulations on the Improvement of the Planned System" put forward 12 reform measures, the heart and soul of which was to narrow the scope of mandatory plans and expansion of guiding plans.

A guiding plan is considered to be "a guiding opinion on the economic activities of the planning executive unit, and a plan mainly using economic leverage to ensure the realization of its objectives" (Liqun and Zhiguo, 1984). The design ideas of it are as follows. First, the central government or the department concerned sets relevant planning indicators or objectives for an enterprise only for reference, not mandatory. Second, the central government used economic leverages such as price, tax, and credit to achieve planning indicators. Third, the guiding plan covered a wide scope of industries and products, but excluded key industries and products. Take for instance the industrial products under the

Table 5.1   Changes of the Products Mandatorily Planned by the State Planning Commission

Year	Products (Categories)	Percentage in the Total Output Value of Industrial Products (%)
1980	120	40
1982	160	20
1992	59	11.7
1993	36	6.8
1994	33	4.5

charge of the State Planning Commission (the predecessor of the National Development and Reform Commission), the categories of mandatory planned products dropped from 120 in 1980 to 59 in 1992. Correspondingly, the proportion of total output value of industrial products controlled by the mandatory plan also dropped sharply from 40% to 11.7% in the same period (see Table 5.1).

There had always been a theoretical disagreement in whether the guiding plan fell within planning regulation or market regulation. Guoguang (1986) argued that the guiding plan was a planning regulation that mainly achieved objectives through market mechanisms. Li (1985) argued that the guiding plan in essence was a market regulation because it, as a plan not binding on the grassroots planning units, only achieved regulation through economic leverages to alter the economic macro-environment and had only indirect effect on the behavior of the microeconomic entities.

Nevertheless, the guiding plan encountered many problems in practice. First, because the guiding plan stressed non-mandate, those enterprises that had long been accustomed to the mandatory plan held a contemptuous attitude toward the guiding plan instead of feeling lucky to have removed the administrative shackles of the mandatory plan. Hence, the guiding plan became something that was dispensable. Second, a problem arose as to who was responsible for the realization of the role as a guide that the guiding plan was designed to play because it was administratively non-mandatory despite deriving from the mandatory plan and remaining almost unchanged in the process of its compilation and implementation.

Third, the difficulty coefficient of planning coordination increased without improving its effect correspondingly because it inevitably was linked to other macro-control institutions such as banking, finance, and taxation due to its emphasis of using economic leverages. Fourth, the guiding plan was de facto mandatory plan because the officials of some enterprises still place more emphasis on planned indicators that seemingly mattered too much to them (Lv, Wei, and Rui, 1992).

The introduction of the guiding plan was, to some degree, a rewarding attempt to reform the traditional planned economic system in the early period of reform and opening up. Theoretically, it reflected the combination of planning and market and practically, it broke through the pattern of the unitarily and mandatorily planning economy. However, it had obvious limitations. First, there was no obvious difference between the guiding plan and the mandatory plan because the former was still designed in the framework of adherence to planned economic system in practice, and hence tingled with the characteristics of the mandatory plan. Second, a narrow understanding of the attributes of the guiding plan misled the practice of it. The theoretical cognition of the guiding plan partly came from the experience of some foreign countries such as France and South Korea. Both of the two market economies achieved satisfactory effects in their plan management because they paid much attention to the guiding role of their plan on the market and enterprises and had no mandatory plan. By contrast, when designing plans, China's central planning management agency divided plans into guiding and mandatory plans, which not only increased the difficulty of the coordination but also intensified the conflict between the general understanding of guidance of the plan and the practice of dividing the plan into two parallel components. Such a dilemma was overcome with the interaction between theory and practice in the second phase: from plan management to macro-control.

5.2 THE SECOND PHASE: FROM PLAN MANAGEMENT TO MACRO CONTROL

Due to the confinement in dogmatic study of Marxist classic works and the Soviet economic model, the failure to transcend planning economy in the theoretical community resulted in a poor understanding of the essence of the socialist economy and the stagnation of the plan management reform for a time. It was Deng who solved the dilemma. As early as in the middle of the first stage of reform and opening up (1987), he asserted that "planning economy is not equal to socialism what market economy is not equal to capitalism" (Deng, 1993). In 1992, he restated this assertion in one of his speeches during his inspection tour to South China, unfettering ideological imprisonment and prompting a giant leap in the understanding of the relations between planning and market in the following aspects.

5.2.1 Planning Economy and Market Economy

Since the 14th CPC National Congress, planning economy and market economy have been no longer viewed as the basic social system, but as a concept reflecting the allocation of resources and economic operation. Any country, be it capitalist or socialist, can use planning and market to allocate resources.

In its narrow sense, planning economy is a means of allocating economic resources whereby the central government uses mandatory indicators to arrange economic activities via administrative instruments, that is, via the planning and management agencies at all levels. This is also called command economy in the West. In its broad sense, planning economy is a socioeconomic operational mode whereby the central government regulates the economy by the administrative command of the mandatory plan and the economic adjustment means of the guiding plan.

Generally, market economy is an economic means of the allocation of resources on the basis of market mechanism, but in the context of modern socialized large-scale production, market economy is on no account a laissez-faire economy, but a market economy regulated and managed by the state.

5.2.2 The Necessity of Plan Management in Socialist Market Economy

Although the market plays a positive role, it is generally believed that it also has a series of drawbacks that cannot be fixed on its own, such as the negligence of social interests, blind production, and excessive disparity in income. All of these deviations can only be settled through plan guidance and macro control. Plans and markets have their own strengths and weaknesses, so it is unrealistic to pursue only one but neglect the other. China should, by fostering strengths and circumventing weaknesses, explore a fair economic system that is suitable for its own national conditions to ensure a high level of market operation and satisfy the majority of its people.

5.2.3 Views on the Relationships between Market and Plan

The views on the relationships between the market and the plan varied. Liqun (1994) asserted that the key to the intrinsic integration of the plan and the market was planned marketization and marketized planning, both mutually inseparable and complementary. Under the condition of the socialist market economy, the plan management was supposed to achieve monist regulation of the market standard on the basis of the market mechanism. The function of the plan was no longer to replace, but to guide and regulate the market and the plan, which was designed to act on the macroeconomy, must be based on the basis of accurate prediction of the macroeconomic environment and the trend of the changes in supply and demand of the market. The function of the market was to regulate the operation and production activities and the state macro control included planning regulation, which mainly aimed at adjusting the percentages of macroeconomy, industrial structure, productivity layout, major projects, and some other deviations in the market. Another view held that planned activities may inadvertently cause negative and uncertain consequences, and thus could be referred to as planned blindness, while unplanned spontaneous activities may also unconsciously produce positive and satisfactory results, and thus could be referred to as unplanned planning. Therefore, the plan and the market were functionally and complimentarily combined without the distinction of being primary and secondary, or superior and inferior. The combination of the two is a scientific attitude toward uncertainties.

5.2.4 Macro Control

The concept of macro control, though introduced as early as in the first stage of reform and opening up, was not a hot issue when planning agencies and the theoretical community were fully concerned about the relationship between the plan and the market, a topic that would become too narrow with the establishment of the goal of the socialist market economic system. The intensity of its research can be revealed from Table 5.2 and Figure 5.1, which clearly show us two upsurges in the discussion of it, the first being between 1994 and 1996 during which the focus was on how to avoid economic imbalances and integrate macro control with the plan and the market amid the weakening of the function of plan management, the second being between 2004 and 2005, during which macro control replaced the dominant position of the state planning management.

Table 5.2 Academic Papers Concerning Macro Control and Macroeconomic Regulations

Year	1986	1987	1988	1989	1990	1991	1992	1993	1994	1995
Number	1	2	9	33	26	33	33	133	986	647
Year	1996	1997	1998	1999	2000	2001	2002	2003	2004	2005
Number	519	370	290	274	196	164	165	159	815	555

Source: Tsinghua Tongfang Full Text Academic Dissertation Database.

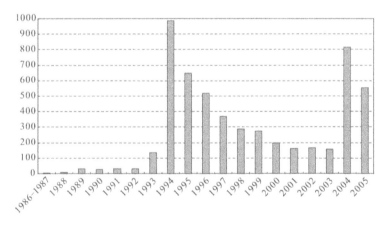

Figure 5.1 Academic Papers Concerning Macro Control and Macroeconomic Regulations

All over the world, planning management exists only in a few market economies, whereas macroeconomic management prevails in many of them. Therefore, it is no wonder that macro control gradually appealed to the attention of the economic intellectuals after the 14th National Congress of the CPC. Initially, macro control was interpreted as planning management in its broad sense merely for the convenience of differentiating it from a narrowly-defined mandatory plan. It came to be viewed as a core proposition in the broad sense of planning management inclusive of not only planning but also of fiscal, monetary, and land policies that were previously neglected in the governmental management. Theoretically, the traditional indirect management based on administrative mandatory plans should be shifted to indirect, diversified, and systematized macro control. In practice, the designers of guiding plans failed to free themselves from the framework of mandatory plans even after the introduction of economic means and economic leverages to achieve the planned goals. Under the condition of a socialist market economy, it was necessary to establish and perfect a macro control system combining plans and policies. Thus, due to a fundamental understanding of guiding plans in the first phase, macro control naturally became the theme of research in the second phase. The replacement of the issue about the relationship between plan and market by the issue about the relationship between macro control and market marked the formation of socialist market economic system.

This replacement took place in the period of preparing the Ninth Five-Year Plan for National Economic and Social Development when the central government proposed that national planning should reflect its macro-, strategy-, and policy-related nature, and the basic requirements of developing a socialist market economy. Specifically, the national plan was supposed to "lay emphasis on the fundamental role that the market plays in the allocation of resources under the national macro control, . . . allow full play to the superiority of socialism in concentrating its strength on ambitious projects. In general, the plan indicators are supposed to be predictive and directive, focusing on the orientation, tasks and corresponding strategies related to socio-economic development and on the aggregate indicators that reflect structural change, major projects of overall significance. Other indicators and projects will be arranged in the forthcoming annual plan" (Li, 1996).

This change in the concept and nature of planning laid a solid foundation for future reform of national planning management.

Thus, the national plan under the socialist market economy came of age. First, the national plan was generally of guidance. Medium- and long-term plans were sketchy (not all-inclusive and exhaustive) and flexible (allowing for fluctuation within a limited range), forming a striking contrast with guiding and mandatory plans in the period of planning economy. Second, the national plan was macroscopic. It highlighted macroeconomic means and overall national economic landscape and interests, differentiating itself from the all-inclusive plans containing specific details. Third, the national plan was strategic. In other words, the national plan was synchronized with national development strategy. The compilation of medium- and long-term plans was practically to design a strategy, quite different from the decoupling of national plan and development strategy. Fourth, the national plan was well-coordinated with national policies. As the guarantor of the attainment of a planned goal, the national policy in the context of socialist market economy, unlike the national plan decoupled from macroeconomic policies in the period of planning economy, was incorporated into the compilation of the national plan.

Due to the efforts in the transformation of a planning economy to a market economy from the beginning of the Ninth Five-Year Plan to throughout the 10th Five-Year Plan, the national plan became increasingly supportive of market economy. Thus, during the 11th Five-Year Plan, the medium- and long-term plans were morphed into medium- and long-term "programming," indicating a pro forma transition from a planning economy to a market economy. Simultaneously, the institutions in charge of planning management have gradually evolved from the National Planning Commission (before 1998) to the National Development Planning Commission (before 2003) to the National Development and Reform Commission (since 2003). Now, in the situational context of Chinese economic development, 规划 (guīhuà in Chinese pinyin, program, or programming) is a more frequent and popular term than its synonym 计划 (jìhuà in Chinese pinyin, plan, or planning), which is now strictly limited in some special cases, although the latter is still widely acceptable in many English versions of academic papers and monographs and journalistic reports on China's economy.

5.3 SUMMARY: INSPIRATION FROM THE HISTORICAL TRANSFORMATION OF NATIONAL DEVELOPMENT PLANNING

Having experienced progressive transformation for decades, China has by and large completed the transition from planned to market economic system. It is now in a steady phase in which institutional innovations, though necessary and constant, are comparatively technical and designed for making it mature. Basically, China has completed large-scale institutional innovations (or transition). Accordingly, after experiencing two phases of interaction between practice and theory, China has also completed the transformation in national economy from the overall planned management to macro control. A management system of national economy with Chinese characteristics came into existence.

Against this backdrop, exploring and improving the planning theory and system of the socialist market economy naturally became the major task of the next development stage, which was designed to change the concept of planning, establish the principle of spatial balance, define the field of planning, straighten out the intra-planning relationship, innovate on implementation institution, expand democratic participation, strengthen planning linkages, clarify decision-making bodies, and accelerate the process of legislation of planning (Yang, 2003).

It must be clearly understood that, in the process of exploring national planning theory and practice under the condition of socialist market system, the achievements in the decades of reform have always been the outcome of the interaction between practice and theory. China did not merely design national economic management on the basis of the theory, but also put a premium on practice. Likewise, China did not merely learn from foreign countries about how to manage market economy but also put a premium on gaining experience from its own practice in the formation and development of market economy.

The following points are noteworthy in the evolution of the transformation from state planning management to macro control.

First, it is still necessary and feasible for China to partly maintain planning and programming management because it still has the basic conditions necessary for planning economy. According to conventional wisdom, state planning management entails three factors: socialized mass production, public ownership of means of production, and the proletarian dictatorship, especially the governance of the Communist Party of China (Li, 1983). Though the reform and opening up over the past three decades have witnessed its achievement of transition from planning to market economy, including the changes of the conditions for implementing state planning management, socialist market economy is still generally operated under the triple conditions of the deepening of socialized mass production, the continuing dominance of public-owned economy, and the ruling of the Communist Party of China.

Meanwhile, unlike what has happened in capitalist market economic countries, defects inherent to the market economy in China necessitates national planning. Some capitalist market economic countries, such as Japan, Korea, and France, promoted national planning economy vigorously and set up a state-planned management department responsible for successive and regular medium- and long-term planning, which, however, was reduced and finally abandoned with the impact of neoliberal ideology. The abandonment, as a matter of fact, was almost equivalent to a loss of counterbalance mechanism, which could be proved by subsequent economic recessions or crises in those countries. Therefore, China should continue to adhere to state planning for a long period of time before market economy comes of age someday in the future.

Second, state planning plays a leading role in the macro control system. For decades, the result of economic transformation is the replacement of planning management by macro control as the main form of national economic management. Some Chinese scholars and officials, having gained some experience from the American model of macroeconomic management, seem to be convinced by the magical power of macroeconomic policies and hence abandon planning, but history shows that simply mimicking macro control is far from satisfactory. In the case of a limited role of macro control and an effective role of planning, why should the former be preferred over the latter in China?

Furthermore, unlike the administratively mandatory planning in the period of planning economy, state planning has altered its role greatly in the course of practice and now serves as an economic charter, which helps to realize coordinated socioeconomic development and solve the double dysfunctions of market and government (Liu *et al.*, 2006). Therefore, planning is on no account a dispensable gimmick, but instead, a fundamental means whereby macroeconomic and other specific policies are formulated and issued. It should be noted that planning under market economy is policy oriented; in other words, it is a set of a spectrum of related policies.

Third, China should continue to lay stress on the comprehensive equilibrium principle and its methodology deriving from the planning theory proposed by Chen Yun, an exceptional economic theorist who had an indelible contribution to planning economy. An adherent to the nature of planning of socialist economy, Chen insisted that it was the productivity that decided that planning should be coupled with market regulation notwithstanding it was part and parcel of China's national economy and that any planning, mandatory or directive, should obey economic rules. Until now, Chen's theory is still a macro-control theory with Chinese characteristics and its brilliance does not fade away with the transformation of economic system, but enlightens the current research and exploration of planning theory.

The comprehensive equilibrium theory emphasizes the principle of Four Equilibria, namely the balance between finance, banking, goods and materials, and foreign exchange. Though altered under the socialist economy, this principle still maintains its spirit and plays a great role in coordinating and integrating major relationships within national economy, such as compiling a comprehensive plan for financial credit that includes budgetary and extra-budgetary funds and bank credit capital in specific accounting plan and preparing a balance sheet of materials and supplies to keep a certain proportion between circulation and storage. The Scientific Outlook on Development emphasizes the Five Coordinated Relations, namely economy–society, rural–urban, interregional, human nature, domestic–foreign relations. Thus, the orientation for the subsequent improvement of planning management should be the establishment of the Five Coordinated Relations that match well with the Four Equilibria.

Fourth, China should base its compilation of economic plans on economic predictions in a scientific and systematic manner. According to Marxist economic theory, the function of economic plan is reflected not merely in the rational use of labor force but also in economizing on time, improving efficiency and increasing social wealth. In developed market economies, economic planning can also be reflected in the expectations of removing uncertainty and ensuring stability and in avoidance of negative effects of fiscal and monetary policies to achieve steady growth and efficient investment. In the context of a market economy, the government serves as a vindicator to protect the rights of the enterprises and individuals involved in market activities, and state planning provides a relatively steady expectation for market subjects, helping those subjects who are well-informed of market environment and latest developments readjust their economic behaviors more rationally.

Therefore, it requires us, when making economic plans or programs, to foresee the prospect of the future. Prediction is becoming even more significant in the age of globalization when a growing number of factors and uncertainties influence socioeconomic development. In the past, planning in market economies was likened to a weather forecast without substantial influence, but now both capitalist and socialist market economies can never be too prudent in predicting the future when planning.

Fifthly, macro control needs improvement. In the era of market economy, the subject of discussion about overall management is no longer planned management but macro control, but the latter has not completely replaced the former. On the one hand, due to the existence of the medium- and long-term planning management and short-term planning, there still exists a poor understanding of the relationship between macro control and planning; on the other hand, with the furtherance of macro control, its understanding is also dynamic.

Historically, China underwent six periods of macro control, including: (1) 1979–1981 national economy readjustment, focusing on the readjustment in economic structure by executive orders; (2) 1986 economic soft landing, attempting to use economic leverage to prevent economic overheating; (3) 1989–1992 governance and rectification, focusing on anti-inflation by various austerity means with administrative ones as the major instruments; (4) 1994–1996 soft landing, focusing on anti-inflation by more austerity means; (5) 1998–2000 stagnation-proof measures, focusing on anti-deflation by expansionary fiscal policies; (6) macro control since 2004, focusing on anti-overheating and anti-overcapacity by a combinational method of credit crunch (stringent fiscal and monetary policies) and strict land policy. Although the goal of macro control has changed over a long period of time — such as the 2004–2006 anti-overcapacity and the 2007–2008 anti-overheating and anti-inflation, it is much more like a temporary intervention against the fluctuation in market economy. Hence, whether macro control is a normal act in national economic management is still a controversial question.

It must be reiterated that the national economic management in a market economy is divided into conventional and unconventional interventions (Liu, 2006). In general, when the market system runs properly, national economic management is necessary, but runs in a conventional, routine, and procedural manner. To be brief, the government collects taxes, approves land use, and spends money as usual. Only when extensive and serious market failures occur is it necessary to transform national economic management into temporary intervention, that is, unconventional national economy management. While Western economic theory views both conventional and unconventional interventions, be they regular or temporary, as government intervention. Since the rise of Keynesianism, there has been a further understanding of the necessity of governmental intervention.

The practices of socialist market economy with Chinese characteristics show that routine national economy management has always existed in its market economy. However, when market dysfunction occurs, a special national economy management, macro control, will be in use. Thus, economic development pattern with Chinese characteristics itself breeds two approaches of national economy management, among which macro control plays a core role and has a special cognitive value. It does not necessarily mean that China should start all over again to build up its own theoretical paradigm of national economy management and macro control in that its reform and opening up have fundamentally terminated conventional theoretical paradigm of planning economy and introduced many Western theories on market economy. It is imperative that China's particularity — which is the starting point of the construction of the theoretical paradigm in issue — should be combined with generality shared by all countries so as to complete the construction of theoretical paradigm of macro control and thus of national economic management with Chinese characteristics.

REFERENCES

Contemporary China's Planned Work Office. *1949–1985 Major Events of the National Economic and Social Development Plan of the People's Republic of China.* Beijing: Hongqi Press, 1987. 当代中国的计划工作办公室. 中华人民共和国国民经济和社会发展计划大事辑要 1949–1985. 北京: 红旗出版社, 1987.

Deng, Xiaoping. *Selected Works of Deng Xiaoping* (Vol. 3). Beijing: People's Publishing House, 1993. 邓小平文选, 第3卷. 北京: 人民出版社.

Li, Peng. *Report on National Economy, Ninth Five-Year Plan of Social Development and 2010 Outline of Long-Range Objective.* Beijing: People's Publishing House, 1996. 李鹏. 关于国民经济和社会发展 "九五" 计划和2010年远景目标纲要的报告. 北京: 人民出版社, 1996.

Li, Tiejun. "Introduction on Some Ideas of Guiding Plans." *Macroeconomic Management*, 1985 (2). 李铁军. 关于指导性计划问题的一些观点简介. 宏观经济管理, 1985 (2).

Liu, Guoguang. "Importance on Respecting Law of Value." *[J] QIUSHI*, 1990 (12). 刘国光. 重要的是遵重价值规律. 求是, 1990 (12).

Liu, Guoguang. *Selected Works of Liu Guoguang.* Taiyuan: Shanxi People's Publishing House, 1986. 刘国光. 刘国光选集. 太原: 山西人民出版社, 1986.

Liu, Guoguang, *et al. No-Loose-Reality and Loosely Achieving.* Shanghai: Shanghai People's Publishing House, 1991. 刘国光等. 不宽松的现实和宽松的实现. 上海:上海人民出版社, 1991.

Liu, Rui. "Macroeconomic Control: Orientation, Basis, Relationship between Active and Passive Bodies, and Law Rationale." *Economic Theory and Economic Management*, 2006 (5). 刘瑞. 宏观调控的定位、依据、主客体关系及法律基础. 经济理论与经济管理, 2006 (5).

Liu, Rui, *et al. Strategies and Plans on Social Economic Development: Theory, Practice, Case.* Beijing: China Renmin University Press, 2006. 刘瑞等. 社会经济发展战略与规划: 理论, 实践, 案例, 2006.

Lv, Ruliang, Wei Wu and Rui Liu. *Investigation Report on Guiding Plans*, 1992. 吕汝良, 吴微, 刘瑞. 关于指导性计划的调查报告, 1992.

Li, Yining. *My Idea on Market Economy.* Nanjing: Jiangsu People's Publishing House, 1993. 厉以宁. 我的市场经济观. 南京: 江苏人民出版社, 1993.

Li, Zhenzhong. *Planned Economics*. Beijing: China Renmin University Press, 1983. 李震中. 计划经济学. 北京: 中国人民大学出版社, 1983.

Ma, Hong. "Further Development on the Reform of Planned Management System." *Outlook Weekly*, 1990 (18). 马洪. 继续深化计划管理体制改革. 瞭望, 1990 (18).

State Planning Commission System Reform and Law Division. *Overview on Ten-Year Plan System Reform*. Beijing: China Planning Press, 1994. 国家计委体制改革和法规司. 十年计划体制改革概览. 北京: 中国计划出版社, 1994.

Song, Tao. "Discussion on Combinations between Planning Economy and Market Regulation." *Academic Journal of Zhongzhou*, 1991 (6). 宋涛, 计划经济与市场调节相结合. 中州学刊, 1991 (6).

Wang, Yawen, *et al. Comparison of Planned Theory, System and Method*. Shanghai: Shanghai Academy of Social Sciences, 1991. 王亚文等, 比较计划理论、体制和方法. 上海: 上海社会科学出版社, 1991.

Wei, Liqun and Zhiguo Han. *Argument on Reform of Planned System*. Beijing: Guangming Daily Publishing House, 1984. 魏礼群. 韩志国. 计划体制改革问题论争. 北京: 光明日报出版社, 1984.

Wei, Liqun, *et al. Reform on Socialist Market Economy and Planned Pattern*. Beijing: China Planning Press, 1994. 魏礼群等. 社会主义市场经济与计划模式改革. 北京: 中国计划出版社, 1994.

Wu, Jinglian. *Planning Economy or Market Economy*. Beijing: China Economic Publishing House, 1993. 吴敬琏.计划经济还是市场经济. 北京: 中国经济出版社, 1993.

Yang, Weimin. *Theoretical Exploration on Planned System Reform*. Beijing: China Prices Publishing House, 2003. 杨伟民. 规划体制改革的理论探索. 北京: 中国物价出版社, 2003.

Chapter 6

Experiences and Lessons in Formulating National Development Plan

6.1 PROCEDURES OF FORMULATING A NATIONAL DEVELOPMENT PLAN

The procedures of formulating a plan, according to the regulations on planning formulation in China, usually include preliminary research, drafting, linkage, verification, examination and approval, publication, implementation, evaluation, and revision.

6.1.1 Preliminary Research

A scientific plan necessitates preliminary research in which a clear line of thinking should be first established. Diligent preliminary research is greatly conducive to subsequent compilation, approval, and implementation. Compared with the past, more attention is paid to preliminary research, which usually begins two years ahead of a new planning period and which includes basic surveys, information collection, subject research, and demonstration of major projects.

6.1.1.1 *Collecting Economic Information*

The collection of a complete set of economic information is the basis for economic forecasting and planning. The success of economic planning largely depends on a good understanding of the actual economic situation.

In addition, the implementation of a plan cannot go without real-time economic information. With the greater integration of global economy and greater dependency of China's economy on the global market, it is also necessary to collect information on international economic development.

6.1.1.2 *Analyzing Domestic and International Economic Situations and Grasping Key Issues*

It is desirable that economic and social maladies and malaises be diagnosed through a systematic causal analysis of the collected information. Only in this way can an effective recipe be prescribed to palliate or cure economic problems and major contradictions. In addition, the compilers should be constantly warned against smug self-satisfaction with previous achievements, but should be forward-looking. By doing so, China can inaugurate a new era of economic construction.

6.1.1.3 *Predicting the Economic Trend and Seeking the Opportunity for Socio-Economic Development*

It is incumbent on decision-makers to have a correct judgment of China's development status quo in the current global economic context so that China can discern what the favorable or unfavorable elements are in the course of aiming at more ambitious goals. In the planning process, it is necessary to make a sound estimate of global political climates, social and economic latest developments, scientific advances, and the possible impact on China's economy in the planning period so that China can avail itself of every possible opportunity to promote development.

6.1.1.4 *Subject Research on Major Issues*

There must also be evaluation of the planning in operation, especially the identification of the objectives and how far theses have been achieved, for the purpose of canvassing the elements that retard economic growth. In addition, there must be subject researches on potential contradictions in the next plan, possible changes in external and internal economic and political environment, basic conditions for further development, optional responses to unexpected and sudden exigencies, and principal guidelines and conception of the development plan.

The planning authorities should assemble a panel of experts populated by insiders and professionals from external agencies. The government should appropriate special funds for planning and break down all major issues concerning economic and social development to ensure that preliminary research can proceed smoothly through the following ways: (1) internal research, that is, organizing internal departments to conduct research on selected subjects; (2) external delegation, that is, organizing scientific research institutions, universities, and industry associations outside government planning authorities to conduct research on proposed subjects; (3) open tender, that is, introducing a competition mechanism to planning research, publishing bidding information on selected subjects and selecting the winning bidders through qualification examination, the evaluation of bidding contents, and the comparative evaluation of bidders; (4) soliciting suggestions from the public, that is, publishing information through the mass media for feedback comment from the public and incorporate carefully sifted opinions into the planning.

6.1.2 Drafting

Drafting a plan is based on systematic analysis and extensive absorption of various proposals. It is a process of pursuing new objectives, approaches, ideas, and countermeasures for economic and social development in the future. It is also a process of innovation by virtue of multidisciplinary knowledge, wisdom, and experience. The planning department should specify the overall goal, the draft of planned indicators and the general framework of policies related to economic and social development. The national development plan is a comprehensive plan, which serves as a guide for all other plans and of which other specialized plans can under no circumstance run afoul of. As for specialized plans within the purview of some special departments, experts should be carefully selected and drawn from many other institutions to participate in drafting or counseling the final draft. After absorbing opinions from major departments, the draft should be submitted to the State Council, which will give suggestions for further revision or modification.

6.1.3 Linkage and Verification

For it to be better linked up with other types of plans, a draft plan should be reported to the department in charge, which will give written opinions within 30 days after receiving the draft plan. Any draft plan shall not be submitted for approval or put into practice unless it has been submitted for linkage with other types of plans. The basic principle of linkage is to subordinate specialized planning and regional planning to the overall planning issued by the same or higher administrative level, and subordinate the planning issued by a lower administrative level to those by a higher level, and actualize the compatibility between specialized planning. When compiling a cross-provincial plan, the compiling departments should take into consideration the overall land use planning and the urban planning.

Verification of the draft plan is an extremely important process to ensure its justifiability. This process includes not only repeated deliberation, demonstration, and modification by the planning department, but also the verification report issued by a panel of experts from various disciplinary subjects. Any draft plan will not be submitted for ratification or put into effect unless it has been demonstrated by experts. Planning demonstration mainly includes the following four aspects.

6.1.3.1 *Feasibility Study*

A feasibility study is an assessment of the practicality of a proposed project. To be more specific, it aims to objectively and rationally reveal the strengths and weaknesses of a proposed venture, opportunities and threats present in the environment, the resources required to carry it through and ultimately the prospects for success. Basically, the successful completion of a plan depends largely on the construction of major projects, which, however, cannot be infinitely expanded because of limited natural resources. A comparative study of the national development plans before and after the reform and opening up shows that a scientifically demonstrated plan will catalyze economic and social development, whereas an erroneous and derailed decision will bring serious disastrous consequences to the society. Therefore, it is necessary to have a feasible study on the planned ventures from all aspects such as social, economic, and political elements and resources.

6.1.3.2 *Compatibility Demonstration*

The national economy is a large and complex system crisscrossed with intricate links. To ensure the smooth realization of the planning objectives, it is necessary to demonstrate coordination between different types of plans. At this stage, the main task is to sort out the relations between the national development plan and its subsystems to ensure a healthy, steady, and sustainable development in the future.

6.1.3.3 *Efficiency Analysis*

China's economic growth is still plagued by high speed, high energy consumption, high pollution, low efficiency, and extensive economic growth mode, which are extremely detrimental to sustainable development. An efficiency analysis of planning is necessary to maximize economic and social efficiency.

6.1.3.4 *Risk Evaluation*

Risks are always concomitant with the formulation and implementation of planning. Based on the conventional wisdom that benefits of economic behavior are proportional to risks. If the growth targets are set higher, the risks tend to be greater. Take the Great Leap Forward in the Second Five-Year Plan as a typical example. An unpragmatic plan will undoubtedly have an extremely negative impact on coordinated economic development. Therefore, a scientific plan is necessary to control risks and benefits within a reasonable range.

6.1.4 Examination and Ratification

In view of its significance in determining development orientation and targets, the examination and ratification stage is a serious matter. The customary practice is as follows: holding seminars to listen to the opinions of different regions, departments, and businesses after the completion of compiling a national medium- and long-term plan; submitting the revised draft plan to the State Council for internal consideration after many substantive deliberations and amendments; submitting it to the National People's Congress (NPC) for consideration and ratification before it becomes a legally enforcing document.

When submitting the draft plan and other relevant documents (such as demonstration reports and administrative laws) to the examining and approving organization, the planning department shall present a description of the planning preparation, including the following items: how the planning preparation has proceeded, how opinion solicitation, linkage and expert demonstration was going, and why did some expert opinions not be adopted?

6.1.5 Promulgation

After the NPC ratifies the national development plan, the State Council shall be responsible for organizing governments, economic management organs, and enterprises at all levels to implement it. The objectives in the plan will be broken down into sub-objectives, which will be delegated top-down from the central government to local governments and enterprises. Unless involving national secrets and otherwise stipulated by laws and administrative regulations, the plan shall be promulgated in time once it has been ratified through legal procedures.

6.1.6 Implementation

As a key stage in the management of the national economic plan, the smooth implementation of the national development plan is the common responsibility of the governments, enterprises, and even all the people. This procedure is guaranteed by the delegation of the decomposed objects to the governments and businesses at a lower level, the utilization of social mechanism for planning implementation, and systematic supervision and examination of how far planning targets have been achieved. The inspection is to track the progress of the implementation so that problems can be detected in time. A good plan is only the first step of the whole planning process, and only effective fulfillment of each objective can consummate this scientific and systematic planning. Inspection and supervision can also help draw lessons and experiences and objectively evaluate the implementation so that the planning objects can be achieved in a methodical manner.

6.1.7 Evaluation and Revision

Evaluation is a systematic and objective analysis of planning targets, economic and social efficiency, political implications, and observance to relevant laws, a procedure that can be conducted in the course of planning or after the completion of it. The evaluation informs the decision makers of how major projects are going, how far the planning targets have been achieved, how great is the impact of the planning on social and economic progress and whether some laws or regulation are violated. In addition, evaluation can also help find problems and get timely information for further revision and future planning. The evaluation can be carried out by the government itself or delegated to other agencies or scientific institutions.

Because the economic situation is always in a state of flux, it is necessary to re-adjust the plan despite the disapproval of making any change to a plan. In the context of market economy, it is unrealistic to keep the plan unchanged. History shows that it was the adjustment of each period that ensured that the plan was consistent with the actual situation and that the net result was relatively satisfactory. As a matter of fact, the formulation of planning is also trial and error. Therefore, it is recommended that decision-makers should not persistently pursue an invariable plan throughout the whole planning period but allow for timely and flexible readjustments when necessary.

After the compilation of the draft plan, it is also necessary to check whether the plan is deviant from the objective reality. If so, the compilers should adopt appropriate remedies to readjust the plan and reset the target. Amendments to a plan are not rare, especially when it is a long-term plan. The longer the planning term, the more uncertainties, the more necessary the amendments.

In the revision stage, it is necessary that a national meeting be held to inform the departments at all levels of the issues as well as to solicit advice from them. Only when the legitimate interests of all parties have been taken into consideration can blindfold actions and difficulties be overcome. Therefore, the exchange of information between the central and the peripheral, planning departments and economic planning management departments, between the state and businesses, can heighten their understanding of social and economic development, give the unpragmatic concept, and make the planning more justifiable, feasible, and democratic.

If the plan needs to be revised after evaluation, the planning department shall prepare a revision scenario and submit to a higher authority for ratification according to the planning procedures, and publish it in time.

6.2 CHOICE OF INDICATORS IN NATIONAL DEVELOPMENT PLANNING

Half of all the 24 planning indicators in the 12th Five-Year Plan are mandatory or compulsory indicators, which are related to livelihood, energy, and environmental protection. In the other half of the anticipatory indicators, only three are related to economic development. Compared with the 11th Five-Year Plan, the central government has significantly increased the number of the mandatory indicators related to people's livelihood and environmental protection and reduced the indicators related to economic growth (see Tables 6.1 and 6.2). However, questions arise as to whether economic targets should be removed from the planning indicators and whether it is operable to transform environmental protection targets into planning indicators.

6.2.1 The Impact of Macro Control Objectives on Planning Indicators

Readers will find, in any textbook of macroeconomics, that the objectives of macroeconomic policies are generally economic growth, price stability, full employment, and balance of payments (BOP). This view is also accepted by China's economic management institutions.[1]

In the century-long practice of government intervention in economic activities, Western developed countries came to realize that the government

Table 6.1 Major Planning Indicators in the 11th Five-Year Plan

Classification	Indicators	2005	2010	AAGR (%)	Attributes
Economic growth	GDP (trillion RMB)	18.2	26.1	7.5	Anticipatory
	per capita GDP	13,985	19,270	6.6	Anticipatory
Economic structure	Percentage of value-added of service sector to GDP	40.3	43.3	[3]	Anticipatory
	Percentage of employment in service sector	31.3	35.3	[4]	Anticipatory
	Percentage of R&D inputs to GDP	1.3	2	[4]	Anticipatory
	Urbanization rate (%)	43	47		Anticipatory
Population	Total population (million)	1307.56	1360	<8‰	Mandatory
Resources	Reduction of energy consumption per unit of GDP			[20]	Mandatory
Environment	Reduction of water consumption per unit of industrial value added			[30]	Mandatory
	Water efficiency of irrigation	0.45	0.5	[0.05]	Anticipatory
	Utilization rate of industrial solid waste (%)	55.8	60	[4.2]	Anticipatory
	Arable land (million hectare)	122	120	−0.3	Mandatory
	Reduction of emission of major pollutants (%)			[10]	Mandatory
	Forest coverage rate	18.2	20	[1.8]	Mandatory

(*Continued*)

Table 6.1   *(Continued)*

Classification	Indicators	2005	2010	AAGR (%)	Attributes
Public service	Average years of schooling (year)	8.5	9	[0.5]	Anticipatory
Living standards	Urban old-age pensioners (million)	174	223	5.1	Mandatory
	Rural cooperative medical service coverage rate (%)	23.5%	>80	>[56.5]	Mandatory
	Urban new jobs over five years (10,000)			[4500]	Anticipatory
	Agricultural labor transfer over five years (10,000)			[4500]	Anticipatory
	Registered urban unemployment rate (%)	4.2	5		Anticipatory
	Urban per capita disposable income (RMB)	10,493	13,390	5	Anticipatory
	Rural per capital net income (RMB)	3255	4150	5	Anticipatory

GDP: gross domestic product.

Note: The values in [ ] are five-year accumulative values.

Table 6.2 Major Planning Indicators in the 12th Five-Year Plan

Classification	Indicators	2010	2015	AAGR (%)	Attributes
Economic growth	GDP (trillion RMB)	39.8	55.8	7	Anticipatory
	Percentage of value-added of service sector to GDP	43	47	[4]	Anticipatory
	Urbanization rate	47.5	51.5	[4]	Anticipatory
Science	Consolidation rate of nine-year compulsory education (%)	89.7	93	[3.3]	Mandatory
Education	Gross enrolment rate of senior high schooling (%)	82.5	87	[4.5]	Anticipatory
	Percentage of R&D inputs to GDP	1.75	2.2	[0.45]	Anticipatory
	Patents per 10,000 people	1.7	3.5	[1.6]	Anticipatory
Resources	Arable land (million hectare)	121	121	[0]	Mandatory
Environment	Reduction of water consumption per unit of industrial value-added (%)			[30]	Mandatory
	Water efficiency of irrigation	0.5	0.53	[0.03]	Anticipatory
	Proportion of nonfossil energy in primary energy consumption	8.3	11.4	[3.1]	Mandatory
	Reduction of energy consumption per unit of GDP (%)			[16]	Mandatory
	Reduction of emission of carbon dioxide per unit of GDP (%)			[17]	Mandatory
	Reductions of emission of major pollutants	chemical oxygen demand			[8]	Mandatory
		Sulfur dioxide			[8]	Mandatory
		Ammonia nitrogen			[10]	Mandatory
		Oxynitrides			[10]	Mandatory

(Continued)

Table 6.2   *(Continued)*

Classification	Indicators	2010	2015	AAGR (%)	Attributes
	Forest coverage rate (%)	20.36	21.66	[1.3]	Mandatory
	Forest reserves (million cubic meters)	13,700	14,300	[6]	Mandatory
Living standards	Urban per capita disposable income (RMB)	19,109	>26,810	>7	Anticipatory
	Rural per capital net income (RMB)	5,919	>8,310	>7	Anticipatory
	Registered urban unemployment (rate (%)	4.1	<5		Anticipatory
	Urban new jobs (10,000)			[4,500]	Anticipatory
	Urban old-age pensioners (million)	257	357	[1]	Mandatory
	Urban–rural medical insurance rate			[3]	Mandatory
	Building of affordable houses (10,000)			[3,600]	Mandatory
	Total population (million)	1,341	<1,390	<7.2‰	Mandatory
	Life expectancy (age)	73.5	74.5	[1]	Anticipatory

GDP: gross domestic product.

Note: The values in [ ] are five-year accumulative values.

could not abandon its control and regulation on the macroeconomic activities in the market economy while allowing the market economic mechanism to adjust the microeconomic activities automatically. After years of research and exploration, economists concentrate on the following four macro-management targets: economic growth, that is, the increase of product output and service quantity, with real gross domestic product (GDP) as the representative index; price stability, that is, countermeasures against various types of inflation, with consumer price index (CPI) as the representative index; full employment, that is, low levels of structural unemployment, unemployment directly associated with insufficient demand and search unemployment during job transitioning after the removal of frictional unemployment, with unemployment rate as the representative indicator; BOP, that is, the records of all transactions made between entities in one country and the rest of the world over a definite period of time, with the accounting of the BOP as the representative indicator.

The mainstream macroeconomic theory represented by Keynesianism constructs the basic theoretical explanations for these four targets. That is, in a closed economic system economic growth is the prerequisite of achieving full employment, but it also causes inflation, which directly affects price stability. The short-run Phillips curve and the long-run curve revised by Friedman more systematically describe the relationship between economic growth, price stability, and full employment. In an open economic system, the stability of a country's economy requires a balance between imports and exports and capital flows. Tinbergen classified economic quantities into targets instruments, and his rule revealed the relationship between them and stress the importance of coordination between them (Tinbergen, 1956: 80). However, the theoretical explanation of the relationship between the four targets does not solve the problems in practice. The stagflation triggered by the oil crisis in the 1970s announced the invalidation of the Phillips curve, and Keynesian mythology stressed strict fiscal policy. The school of money supply represented by Friedman simply attributed stagflation to ill management of money supply and argued that exchange rate stability, economic growth, full employment, and price stability could be achieved by increasing money supply at a fixed ratio. In the 1980s, the German federal government even abandoned its target of pursuing economic growth and intensified its intervention in monetary policy (Yang and Li, 1988: 25). However, this theory cannot explain the outbreak of the global financial crisis in 2008.

From the practice of Western advanced nations, there are two basic principles in dealing with the relationship between the four targets. The first is to set for each target a quantitative control standard. For instance, the United States keeps economic growth rate, inflation rate, and unemployment rate, respectively, within 3%, 3%, and 4% and roughly keeps the BOP in equilibrium. Second, the government arranges the four major targets in the order of importance or urgency in case it is unable to give balanced weight to each of them. For instance, in the response to the international financial crisis in 2008, the United States prioritized the increase of employment. In addition, with the spread of the concept of sustainable development in the new millennium, Western developed countries have actively coordinated environment protection with the macro-control indicators.

After its formal choice of market economy in 1992, China followed the path of the Western advanced nations in its intervention in the market economy. In view of its distinct institutional background and national conditions, its selection of macroeconomic indicators is quite different from those of Western countries, both in goal setting and the number.

First, China's macro-control indicators are a binary target structure, including aggregate and structural indicators, which are quite different from the unitary target structure of Western advanced nations. In the West, a mature market economy provides the basic premise for macroeconomic management; the economic integration resulted in a unitary management model, and all four targets are aggregate. In contrast, China's macroeconomic management is dual since its economy has been in a dual-sector model (capitalist and subsistence sectors) constructed by W. Arthur Lewis for a long time. The Chinese government sets aggregate targets to deal with aggregate imbalance while setting structural target to deal with structural imbalance. Looking back at every major macroeconomic regulation and control since the late 1970s, we find that China has always put economic restructuring in the foremost or extremely important position and juxtaposed it with other targets related to economic stability. This is not so much a preference as the last resort of China's macro control management. For a long time, China has been in a binary or trinary economic structure in which all economic aggregates are intertwined with economic structures.

Second, China determines not only the goals of economic regulation, but those of social regulation. Since the 1980s, the national plan, as the most important instrument of macro control, has been renamed as the economic and social development plan. In other words, the social macro control has been added to the plan. For instance, the main indicators in the 12th Five-Year Plan included economic growth, science and technology, education, resources and environment, and people's welfare. The main goals in the 2011 Government Work Report were GDP growth at 8%; further optimization of economic structure; CPI control below 4%; creation of over 9 million new jobs in cities and towns; registered unemployment rate within 4.6%; improvement of BOP. The fundamental task was to create a good environment for transforming the mode of economic development and guide all parties to focus on the acceleration of economic restructuring, the improvement of development quality and efficiency, the creation of new jobs, the improvement of people's well-being and social harmony. The juxtaposition of economic and social macro control is of great significance both theoretically and practically (Hu and Liu, 2009).

Third, China sets more than four macro-control targets and flexibly decides the order of priority in accordance with the changes of domestic and international economic situation. By contrast, there are only four targets in Western countries, and whatever happens, full employment is always prioritized, followed in turn by price stability, economic growth, and BOP. In China, structural readjustment is also an important target, and since the beginning of the 21st century, energy conservation, emission reduction, resources conservation, and environment protection have also become the important target of macroeconomic management. In each planning period, some other targets will also be added, such as the cleaning up of development zones in 1993 and 2004, the reduction of overcapacity in 2004, and the regulation of real estate in 2007. These specific and practical regulatory targets are difficult to be written into the standard textbooks of Western macroeconomic theory. It may be controversial, but the Chinese government's pragmatic attitude and sense of responsibility are the basic guarantee of its successes in macroeconomic control.

Finally, China's selection of macroeconomic control targets is flexible but not doggedly limited to an economic or political cycle. However, in the Western developed countries, all regulation measures to cope with changes in an economic cycle are regarded as short-term control. The typical example is Keynesian management, which focuses only on short-term regulation but not on medium- and long-term regulation. In general, short-term regulation can only choose aggregate and emergency targets. But for those medium- and long-term structural targets, it usually takes three to five years to achieve them, during which the cabinet or administration may be reshuffled and no politician may consider the macroeconomic regulation targets for the next cabinet or administration. Western political arrangements compel the government to consider only the short-term regulation targets but leave the long-term regulation targets to the next cabinet and political adversaries. For example, in 2008, when the outbreak of subprime mortgage crisis coincided with the U.S. general election and the end of the second term of the presidency, President George W. Bush extricated himself by quickly signing the *Emergency Economic Stabilization of Act of 2008*, a bailout of the U.S. financial system, which focused on toxic securities and problematic financial institutions, leaving to the Obama administration the structural problems such as the rejuvenation of real economy and creation of new jobs. However, this expedient emergency program delayed the solution to the crisis.

On the contrary, the stable political system of China guarantees continuity of target selection in its macroeconomic control. Due to no political pressure for a new term or a new generation of leadership, the government can devote itself to the realization of the macroeconomic regulation targets in a stable political environment. Besides, the government has more freedom to choose from diversified and flexible control targets instead of locking merely on the four targets. Even in the case of failure of macroeconomic control, the problem seldom lies in inappropriate selection of target but in other aspects.

To sum up, the macro-control objective has been clearly specified in China and the planning indicators of national economic and social development are gradually forming a system (Table 6.3).

Table 6.3 The System of Indicators for National Development Planning in China

Attribute 1	Indicators	Attribute 2
Economic indicators	1. GDP growth	Aggregate
	2. CPI stability	Aggregate
	3. Reduction of energy consumption per unit of output value	Structural
	4. Service growth	Structural
	5. Development of strategic emerging industries	Structural
	6. Equilibrium of Balance of Payments	Aggregate
	7. Increase of ratio of R&D investment to GDP	Structural
	8.	
Social indicators	9. Decrease of registered urban unemployment rate	Aggregate
	10. Increase of per capita income	Structural
	11. Population control	Aggregate
	12. Pollutants control	Aggregate
	13. Decrease of major safety accidents	Structural
	14. Increase of social insurance coverage rate	Structural
	15.	

GDP: gross domestic product.

Note: (1) The dots ...... indicate that other indicators may be chosen according to actual situations. (2) Though structural indicators are not easy to define, economists often count the transformation of development mode, optimization of economic structure, and institutional reform.

6.2.2 Controversies About Planning Indicators

6.2.2.1 *GDP: A Planning Indicator?*

Traditional macroeconomic theories regard economic growth as the main objective, which is typically indicated by GDP growth rate and per capita GDP. After the Asian financial crisis in 1997, China set the benchmark of GDP growth rate as 8%. However, GDP has become the target of critics who believes that officials' obsession with GDP growth is simply for political promotion and the culprit of their failures in energy conservation and environment protection. Besides, the academic circles are somewhat disappointed at this indicator, trying to replace it other indicators such as happiness index and green GDP.

From a realistic perspective, GDP growth rate should continue to be used as a planning index. First, imperfect as it is, GDP is still the most useful indicator to measure the economic development of a country or region. According to the System of National Accounting (SNA) recommended by the United Nations to all countries in the world, GDP is usually the sum of the final products and services produced by a country or region in a year. As a measure of the total amount of economic activities of a country or region, it only reflects the scale of wealth creation. Even the per-capita GDP can neither reflect whether we are friendly to environment or whether the distribution of personal income is reasonable nor answer the question as to whether people are happy. Most economists agree that GDP, in its strict sense, can by no means carry any extra-economic information and value request. Second, it is justifiable for a rising developing country to achieve a high-speed GDP growth. China used to be the largest economic power in the world with the greatest accumulation of wealth, but it began to decline after the mid-19th century, and it was not until four decades ago that it began to achieve economic growth in a modern sense. It would be absurd if we ignore GDP growth in the early stage of socialism construction. Third, other indicators cannot replace GDP. There is a groundswell for public opinion in favor of green GDP and gross national happiness (GNH) index (Shen and Ura, 2011). However, the problem is that the green GDP indicator cannot solve a series of technical problems under the current statistical system, such as the measure of environmental costs. In addition, the practice of including the investment in environmental restoration and protection would distort the principle of production calculation based on market transactions. Likewise, the substitution of GNH index for GDP would render this aggregate indicator not objective and incomputable. Well intended as it is to reflect more accurately people's gains from social progress, this alternative indicator cannot really reflect economic activities, which, according to historical materialism, as the material basis of all human activities, should maintain its objective independence and final decisiveness. As superstructure and other activities, although remaining relatively independent and reacting to economic activities, are always decided by economic activities, a dogged insistence on incorporating all these activities into a comprehensive index would inadvertently have an adverse effect on planning and obliterate the dual attributes of human activities.

It is necessary to maintain GDP growth as a planning indicator, but it should be combined with the scientific outlook on development. First, China should take the transformation of development mode as a long-term task and align it with the realization of the structural objectives. The transformation of development mode is the optimization of structural objectives such as demand structure and industrial structure. Therefore, China should sustain its stable and steady GDP growth through transforming the development. Second, China needs to form a more scientific and rigorous system of planning indicators by supplementing other indicators such as Gini coefficient, Engel coefficient, energy consumption coefficient, and GDP growth rate. These indicators may help people have a more comprehensive judgment of economic growth and other concomitant results. Third, the Chinese government should avoid evaluating local officials' political performance with the single indicator of GDP.

6.2.2.2 *CPI: How to Control?*

CPI is a target index widely accepted by market economies to measure the living conditions of the residents. Public opinions often complain that the CPI published regularly by the government does not reflect the real livelihood of the people while the academia holds different views on the composition of it.

Maintaining the stability of the aggregate price level is undoubtedly one of the regulatory objectives in all countries. Stable aggregate price level can comparatively ensure a stable expectation for the operation of market economy and keep social and economic life in a normal state. Nevertheless, due to various factors in market economy, price fluctuation within a reasonable range is unavoidable. Price, as the monetary expression of commodity value and the interaction between supply and demand, is formed spontaneously under market economy and can sensitively reflect the direction and change of market resource allocation. It is through price fluctuation that people adjust their economic behaviors. The price formed spontaneously becomes one of the levers to regulate the operation of market economy and improve the efficiency of resource allocation. The failure of planning economy in the past was attributable to the arbitrarily fixed price. The rigid price mechanism distorted resource allocation. Although it is necessary to retain administrative pricing in "blind spots," we should basically regulate the overall price level by observing the law of value and the law of supply and demand.

As to the price level regulation in 2011, we need to understand it from the following aspects. First, we should adjust the overall price with various implements. What causes the rise of the aggregate price level, monetary, or nonmonetary factors? As far as we can judge, nonmonetary factors are more responsible for it. In this case, a mix of implements is needed; otherwise, it is difficult to achieve the goal solely by monetary policy tools. It is unrealistic to believe that the overall price will fall accordingly as soon as the interest rates and the reserve requirements are raised. Second, we should distinguish different types of increases in price and determine what is the most important in price regulation. The main problem is not hard to divine. A careful observation reveals the following basic facts: the long-term upward trend of the costs of both resource products and labor; the short-term and cyclical price rise of fresh agricultural and sideline products; the short-term speculation of bulling the market; the potential and uncertainty of increases in price caused by excessive liquidity of monetary funds; and the offset between the increases in price of bulk imported commodities caused by the excessive U.S. dollars and the appreciation of Chinese renminbi. This requires that price regulation should resolutely suppress short-term speculation, prevent potential increases in price from becoming reality, and have a tolerant attitude toward long-term steady increases in price. Third, any policy measure to regulate market prices has a time-lag effect, so it is necessary to allow for an observation period. It is inadvisable to introduce various regulatory measures intensively within a short term. Fourth, price regulation should be forward-looking so as to prevent spiral inflation. An increases in price breeds a tendency to peg nominal income and other welfare benefits with CPI for the sake of avoiding the decrease of real income. In fact, the increased income will eventually be countervailed by the cost of products, thus triggering a new round of price increases and plunging into never-ending spiral inflation. Some countries adopted this practice in the times of severe inflation and even temporarily froze prices, but later the price rebounded. Obviously, this practice lacks foresight.

6.2.2.3 *Energy Consumption Per Unit of Output Value: How to Actualize?*

Energy consumption per unit of GDP has been determined as an important indicator since the 11th Five-Year Plan, and the mandatory aggregate indicator of reducing 20% over five years has been decomposed five sub-targets in annual plan. The 12th Five-Year Plan further firmed up this indicator and added other indicators related to energy conservation and environmental protection to the overall objective of macro control. The purpose is to achieve sustainable development characterized with environmental friendliness, green growth, low-carbon economy, circular economy. By far, the results show that it is incumbent to make improvement.

First, China is still adopting the traditional practice of using coal consumption as the standard measurement of energy consumption, while in the West it has been replaced by the consumption of petroleum, electricity, or photovoltaic power. Although the adoption of which standard measurement depends largely on the energy consumption structure of a nation, it is undeniable that these measurement methods reflect the energy consumption of new industrialization. The proportion of coal in total energy consumption is as high as over 60%, but other sources of energy will be in a dominant position in the future. In addition, the adoption of standard coal as a comprehensive unit of energy consumption measurement is misleading. Despite the downward trend of energy consumption of per RMB10,000 of output value since 2000, China is still a major energy-polluting country, with carbon emissions ranking first in the world. Obviously, the use of industrialized comprehensive energy consumption standards can no longer reflect the situation of new industrialization. The adoption of noncoal standard measurement is conducive to promoting the energy revolution.

Second, the comprehensive energy consumption index needs to be decomposed and refined into sub-indicators that are more easily quantified. According to mass media, in the late stage of the 11th Five-Year

Plan, local governments were obliged to pull the switch for power rationing for fear that the target of 20% reduction in total energy consumption over five years could not be achieved, forcing many enterprises to be equipped with diesel engines to fulfill production orders. For a time, there was a shortage of diesel, and the air pollution caused by diesel power generation was also aggravated. This case shows that this practice needs improvement. Energy consumption of per unit of output value is a comprehensive indicator, specifically involving the consumption of coal, gasoline, diesel, kerosene, thermal power, hydropower, and nuclear power. Therefore, it is difficult to control energy consumption through only one index. Since the 12th Five-Year Plan, the indicators for controlling environment have included the reduction rate of the emissions of carbon dioxide per unit GDP, chemical oxygen demand, sulfur dioxide, ammonia nitrogen, and nitrogen oxide. Nevertheless, the realization of these sub-targets depends on effective means and the chief executive accountability system of the head does not suffice.

6.2.2.4 *Balance of Payments: How to Achieve Equilibrium?*

Under the open economy, it is necessary to maintain the BOP. BOP helps the domestic economy countervail the external economic brunt. However, in the trend of economic globalization, it is not easy for a nation to achieve BOP. As a matter of fact, China has never succeeded in doing so and the current account and capital account in the BOP both have always run surplus since its opening up in 1978. The direct cause of this disequilibrium is the perennial surplus of China's goods trade, which has accumulated trillions of dollars of foreign exchange reserves year by year under the compulsory foreign exchange settlement system. This exposes China to the risk that once the foreign currencies (U.S. dollar, Japanese yen or euro) depreciate, China's foreign currencies will shrink. If China continues to maintain the current mandatory foreign exchange settlement system, then the same amount of RMB supply will assuage inflationary pressure. Although the imbalance of international payments will not result in the collapse of China's economy as some foreign comments have predicted, it is really a serious problem. The annual government work report is always emphasizing the improvement of positions of payments instead of the achievement of the BOP. Obviously, China is in a disadvantageous situation in choosing this as a macro control target.

There are several ways to achieve the flexibility of the BOP, but none of them are ideal choices. First comes the improvement of the elasticity of RMB exchange rate. Admittedly, the free fluctuation of RMB exchange rate in the international market will naturally create its elasticity for maintaining the BOP. However, since China's international competency mainly depends on price advantages, it is not wise to voluntarily abandon control over RMB exchange rate without any intervention. Second, the abolition of the compulsory foreign exchange settlement system can defuse the inflation pressure, but large amounts of new foreign exchange reserves are also exposed to risks. In case the capital account is not open, new foreign exchanges flow to foreign markets, which denotes capital outflow; in case capital account is open, new foreign exchanges will form domestic investment demand. Third, the change of the export-oriented development model can fundamentally resolve the long-standing surpluses of current account and capital account. However, this requires a series of structural readjustments which can only be completed in the medium and long run.

The fear is that China has not yet formed a mature policy consideration on achieving the equilibrium of BOP. This is the greatest danger that potentially roil China's healthy economic globalization in the future.

6.3 SOCIAL PARTICIPATION IN NATIONAL DEVELOPMENT PLAN

How to mobilize the public to participate in the formulation of the national development plan that is highly technical in an appropriate way is an important task of planning. In some market economies with planning experience, one of the main tasks of planning agencies and staff is to organize public participation in planning.

6.3.1 The Implications of Improving Public Participation

Social participation in planning reflects democratic decision making and the scientific outlook on development. Social participation is a process of research, drafting, compilation and review of government planning by social institutions, NGOs, democratic parties, overseas institutions, and individuals. The implications of improving the degree of social participation are reflected as follows.

6.3.1.1 *The Requirement of a Sound Market Economy*

There is a consensus among the government, enterprises, and all sectors of society that the formulation of the national development plan is a process of social participation. This is decided by the coexistence of state-owned economy and other various economic components since reform and opening up. The fact that the whole planning process is led by the government does not necessarily mean that the government undertakes the whole planning process. The national development plan should take into account the interests of the economic entities. It is through the planning process that all sectors of society reach a consensus and that the interests of various social groups can be coordinated. By doing so, the national development plan has a solid social foundation and the quality of planning is improved. Motivating enterprises' enthusiasm to participate in planning is particularly important because this is helpful to keep the goals of the enterprises congruent with those of the state and thus reduce the difficulty to carry out the plan in enterprises.

6.3.1.2 *The Requirement of a Guiding Plan*

In the new era, with the salience of the guiding role of planning, the planning indicators, and planning projects are more concentrated on macro control, social progress, ecological environment, economic efficiency, economic structure, and so on. With the reduction of the number of traditional indicators, planning outline has replaced planning indicators. This change means the shift of national planning from the emphasis on economic development to giving full play to the governmental function as a guide. The national development plan should give more prominence to its strategy, macro control, coordination, and economic forecast. In order to give full play to the role of planning in providing information and coordinating interests, planning should be formulated in an ambience of democratic consultation to enhance social participation. Social forces, especially the experts and representatives from the business and social groups, should be organized to participate in planning to ensure a democratic, open, and normative decision making and further improve its transparency.

6.3.1.3 *The Requirement of a Scientific Plan*

The formulation of a scientific plan requires information from different sources and channels a large amount of economic and social information, which will then be carefully filtered and processed for subsequent prediction, drafting, and decision making. Without a sound social participation system, it would be difficult to ensure that the planning has a solid information base. Social participation in planning formulation and implementation is a prerequisite for ensuring a scientific and feasible plan. Only through active and broad participation and cooperation can all sectors of society be marshaled for an open, democratic, and transparent plan, breaking the stereotyped pattern in which experts make predictions and the officials make decisions. This innovative arrangement helps all sectors of society arrive at a consensus over major issues and further guarantees the realization of the objectives prescribed in the plan.

6.3.2 Social Participation in Planning in Japan, France, and South Korea

In order to rehabilitate the ravaged post-WWII economy, Western market economies and some newly industrialized countries such as Japan, France, and South Korea, respectively, introduced their own planning coordination and consultation mechanisms to motivate the social participation in planning formulation.

6.3.2.1 *Japan: Consultation System*

In the formulation of its plan, Japan adopted the consultation system through which Japan achieved wide social participation in planning by channeling vertical exchange of information and strengthening cooperation between officials and the public. Before making the plan, the Prime Minister of the Cabinet consulted with the Economic Deliberation

Council, which was responsible for investigating and deliberating the formulation of the plan and major economic policies and drafting the plan in cooperation with the relevant departments such as the Economic Planning Agency. The Council submitted the draft plan to the cabinet for reconsideration before its publication to the public. Obviously, Japanese planning was mainly centered on the Economic Deliberation Council, an affiliate to the Economic Planning Agency. This Council was populated by about 30 influential representatives from industrial, financial and academic communities, trade unions, mass media, and consumer groups. Entrusted by the Prime Minister, the Council mobilized hundreds of regular members, senior specialists, and provisional members to form many subcommittees that were respectively responsible for investigating and deliberating the objectives, policies, and guidelines of the plan. During investigation and deliberation, the Council collected the necessary information, conducted model analysis, and consulted with major enterprises. Japan's unique tradition of government intervention made enterprises feel it an obligation to report to a higher authority and therefore vertical information exchange became an effective form of close cooperation between the government and the business community. In Japan, the successful launching of any plan was preceded with a consensus of all parties organized by the Economic Deliberation Council after repeated consultation, bargaining, persuasion, and counter-persuasion. It usually took nearly one year for a plan to go through the whole process from its conception to final promulgation. Such a plan could hardly face any resistance.

6.3.2.2 *France: Counseling Principle*

In France, the counseling principle referred to the consultation and dialogue between government officials and social partners — the representatives from all walks of life — for the purpose of completing the compilation of planning. The Modernization Commission (later renamed the Working Committee of Planning), the main consultative organ for planning, consisting of special professional teams and populated by 20–50 officials, experts recruited by the government, and representatives from trade unions, was directly under the General Commission of Planning. Its paramount task was to formulate a plan that could full embody the interests of all parties of the society. The Modernization Commission had affiliates, such as committees organized vertically according to the classification of industries, cross-sectoral committees, and the committees for collective affairs and regional development. Both public and private enterprises could directly participate in the formulation of the plan, either by sending representatives to the Modernization Commission or by maintaining direct contact with some departments under the General Commission of Planning. This helped enterprises understand the intention and content of the national planning. Based on the plan report drafted by the Modernization Commission, a general plan outline was drawn up by the General Commission of Planning and then became a common action program to guide the behaviors of economic entities. This institutional design could help the French government smoothly maintain its national planning in operation and achieve desired objectives.

6.3.2.3 *South Korea: Encouragement of Private Innovative Ideas*

The Economic Planning Board, a state bureaucracy pilot agency now merged with the Ministry of Finance as the Ministry of Economy and Finance, was responsible for the compilation of planning. Before the draft plan was submitted to the cabinet for consideration, opinions on planning objectives and policy trends were widely collected from the public and sent to the government departments after approval. The Economic Planning Board not only consulted with relevant departments but also encouraged public and private enterprises to propose their own innovative ideas on the external environment and the objectives of economic development and the policy orientation in the planning period. In the formulation of departmental planning, the government held seminars to solicit opinions from experts and public and private enterprises. These seminars not only helped planning officials have a better and more comprehensive understanding of economic development but also helped private enterprises have a better understanding of the government's intent for economic prospects and macro-policy orientation. What's more, after keenly aware of the goals that the government tried to achieve through policy intervention, private enterprises could formulate their own planning.

Through wide discussions, consultations, and seminars by pooling ideas and information from the public, private enterprises had a clear understanding of the macroeconomic issues.

To sum up, Japan, France, and South Korea emphasized that planning was not only a matter of the government and economists but a wide social participation. The combination of the scattered goals of families, enterprises, communities, and regions into collective and social goals greatly improved the public's consciousness and initiative to carry out the national planning.

6.3.3 Establishing a Sound Social Participation System

It is an urgent task to establish a system of social participation with Chinese characteristics featuring wide consultation and dialogue and normative organizations through summing up historical experiences and drawing lessons from the relevant practices of foreign nations. The government should encourage the public to take an active part in the formulation of a scientific and systematic plan by collecting topics, inviting tenders for topics, setting up expert committees, holding seminars and symposiums to reach a consensus on major issues.

6.3.3.1 *Consultation and Dialogue*

First, the planning agency should consult with experts and socials groups, especially allowing full play of the research institutes in counseling on the formulation of planning. Second, the government should encourage enterprises to take part in the discussion of environmental protection, objective setup, and policy trends. Third, the current "half-open" or unilateral counsel-seeking should be replaced by a normative bilateral consultation in which official information, consultancy, and research agencies conduct a dialogue with the nongovernmental chamber of commerce, sectors of industries, and state-owned, collective, and private sectors of economy in a democratic ambience. Finally, it is necessary to strengthen consultation and dialogue with enterprises, especially conglomerates. In the planning stage, the state functional departments should request enterprises to provide predictive and computational data as a reference for planning and inform enterprises of macroeconomic objectives, planning ideas, and major measures. In a word, the government planning department should reform the past practice of mapping out a plan only by the government departments and establish a normative, institutionalized, and democratic system of social participation.

6.3.3.2 *Coordination*

China's new planning system is a synthesis of comprehensive economic aggregate indicators consisting of many quantitative indicators and industrial policies, especially many regulations concerning economic and technological development. Planning coordination aims to actualize the congruity of indicators, unity and continuity of policies and regulations, and the compatibility of policies and indicators. Various coordination meetings should be held to ensure the smooth implementation of the plan. It is necessary to establish a strict system of joint coordination meetings, according to which the government planning agency should first seek advice from the competent economic departments and a panel of economists (in the form of planning consultation meetings) and propose a preliminary conception. Then it should convene joint meetings of different regions or departments for coordination. It is also necessary to coordinate the relationship between the government and enterprises. Before formulating the planning objectives and economic policies, the government should hold meetings to exchange opinions with trade associations, large backbone enterprises, and relevant experts. For the specific requirements of some specific tasks in a plan, such as the economic scale of an industry, the timetable for technological transformation, and equipment renewal and the issuance or cancellation of a protective policy, the planning agency should take into consideration the opinions of experts. This is the guarantee for the feasibility and effectiveness of the plan.

6.3.3.3 *Exchange of Information*

Due to their irreplaceable role in achieving planning objectives, the government planning agency should establish a system of direct information exchange with key enterprises, industries, social organizations, and economic development zones, which are required to provide sufficient economic information for accurate prediction and tailored macroeconomic control and which can in turn be well informed of the macroeconomic objectives, planning conceptions, policy trends through departments in charge and channels, and thus make their own autonomous decisions congruous with the national development plan. In the stage of planning implementation, accurate information should be collected, transmitted, and feedbacked quickly and completely for reference for subsequent adjustments or for future planning. In the stage of planning completion, experiences and lessons should be summed up. It should be noted that in the era of knowledge economy, of information and of economic globalization, China should pay close attention to the global economic operation and development trend, especially to the development and policy change of those nations and regions closely related to China's economic development. It is recommendable that the government reconcile domestic development and foreign trade, internal and external equilibrium, and value the transmission effect in the international economy.

6.3.3.4 *Counsel*

Counseling is of great significance to scientific and democratic macro decision making. Planning counseling includes counseling on policy and decision making, engineering projects, technical problems, foreign affairs, social audit, accounting, pricing, market changes, and various sources of information, among which the first two are most closely related to the formulation and implementation of national development planning. In addition, foreign experts can be invited to counsel on certain issues. Various analysis and evaluation groups can be formed to make empirical judgments and quantitative analyses based on large quantities of information and model methods. The government planning agency should hold advisory seminars and deliberations at different levels according to the progression of planning implementation and organize representatives from industrial and commercial groups, trade associations, market organizations and intermediaries, consumer groups, economic research and counseling institutions, and universities to participate in the process of planning or directly provide decision makers with the "expert version" of development plan or evaluation report for reference. For instance, the Shanghai Academy of Social Sciences took the lead in compiling the expert version of the 11th Five-Year Plan. In the process of compilation, these experts widely sought advice from all sectors of society, especially from the business community. Since there was no stake in giving advice and no financial constraints, the advice was more transparent and objective than expected. The Shanghai Municipal government believed that the expert version had a great significance in its planning.

In addition, it is necessary to handle the relationship between the government and the market in the process of improving social participation in planning. For instance, industry associations participated in the formulation of "Revitalization Plan for Ten Industries" of 2008. Although it was an exception, it was still a rewarding attempt because the industry associations themselves know better about the actual situations.

6.4 IMPLEMENTATION AND MONITORING OF PLANNING

The national development plan, no matter how well it has been formulated, would become nothing but a dead letter if there was no regulation guarantee of implementing it.

Under planning economy, the implementation of the plan was not a problem because the plan was mandatory, and the overall objective was decomposed into many indicators. By contrast, under the market economy, market entities have the freedom to manage their own business and enterprises are no longer the basic units of the national plan. Therefore, the implementation of the national development plan has become a somewhat thorny question.

Because the implementation of any plan may deviate from its original expectations and different enterprises have strong or weak execution performances, it is necessary to establish a system of inspection and monitoring. Planning monitoring, an important part of national economic monitoring system, is a means by which to make timely and accurate analysis and judgment of the development situation as required by the national development plan and the interrelationship between various indicators of economic and social development so that the competent authorities at all levels can adopt appropriate measures to make adjustments in time lest excessive deviation may happen in the future.

6.4.1 Implementation and Management

Implementation has been a relatively weak link in planning for a long time. The problem of "giving too much concern over compilation but making little of implementation" is quite common, and as a result, the implementation of a plan is decoupled from planning itself and some indicators have remained mere words on a scrap of paper. Such being the case, more attention should be paid to the implementation in the future.

6.4.1.1 *The Transformation of Implementation Mode*

Under planning economy, the national development objectives were decomposed into mandatory indicators to be assigned from the central government to each administrative region and down to the grassroots units (local enterprises), which would unconditionally complete the tasks delegated to them by superiors. By contrast, under socialist market economy, the national development plan is more a guide than an authoritative command, which denotes a fundamental change in the mode of implementation.

A guiding or policy-oriented plan emphasizes the direction and objectives of development and has no administrative binding force on enterprises. Its main function is to provide enterprises with information, and the decomposition of a few anticipatory indicators is only to provide them more detailed economic information. By doing so, the plan shows the governmental intention that is to guide enterprises in making production and management decisions compatible with macroeconomic objectives.

It should be noted that the objectives and tasks stipulated in the national development plan have administrative-binding force on governments at all levels, which, alongside with central special and comprehensive management departments, are the organizational guarantee for the completion of the national development plan.

The objectives and tasks that the national development plan requires the governments at all levels and the competent central authorities to complete should be the fundamental basis on which to formulate economic and social policies, use economic adjustment instruments and adopt macro control means.

History shows that the smooth implementation of the national development plan requires at least the following safeguards: government supports at all levels; basic policies and measures pertinent to the implementation of the plan; the successful completion of major construction projects blueprinted in the plan; necessary resource guarantees, especially the support from the national monetary and financial institutions; public cognizance, recognition, and active participation; the institutionalization of the planning process including formulation, implementation, readjustment, revision, supervision, and evaluation; and guarantee of other objective conditions, such as a favorable international environment and freedom from mishaps and natural disasters.

6.4.1.2 *Instruments*

• Publication and propagation of the plan

Once ratified, the national development plan will be published, except for those involving confidential information stipulated by relevant laws and administrative regulations.

There are no clear legal provisions except some official documents for how and when a plan is published by which department. The following basic principles are usually observed. The authority of planning publication belongs to the organ of examination and ratification authority. The national master plan ratified by the NPC shall be promulgated by the NPC Standing Committee. The national specialized plan and regional plan shall be issued by the State Council. The forms of publication include documents, official newspapers, websites, and other mass media. These principles are also applicable to plans at provincial and city–county levels.

The propagation of the plan through meetings, documents, newspapers, television, radio, and the Internet is helpful for the officials and the public to arrive at a consensus that the plan should be translated into action. It is not enough to publicize the plan as it is. Much attention should also be paid to the clarification of the progression of the planning, supporting materials, assessment of the situation, and the goal to attain so that the mass of people can be inspired, educated, and mobilized to strive for the goal.

• **Decomposition of indicators and execution**

Governments at all levels should be responsible for breaking down the overall objective into indicators and for the delegation of the indicators to the lower administrative organs and down to the enterprises and other basic units. It should be noted that the breaking down and delegation of indicators under the socialist market economy are fundamentally different from those under the planning economy system. For instance, it is not necessary to break down and delegate the forward-looking and anticipatory indicators in the national development plan to each region and each enterprise. The principal responsibility of the governments is to handle the indicators they held responsible for and ensure the attainment of the indicators by rationally allocating public resources and utilizing administrative forces.

• **Practicable safeguards**

First comes the promotion of the national development plan through annual plans. Little attention was paid to the combination of the five-year plan with annual plans in the process of implementation. As a matter of fact, each individual annual plan should become an important means of implementing a medium- or long-term plan. The targets in the five-year development plan can be decomposed and then placed into five annual plans so that they can be attained year by year. More importantly, through the monitoring of annual plans, problems, and deviations in the implementation of the medium- and long-term plan could be diagnosed so that timely remedies could be prescribed for a healthier development.

Second comes the assurance of the implementation of major projects predetermined in the plan. A reasonable arrangement of the construction of major projects buttresses the success of a plan. Whether they are in an overall plan or in a specialized plan, the main indicators are all achieved through specific construction projects. Endeavors should be made throughout the whole construction process to ensure that they are completed as scheduled.

Third, policy guidance is an instrument for the government to guide, in the context of market-oriented development planning, the behaviors of enterprises to attain the planned objective. These policy instruments are a mixture of financial and monetary means and the economic leverages, such as pricing, taxation, interest rates, and exchange rates. Policies may be flexible and be in line with the changes in the macroeconomic environment. The government should also track the effect of policies so that it may change or stick to the policies according to different situations.

6.4.2 Monitoring System

The monitoring system, a guarantor of a scientific and effective plan, includes the following.

6.4.2.1 *Periodic (Quarterly, Monthly) Monitoring*

In most cases, macroeconomic monitoring is periodically conducted on a monthly or quarterly basis. After being processed technically, the monitoring data are collated with the preset alarm values. During the period of frequent economic fluctuations, some indicators central to macroeconomics should be monitored on a 10-day basis. Monitoring is also necessary for the supply and demand of the undersupplied products that restrict national economic development and products with a larger elasticity coefficient. Regular monitoring should also be targeted at the international market of the imports and exports that have a great impact on domestic production. Meanwhile, monitoring can also be directed at a region or an industrial sector.

6.4.2.2 *Ex-ante, Interim, and Ex-post Monitoring*

Ex-ante monitoring, precautionary before the implementation of a plan, is designed to monitor whether the plan is rational and feasible. Interim monitoring, a routine examination in the process of the implementation, is designed to find out whether the plan deviates from expectations and pinpoint the reasons for the problems. *Ex-post* monitoring is a measure of the past performance in executing the plan. *Ex-ante* monitoring is typified by the consideration and ratification of the national development plan by the NPC, *ex-post* monitoring typified by the consideration and approval of the progression of executing the plan, and interim monitoring by the periodical analytical report about economic performance issued by the national comprehensive economic department.

6.4.2.3 *Monitoring by the State, Society, and People*

The state organs can wield power authorized by the state to monitor the implementation of the plan. Monitoring by the state is the most authoritative and effective means. In addition, social groups and the public also have the authority or right to do so. The public are entitled to monitor the implementation process of a plan through complaints, petition letters, and news media. Monitoring by society and people is complementary to monitoring by the state.

6.4.2.4 *Internal and External Monitoring*

Internal monitoring within an economic entity includes two levels of monitoring. One is the inspection and control of its own behavior by the economic entity itself and the other is the monitoring within the same economic entity or between the subordinate units of the same department. Although internal monitoring can regularly provide timely and comprehensive information, it is subject to intervention from the executive leaders. External monitoring refers to the monitoring of economic activities of enterprises by state organs or social organizations. The feedback information from external monitoring is usually objective and fair.

6.4.2.5 *Intensive and Extensive Monitoring*

Extensive monitoring refers to a comprehensive supervision and inspection over economic operations, while intensive monitoring aims at a special inspection over a particular economic entity or a particular economic activity as required by the state or by the public tip-offs.

In addition, a monitoring system can also be set up on the basis of nature of industry, the methods of planning management, and the aspects of social reproduction.

6.4.3 Content Design of Planning Monitoring

6.4.3.1 *Major Objectives and Parameters*

The major macroeconomic objectives and parameters include the balance between total social supply and total social demand, economic growth rate, the objective of the transformation of industrial structure, income distribution structure, scale and structure of domestic and foreign trade, price index, unemployment rate, BOP, economic benefits, and the rationality and feasibility of relevant major policies.

6.4.3.2 *Macroeconomic Climate Index*

An analysis of the changes of some macroeconomic indicators and the regularity of macroeconomic climate index helps economist forecast economic prospects. Economic undulations, which are inevitably frequent for various reasons under market economy, have a great impact on the choice of national macro-control policies. Therefore, monitoring macroeconomic climate is of great importance to the formulation and implementation of the national development plan.

6.4.3.3 *Capital Operation*

It is urgent to monitor capital operation of the whole society for the purpose of optimizing capital structure, improving capital utilization efficiency, and sustaining a coordinated development of national economy. Monitoring should focus on how the use of funds in various department is related to the overall arrangement of social funds, and how financial and monetary departments operate and allocate funds when they cooperate with planning departments. Besides, attention should also be paid to the stock, flow, and distribution structure of various types of social funds. The government should strengthen stringent fiscal discipline and economic accounting, improve capital distribution structure, reduce losses and waste, and improve economic efficiency.

6.4.3.4 *Market Operation*

Under socialist market economy, the market plays a fundamental role in allocation of resources only when it operates normally and orderly and the behaviors of the market subjects are normal. The purpose of monitoring market operation is to protect legitimate transactions, ban illegal practices, safeguard fair competition, and maintain normal operation of the market. The monitoring of market operation should focus on the legitimacy of the business activities of the buyers and sellers, the quality, safety, environmental standards of the trading objects, and the legitimacy of listings, trading prices, measurement means and standards, trademarks, and so on.

6.4.3.5 *Foreign Trade*

The trend of economic globalization and integration may bring about opportunities on the one hand but pose a threat to a country's economy on the other. One of the important tasks of macroeconomic management is to seize these opportunities to facilitate the development of national economy in the international economic environment. At present, China's imports and exports, labor export, foreign cooperation, inbound and outbound investments are on the increase, and the domestic economy is increasingly dependent on the global economy. Foreign market expansion and utilization of foreign resources have become an important subject for furthering economic development.

In addition, the degree of the implementation of major policies and the impact of some emergencies on the implementation of planning should also be included in the system of planning monitoring.

6.4.4 Methods of Planning Monitoring

Monitoring of planning implementation depends more on data indicators. Therefore, the first step is to determine a scientific and reasonable evaluation index system, through which a fair evaluation conclusion can be drawn. Generally, the indices should be typical, and the sources of data should be stable and reliable. Second, information channels for better monitoring should be established. It is necessary to strengthen the vertical information exchange between the competent departments at all levels, the horizontal information exchange between the planning departments in charge and the monetary, financial, statistical agencies at the same level, and the connection between monitoring stations like central cities and key enterprises and important markets. Planning authorities at all levels should ensure the sharing and full use of monitored information. Finally, the collected information should be processed with various methods including macroeconomic models, especially macroeconomic monitoring models and forewarning models. The specific safeguards for planning monitoring are as follows:

Information collection: Focusing on the key sections and links of the chain of monitoring and collecting the most typical information by the direct or indirect investigation.

Quantitative accounting: Providing comprehensive, systematic and accurate accounting data by integrating and processing data obtained from accounting, statistical and commercial departments.

Checkup: Ascertaining the truth through policy checkup, on-the-spot checkup, and financial checkup, and drawing conclusions.

Causal analysis: Determining the reason by analyzing accounting and checkup results.

Deviation correction: Pinpointing the deviation and determining when and how it should be corrected.

6.5 EVALUATION AND REVISION OF PLANNING

In the implementation of a plan, a series of problems will inevitably arise. How is the plan going? What effects have policies and regulations exerted on the formulation of the plan? Has there been any serious aberration? Is it necessary to make any adjustments? These questions have a stake in smooth promotion of the plan and the solutions to these questions largely depend on evaluation and revision of the plan.

6.5.1 *Ex-ante*, Interim, and *Ex-post* Evaluations

The planning evaluation can be divided into *ex-ante* evaluation, interim evaluation, and *ex-post* evaluation. As the names suggest, *ex-ante* evaluation refers to the evaluation before the implementation of the plan, interim evaluation to the evaluation at any point of time somewhere between the beginning to the end of the event, and *ex-post* evaluation to the evaluation after the event.

Ex-ante evaluation is an assessment of the feasibility of planning on the basis of historical and empirical data, some of which are speculative and predicative. Interim and *ex-post* evaluations are relatively independent and interrelated since they have both similarities and differences. Interim evaluation is designed to check the quality of *ex-ante* evaluation or evaluate major changes in the implementation process and relevant impact so that difficulties can be overcome. Its core is to assess whether the progression of the plan is consistent with the established objectives. *Ex-post* evaluation aims to check whether planning formulation is practical and how far the expected goals have been achieved by comparing the actual completion of the planning target with the expected goals as well as to propose remedial measure for future planning by causal analysis of success or failure. The results of *ex-post* evaluation should be feedbacked for improving future planning management level. Interim evaluation and *ex-post* evaluation are both based on realistic data and the evaluation objects in them are nearly the same. Interim is the basis for *ex-post* evaluation and the latter is the continuation of the former.

In China, *ex-ante* evaluation is relatively common while *ex-post* evaluation is too simplified and interim evaluation is very few and far between. The evaluation of the planning implementation in discussion in this chapter refers to interim evaluation and *ex-post* evaluation. The duration when interim evaluation is involved in a five-year planning is usually the time from the beginning of the implementation the third or fourth year, as interpreted by the National Development and Reform Commission.

6.5.2 Content Design of Planning Evaluation

Planning at all levels extensively covers all areas of national economic and social development, but the content design of evaluation cannot be inclusive of them all. Generally, the evaluation of planning implementation should include the following four aspects.

6.5.2.1 *Target Evaluation*

Once a plan has been put into practice, what concerns people most is the completion of the planning targets, most of which can be observed and analyzed because their quantitative changes can be reflected by indices. Because the progression of implementing the plan is inevitably affected by many invariables, the actual results may be at variance with the expected values. Therefore, a reliable evaluation of how fast and how far the plan has been carried out mainly depends on making a systematic analysis of the variances between the actual results and expected goals. The systematic analysis should solve the following questions: what deviations have happened? When and where and why have they happened? How serious are they?

6.5.2.2 *Efficiency Evaluation*

Efficiency evaluation is an analysis of the ratio of planned input to actual output. It includes the evaluation of the planning input–output ratio. From the planning output, we can evaluate the impact of planning on the national economy, namely the contribution rate of planning to national economy; from the planning input, we can evaluate all the costs inputted to the planning and the input structure. Meanwhile, it also includes an analysis of the input–output ratio of the whole national economic efficiency, a region or an industry. Of course, input–output ratio analysis is not applicable to noneconomic fields such as education and healthcare. The efficiency evaluation for different sectors should focus on different factors and the key is to find out the reasons for high or low efficiency.

6.5.2.3 *Impact Evaluation*

The impact of the development on a nation can be quantified from environment, income, and employment, or can be estimated by social measure of value. For instance, an overall plan is more concerned about its impact on the degree of equality of regional development, urban and rural resident income, employment, and environment protection. Impact evaluation is becoming more important because the concept of sustainable development has lodged itself in the public mind.

6.5.2.4 *Evaluation of Observance of Laws*

Besides concerning itself with how far the objectives have been achieved and how much efficiency has been improved, evaluation should also deal with how these objectives have been achieved and whether market entities have observed the laws or regulations related to planning. This is particularly of great realistic significance in the case of imperfect legal system in the current China. This mainly includes the allocation and use of planning funds, equipment procurement, congruity between planning regulations and national laws.

Each of the above evaluates economic activities of planning from different aspects. In the actual evaluation, it is essential to combine all of them and make a comprehensive and systematic evaluation.

6.5.3 Safeguards for Planning Evaluation

6.5.3.1 *Organizer and Executor of Planning Evaluation*

Planning evaluation is so onerous that it should be organized and conducted by special departments.

The organizer should be decided by the nature of evaluation. Generally, planning evaluation mainly involves the evaluation of the plan itself, which focuses on whether the plan is suitable to actual situations and of the implementation of the plan, which focuses more on how far each target has been achieved and how well the departments in charge have fulfilled their responsibility. Theoretically, the compiling departments should be responsible for organizing the evaluation of the plan, and the approving agencies for organizing the evaluation of the planning implementation. Therefore, the organizer of planning evaluation may be the examining and approving agency or the compiling department. At present, whoever compiles the plan is responsible for the organizational work of evaluation. In the long run, it should be stipulated by law.

To whom is the planning evaluation entrusted? This also depends on two situations. One is that whoever organizes evaluation is responsible for specific evaluation work, that is, internal evaluation in the form of administrative evaluation. Nevertheless, this design has the disadvantages of insufficient human resources, limited scope and depth of evaluation, and less objective and fair evaluation as a result of internal monitoring although it can benefit from rapid feedback of information and relatively low cost. The other is to entrust evaluation to external agencies, such as investment consulting corporations and professional evaluation agencies. This entrustment guarantees a more accurate and objective evaluation. However, the cost to recruit external agencies is relatively high and the evaluation agencies are prone to encounter resistance when they attempt to cooperate with the departments in charge of planning implementation.

The determination of what means should be applied in evaluation depends on the purpose, content, workload, time requirement, and financial position of planning evaluation. In China, internal evaluation is more widely applied than external evaluation. It is recommendable that the departments should recruit outside experts and encourage public opinions for a more reliable, objective, and fair evaluation. In the long run, planning evaluation should be entrusted to external agencies.

6.5.3.2 *Procedures for Evaluation*

Specifying objectives: The planning evaluation organizer determines evaluation objects and proposes main tasks and basic requirements.

Inviting sponsors: The organizer entrusts evaluation to outside expert agencies through negotiation, invitation for bid, or setting up an evaluation agency.

Formulating a work program: The sponsor, after accepting the evaluation, formulates a work program, which includes personnel structure, time schedule, evaluation methods, forms of results, budget, and so on.

Evaluating: The sponsor carries out a comprehensive survey, collects information, verifies data, identifies the existing problems by scientific demonstrations and rational evaluation methods. Besides, the sponsor should also propose corresponding suggestions.

Evaluation report: The sponsor researches and aggregates each evaluation result and then forms an evaluation report which will be submitted to the organizer or higher authorities.

6.5.4 Revision of Planning

Economic aberrations from the planned targets that are attributable to the failure of macroeconomic control can be remedied by the issuance of more supplementary regulations and laws. If it is the outdated plan or misjudgments in formulating the plan that resulted in the aberrations, the plan should be revised.

6.5.4.1 *Necessity of Revising a Plan*

The necessity to make flexible readjustments or revise the plan during the implementation of national development plan is reflected in the following three aspects.

First, revisions and readjustments can ensure the adaptivity of the plan to the ever-changing development environment. Many planned objectives are directly and highly correlated to environmental variables. If no revision is made according to the changes of actual situations, many objectives may not be achieved.

Secondly, revisions and readjustments can safeguard the scientific and systematic plan. The adjustment of planning can countervail the impact of negative environment and improve the independence of planning from within so that the net results of planning are not subject to external environment. Therefore, it is advisable to handle the problems unexpectedly emerging from the implementation of the plan with a foresighted attitude lest we might be stereotyped.

Third, the ultimate purpose of revising and readjusting the plan is to more smoothly promote the realization of the national development goals. When the significant internal and external changes retard the progression of the plan, revising and readjusting the plan becomes inevitable.

6.5.4.2 *Precautions*

Planning revision, which has a stake in the success of the national development plan, should be conducted discreetly and timely. There are a few precautions should be noted when revising the plan.

First, there must be a justification for revising the plan. The main reason for planning adjustment is the changes in the actual situations, such as changes in the international political and economic environment, the domestic macroeconomic situations, emergencies, special opportunities, and problems caused by the implementation of some major policies and measures. All of these should be discreetly evaluated before conclusion can be drawn.

Second, revision should go through statutory procedures. Legal procedures cannot replace the will of officials.

It should be regulated and restricted by law and system. Some planning contents that need to be adjusted and revised shall be put forward by the original planning units in accordance with the legal procedures for adjustment and revision, and shall be publicly released after being deliberated and approved by the departments with legal authority. Attention should be paid to continue to reassess and remonitor the adjusted plan. The environment of economic operation is always changing. No plan can be implemented once and for all. The implementation after adjustment is relatively smooth. Implementation is always a dynamic process, from implementation, monitoring, evaluation and adjustment to reimplementation, remonitoring, and reevaluation, and if necessary, readjustment. Therefore, the adjusted plan also needs to be remonitored and reassessed in order to find new problems in a timely manner and take measures to solve them. The planning revision includes two aspects: revision of the planning objectives and revision of policies and measures. Planning revision should be carried out in strict accordance with legal procedures to safeguard the seriousness and authority of national planning. Meanwhile, attention should also be paid to the comprehensive balance of planning, so as to ensure that the revised plan remains a systematic, coordinated and complementary overall system.

REFERENCES

Hu, Zucai, and Rui Liu. *Macro Control in Social Development: Theory, Practice and Innovation.* Beijing: China Market Publishing House, 2009. 胡祖才,刘瑞. 社会发展宏观调控：理论-实践-创新. 北京：中国市场出版社, 2009.

Shen, Hao, and Karma Ura. *National Happiness: An Index of a Nation's Development.* Beijing: Beijing University Press, 2011. 沈颢, 卡玛•尤拉. 国民幸福: 一个国家发展的指标体系. 北京: 北京大学出版社, 2011.

Tinbergen, Jan. *Economic Policy: Principles and Design.* Amsterdam: North-Holland Publishing Company, 1956.

Yang, Zhongwei, and Bo Li. *Planning System and Macroeconomic Policies in Federal Germany.* Zhengzhou: Henan People's Publishing House, 1988.

NOTE

1. In his online communication with netizens over the interpretation of the Report on the Implementation of the 2010 National Economic and Social Development Plan and the Draft National Economic and Social Development Plan for 2011 on March 8, 2011, Li Pumin, Deputy Secretary-General and Press Spokesperson of the NDRC, remarked: "It is universally accepted by all countries that economic growth, price stability, full employment and balance of payments are the four major macroeconomic objectives."

Chapter 7

Improving Regional Planning

Regional economic adjustment made according to the regional economic plan is the key to the realization of macroeconomic control. For many market economies, the bulk work of national economic planning involves regional economic planning (REP), but that is often overlooked in China. At the turn of the century, especially in the face of a global financial crisis, China is at a critical stage of development. Against this background, it is particularly relevant to examine the trends and characteristics of REP, to take stock of the lessons of previous regional planning practices, and to update the theories.

7.1 DEFINITION OF REP

REP involves the drafting of a land utilization or development plan, which coordinates the development of population, economy, natural resources with the protection of the environment, and harmonizes regional relations. REP, a manifestation of the regional development strategy, helps to optimize the economic development of the whole country, and is an effective mechanism to solve regional development conflicts.

REP, which is aimed to achieve sustainable development of the region concerned, is based on a thorough understanding of the economic, resources, social, and environmental factors of a specific region. It consists of two levels of planning: trans-regional and regional planning. The former addresses the problem of uneven development between different regions, or for achieving an optimized division of labor between the regions, and the latter is a comprehensive plan for social and economic development of a certain region. REP involves the planning of major infrastructure projects, industry deployment distribution, environmental conservation, natural resources development, and many other issues. In short, it addresses specific economic issues of a certain region.

REP is a means to achieve coordinated and sustainable development of different regions, and an effective vehicle for allocating resources to materialize the development strategy laid out by the government. To draft an REP, one needs to determine the economic regions from the following five perspectives:

(1) Administrative districts: An administrative district is a unit for carrying out the functions of the government in a specific hierarchy. A regional plan for an administrative district or several districts can be executed more efficiently by the relevant governments.

(2) Economic zones: Economic zones are geographic areas that have similar or integrated economic operations. Common economic zones include urban areas, industrial development zones, tourism development zones, or rural development zones. To define a region by economic activities is to give a clear division of economic operations of these zones according to their economic strengths and potentials, or in other words, their individual comparative advantages. A majority of REP involves an economic zone that encompasses several administrative districts.

(3) Geographic areas: A geographically based REP is used as drafted for the utilization or development of certain natural resources, such sea, island, river, and lake, or for addressing ecological issues in those areas.

(4) Problems: Areas confronted with similar problems or obstacles in the process of economic development can be defined as a region. Common problems include the development of poor and backward areas, reformation of old industrial bases and the like.

(5) Special economic projects: REPs of this kind often involve the planning of special economic zones, economic and technological development zones, bonded areas, and so on.

7.2 THE ROLE OF REP

China's socialist market economic system has been improving steadily, and its macroeconomic control practice has undergone fundamental changes. Noticeably, regional planning and policies are playing an increasingly important role in China's macroeconomic control system. In fact, REP is highlighted in the 11th Five-Year Plan, which outlines the development strategies, the focus of structural adjustment of regional economy. The role of REP can be summarized as follows:

First, REP is an important means to promote coordinated development of different regions. In a market economy, the market tends to expand rather than narrow the economic gap between regions. In order to promote a coordinated development of different regions, Western market economies have to formulate REP and policies to address the issue. China is a vast country and due to the uneven distribution of natural, social, and cultural resources, the imbalance of regional development is more prominent. Drawing on the experience of Western countries and taking into consideration the current reality of the country, China, as a socialist market economy, has to formulate and implement regional planning and policies to promote a coordinated development of different regions.

Second, REP contributes to the building of a well-off society in an all-round way. Coordinated development of all the regions in the country and a gradual reversal of widening regional disparity are indispensable with REP. At present, the major issues involving regional development, such as the formulation of key regional development strategy, the arrangement of regional economic activities, and the construction of key infrastructure and ecological environment projects, need to be coordinated through regional planning.

Third, REP helps to improve China's economic management practice. Traditionally, the economic management of China focuses on the assessment and approval of key projects and the economic activity of individual administrative district, which often overlooks the provision of comprehensive supporting facilities and the interaction between the projects and their surrounding environments. This negligence has brought adverse effects on the optimization and sustainable development of regional productive forces. In contrast, REP pays attention to the rationality of the spatial distribution of regional comparative advantages and factors, and the coordination of economic and social development with people and natural resources. Thus, REP is conducive to the improvement of China's economic management practice and its integration with the international modern economic management system.

Fourth, REP promotes the improvement of China's planning practice. At present, macroeconomic management is plagued with an absence of relevant legislation. There is also a lack of legal basis for planning. Due to the lack of legislation on regional planning, when regional planning, urban planning, and land use planning conflict in objectives and contents, disputes among the stakeholders will rise. Therefore, pushing forward with REP will give an incentive for the legislation of China's planning system.

7.3 THE TASKS AND CONTENTS OF AN REP

REP, a strategically spatial and mandatory planning aiming to tackle specific economic issues of a certain region rather than a guiding and anticipatory plan, basically specify the following components.

7.3.1 Development Orientation

To define the development orientation is the primary task of REP and the planners need to take the following five aspects into consideration. (1) The trends of the economic and social development of the country at the time. The focus, speed, and policy of regional economic and social development are determined to a large extent by those trends. (2) The level of economic strength and the natural resources of the region in concern. (3) The current economic status of surrounding regions and their interaction with that of the region in concern. (4) The principle of sustainable development. The purpose of regional economic development is to achieve the best economic, social, and ecological benefits. Therefore, to define the purpose of regional planning, the principle of sustainable development must be followed. (5) The trend of science and technology. Regional development is dependent on the development of science and technology. A clear understanding of current science and technology helps to ensure that the region in concern can catch up with that trend.

7.3.2 Defining Goals and Objectives

A comprehensive evaluation of the development conditions, a correct understanding of the strategic position, and division of labor of the region are important factors for the formulation of regional development objectives. To accurately predict the future economic and social development of a region, qualitative and quantitative analysis should be used to scrutinize the factors that may affect the future development of the region.

The planners make sure that the objectives are achievable, detailed, and tailored to a specific region. In addition, the objectives must reflect the various aspects of regional development, and the time for achieving the objectives should be clearly specified.

7.3.3 Identifying the Key Sector, Area, and Projects for REP

A good REP identifies key sectors and regions, so they can serve as the economic growth engine of the entire region. When economic, human, scientific, and technological resources are working as a whole, they can give a full swing to economic development of the region.

Identifying the key sector comes first. There is no fixed formula for selecting the key sector in a certain region at a particular period of development. The planners have to take the specific conditions of the region into consideration before making the final decision.

A general rule is to prioritize leading industries that can spur the development of supporting industries and infrastructure building. Then comes the selection of key development areas. The key to successful regional planning is to draft phased plans that suit the specific conditions of the area. The selection is based on the research of experts.

Finally, the selection of key projects. Infrastructure construction projects are often proposed by the government, while industrial projects are often proposed by the enterprises. To best guarantee the effectiveness of the plan, the planners should conduct initial feasibility research to ensure the projects proposed can promote the development of the area in question. The projects must be in line with the overall plan and the arrangement of the governments and the development goals of the enterprises within the area. The projects must follow a timetable that suits the development objectives of the area.

7.3.4 Designing the Layout of the Industrial Area

The core mission of REP is to determine the regional development mode, optimize the regional spatial structure, and achieve reasonable productivity distribution via a comprehensive assessment of the advantages and constraints of the region, the interregional economic ties, and market needs.

As for an REP for a larger region, the planners should take into consideration spatial structure, including relationship between the central and peripheral regions, infrastructure construction, and the distribution of industrial functions. As for an REP for a smaller region, the planners should incorporate the distribution of public facilities such as education, medical care and health, commerce, culture, sports, entertainment, and tourism into the planning. Besides, the REP should make specific proposals about conservation of natural environment, water sources, public hygiene, and countermeasures in case of emergencies.

7.4 REP VERSUS OTHER TYPES OF PLANNING

REP, national economic and social development planning, urban planning, and national land planning are related and can be overlapping. Regional planning is often the middle ground where all other types of planning interact. Therefore, it is necessary to identify the relationship between regional planning and other types of planning.

7.4.1 REP Versus National and Social Development Planning

The national economic and social development plan is designed to achieve the growth objectives of the national economy along a timetable by coordinating the work of all departments or sectors. The regional planning, however, is designed to optimize the natural and human resources of a specific region or area to speed up the economic development of that region. China's national economic and social development plan basically involves the administrative districts at or above the county level, while regional planning mainly involves economic regions across administrative districts. A regional plan may involve several provinces, cities, and districts. In addition, due to accelerated economic globalization and regionalization, regional planning involves not only some regions of China but also some neighboring nations.

The national economic and social development plan is the governing plan for regional planning. In fact, regional planning is an implementation of the national economic and social development planning. Regional planning aims to regulate the allocation of spatial resources and gradually shift down-to-earth spatial control from a theoretical control. More importantly, it proactively revises the irrational parts of national social and economic plan through "space access," such as spatial affordability and the constraints of subregional development. In a word, regional planning reflects not only the national economic development policies and the social reformation intent in the construction of spatial environment but also puts forward proposals for social objectives.

7.4.2 REP Versus Urban Planning

The history of worldwide planning shows that urban planning preceded regional planning. Both regional planning and urban planning are directed at a synthetical arrangement of social and economic development in a specific territorial space. In a broad sense, the planning for a large city and its suburban towns and county-level cities is regional urban planning, typically represented in China by the urban planning of large cities such as Beijing; Shanghai; Guangzhou; and other metropolitan cities, the Planning for Urban Agglomeration in Central China; and the Changsha–Zhuzhou–Xiangtan Urban Agglomeration Planning. In a stricter sense, the planning for a single city or town is urban planning, which will be conditioned by regional planning. From the perspective of the single point of a city and a broader scope of a whole region, regional planning is the important basis for urban planning and the latter should be congruous with the former. In this sense, urban planning is the concretization of regional planning and in turn regional planning will be gradually pushed forward with the implementation of regional planning.

In China, urban planning is less comprehensive than regional planning because the former is headed by the Ministry of Housing and Urban–Rural Development, a specialized rather than a comprehensive management department, while the latter is usually an interregional or interprovincial planning and thus comprehensive. From the perspective of planning at the spatial level, regional planning is higher than urban planning though the former evolved from the latter in time sequence.

7.4.3 REP Versus National Land Use Planning

National land use planning is designed to optimize the exploitation, utilization, conservation of the land as a whole in accordance with the national social and economic development plan and the natural; social; economic; scientific; and technological conditions of the region in question. Therefore, national land use planning and regional planning share many similarities. Comprehensive and forward-looking, both national land use planning and regional planning address the across-the-board issues in a particular geographic region that are related to natural environment, socio-economic development, and technological factors that only a multidisciplinary team of experts can do justice. From the perspective of spatial planning, both aim at a coordinated economic and social development by rationally utilizing spatial resources. Regional planning is formulated by the National Development and Reform Commission, and the national land use planning is headed by the Ministry of Land and Resources. The Ministry and the Commission should strengthen communication over the coordination of planning although they fall within different administrative departments.

However, land use planning focuses on the overall planning for the land development, utilization, and conservation of a single administrative region and therefore cannot guarantee the maximization of economic and social benefits of the region and its neighboring administrative regions. By contrast, regional planning is designed to achieve a coordinated development of geographically adjacent administrative regions to maximize the overall economic growth.

7.4.4 REP Versus Major Function-Oriented Zone Planning

The major function-oriented zone (MFOZ) planning and regional planning are both tailored for different regions so that regional specialty economies can prosper and further coordinate national economy. MFOZ planning, basically a regional planning, emphasizes planning the main economic functions in consideration of the advantages and disadvantages of natural resources, population distribution, layout of major infrastructures, public service facilities, and regional policies. Therefore, it has an innovative influence on regional planning in terms of theoretical system, concept, contents, spatial system, and implementation safeguards. MFOZ planning, a strategic and fundamental planning that has binding effect, can be redeemed as the optimization of regional planning.

In addition, MFOZ planning is a phased action plan for the promotion of dividing MFOZs. Unlike the region involved in regional planning based on administrative regions, natural reserves, or economic zones, an MFOZ is one of the spatial units partitioned out of the whole national territorial space in consideration of the affordability of natural resources, potential development density, population distribution, economic layout, land use, and urbanization. Nevertheless, an MFOZ still often centers on a single administrative region in practice although it involves more than one administrative region. In the four major types of MFOZs (see Chapter 9), restricted and forbidden development zones, key functional planning involving cross-administrative districts is practiced.

7.5 THE PROSPECT FOR REGIONAL PLANNING

Regional planning (RP) should be continuously innovated with the more penetrative economic globalization to better suit the changing social and economic development demands.

7.5.1 Features of Future Regional Planning

7.5.1.1 *Coordination*

The core mission of regional planning in the new era is to achieve the common development of different regions by comprehensively coordinating the relationship among the stakeholders, including the regions and the regional government departments, enterprises, and social groups, who inevitably have different interests and demands under the market economy. The comprehensive coordination not only deals with the relationship between national economic departments but also tackle the interests between the central government and local governments and between the collective and the individual. It also involves the solution to the conflict between economic benefits and social and ecological benefits.

7.5.1.2 *More Binding Force on the Local Governments*

Regional planning (RP) has binding force on the local governments. Regional plans are designed to specify the functionalities of a region so that supporting infrastructure projects can be tailored. It is the basis for spatial planning such as urban planning and land use planning. As a mandatory planning, regional planning chalks up the "red lines" for certain development activities and sets out policies, consultation mechanisms, arbitration bodies to ensure that all issues or disputes concerning the implementation of the plan can be effectively solved.

7.5.1.3 *Openness*

In the new era when regional development is becoming more closely bound to the global economy, regional planning in the traditional sense of developing a small region cannot properly guide regional economic construction, and therefore the planners should set regional planning in the broader context of national and international economic development and breakthrough the bondage of the fragmentation of administrative regions so that more rational division of labor and comparative advantages can truly play a decisive role in regional economic development.

7.5.1.4 *Guidance*

Traditional regional planning, as a rigid qualitative arrangement for resource allocation, the spatial layout of productivity, transfer of population, urban and rural development, and function positioning through governmental mandatory decrees, finds itself hard to suit the flexible yet fickle market economy. Therefore, future regional planning must give more weight to the formulation of regional economic and social development policies, and the establishment of mechanisms for sharing regional resource and infrastructures, highlighting the governments as a guiding force and a coordinator rather than simply a commander.

7.5.2 Updating Regional Planning Concepts and Theories

In addition to a viable working mechanism, effective RP for the new era calls for innovation of theories and concepts. The following are a few proposals.

7.5.2.1 *The People-Centered Planning Concept*

With the continuous advancement of human civilization, the well-being of humanity has been given unprecedented priority. Under the guidance of the scientific concept of development, human-centered planning is becoming increasingly recognized. That means putting the public interests, such as cultural needs and people's interaction with the environment, first in drafting the RP. The planners have to break the tradition of putting the demands of the officials or government first. The plan needs fully reflect the needs of the public, maximizing the interests of each individual of the society and each social group, and make public satisfaction a fundamental criterion for measuring the merits of the plan. Specifically, a people-centered plan covers the following aspects.

First, a people-centered REP must prioritize the needs of the people. The people-centered concept requires that planning satisfy the people's needs and bring felicity to them from the human scale, human needs, human affection, and human perception. The ultimate goal of all development planning is to "better the livelihood" of all human beings.

Second, people are entitled to the right to get access to the plan and make comment on it. People living within the planned area should be well informed of the planning status quo and planning orientation and design in the future so that they can respond to or participate in the plan in their own way.

Third, the public must be mobilized to weigh in on formulating planning because local residents are, to some degree, more familiar with their own environment than the planners and government officials and their participation can ensure the effectiveness and feasibility of the plan.

7.5.2.2 *The Concept of Sustainability*

Sustainable development seeks to improve the living standard of the humanity infinitely for current generation and posterity through coordinating the conflicts between economic and social development and resource depletion and environment pollution. The core of sustainable development is social and economic development, which balances human population, living standard, and environmental conservation. In drafting a regional plan, the concept of sustainability should serve as a guiding principle.

In making plans, planners should take into consideration economic growth and social progress as well as social justice and environment protection. They should also incorporate social and cultural development in regional planning. A sustainable regional planning has to balance current and long-term gains, the interest of the region concerned and the interest of the whole country or even the whole world. Supportive measures must be given to economically backward areas, and the needs of different social classes should be carefully weighted so that the interests of the vast majority of people are secured.

7.5.2.3 *The Concept of Coordinated Regional Development*

For a long time, the cities within a region, though are close to each other in terms of space, are alienated in administrative management. To put into another way, all development plans for the cities do not go beyond their respective administrative boundaries. However, the increasingly frequent interregional interactions make it necessary and urgent to coordinate planning across administrative regions. Therefore, in regional planning, it is necessary to follow the concept of coordinated regional development. The concept helps to maximize the comprehensive comparative advantages of the whole region, and in turn gives the region an edge in participating in the international division of labor and promote the overall economic and social development. To put this concept into practice, the planners need to take into consideration the following aspects:

First, to coordinate spatial planning and social and economic development planning. Space is the carrier of economic and social progress, which, in turn, provides powerful engine for the evolution in the space. It is obvious that coordinated regional development requires the coordination of spatial planning and social and economic planning.

Second, to coordinate the inter-department relations. A mature regional planning is the product of the exchange of ideas between different administrative departments related to planning work.

Third, to coordinate relations between different administrative regions. A holistic approach that takes into account the interests of all stakeholders should be adopted lest a planned region composed of many administrative regions fragments in the process of formulating a regional plan. This could lead to chaotic regional planning.

Fourth, to coordinate the time schedule of the plan. An effective RP often encompass a long time span and many sectors; therefore, the timetable for development has to be negotiated and coordinated among the participants and there must be room for adjustment for discrepancies between the goal and the actual conditions of all factors involved.

7.5.2.4 *The Concept of Dynamic Comparative Advantage*

The traditional concept believes that natural resource advantages of a region determine the capacity and potential of regional development. But this logic is based on traditional economic production mode. With the advent of information-based economy and postindustrial era, this natural resource determinism has been gradually challenged. Instead, intellectual resources, informatization level, and comprehensive social environment have become the new determinants of regional development. Comprehensive competitive advantages have replaced natural resource advantages to a certain extent. Regional development is more dependent on "what this region is capable of doing" than on "what natural resources a region is endowed."

As the natural resource advantage of a region is giving away to its comprehensive competitive advantage — which is always in a state of flux, RP that focuses on the latter must allow enough room for innovation. The development of a region will be affected by many external factors, which may speed up or slow down the development of a region, so an effective RP must be open and elastic, that is, the RP gives future development plenty of leeway for population growth, infrastructure expansion, and more industrial facilities. In a word, regional planning must also be economically, politically, and technologically feasible.

7.5.3 Innovations on Regional Planning Contents

7.5.3.1 *Spatial Planning*

Regional planning is not only a planning for promoting economic and social development, but also a regional spatial planning mainly regulated by the allocation of spatial resources. To put it in another way, the purpose of RP is also to set up a "space access" threshold to the natural resources available for the players of the economy. It is a new trend to replace the traditional regional planning featuring the layout of productivity and urbanization with spatial planning focusing on the allocation of spatial resources. The future regional planning will proactively regulate social and economic development through "space access" and modify unwanted or improper social or economic development. This new planning method is aimed to both materialize the purpose of national development and have the purpose itself watched and amended when it is appropriate.

7.5.3.2 *Shift from Comprehensive Planning to Problem-Based Planning*

Because a region is complex in a state of flux, an across-the-board planning, which takes up every aspect of the developments of a region, has a tendency to adopt a scattershot approach to affairs and thus render the planning uncontrollable. Many regions in China now are confronted with problems in development, so it is necessary to shift from detailed comprehensive planning to problem-based planning so that recipe for economic malaise and malady can be prescribed. In this regard, Japan has set up a good example. Japan's first territorial spatial plan was well directed at optimizing the economic productivity; the second and third plans were directed at the solution to the imbalance of regional economic development; the fourth stressed the development of informatization and internationalization, and the solution to population aging; the fifth focused on enhancing Japan's competitiveness in global economic and social development, and building the country into a cultural highland.

7.5.3.3 *Shift from Urban Planning to Integrated Urban–Rural Planning*

Dualistic cleavage was very obvious in the conventional regional planning, which had its eye on economic production activities of the economic centers (cities and towns) in the region and regards other areas such as nature reserves, rural areas as the base for urbanization. With economic development, the urban–rural cleavage is becoming increasingly blurred and urban and rural areas are more closely tied. The countryside is not merely a base that provides production factors for cities and towns but a guarantor of urban sustainable development with the rediscovery of its economic, social, and ecological values. The innovation mechanism of economic development facilitates the development of the rural areas and the unidirectional radiation from cities to the countryside is changing to bidirectional. Therefore, in the future, integrated regional planning is the major content of planning.

7.5.3.4 *Shift from Objective-Based Planning to Process-Based Planning*

Compared with other types of planning, regional planning is more macroscopic, long-term, and strategic. Therefore, transforming the "ultimate and reasonable goals" of regional planning into concrete and feasible "action processes" is the key to the success of regional planning. It is necessary to stress the implementation steps and measures. The market-based space control guarantees the smooth implementation of regional planning through the allocation of regional construction funds, preferential policies, and the construction of infrastructure.

7.5.4 Improvement of Regional Planning Auxiliary Technologies

Regional planning requires the collection, storage, and analysis of large amounts of economic and social information. Modern information technology and scientific survey methods will play an irreplaceable role in the formulation and implementation of regional plans. Comprehensive use of remote sensing (RS), geographic information system (GIS), global positioning system (GPS), and other high tech in regional planning are musts. RS is used for imaging information, GPS for precise measurement, coordinates, and geometric rectification, and GIS for regional analysis. The combined use of GIS and Internet can provide the public with electronic maps so that social participation can be mobilized. In addition, mathematical modeling can also be complementary to the application of the traditional qualitative method so that a more scientific regional development model that is helpful for more accurate prediction can be established.

7.6 COORDINATION OF INTERESTS IN REGIONAL PLANNING

A regional plan often involves an economic zone that may cover several counties, cities, provinces (autonomous regions and municipalities). The coordination of interests between these administrative regions exerts influence on the implementation of the plan.

In China, a regional plan within a single province (autonomous region, municipality), for instance, the "Regional Plan for Changsha–Zhuzhou–Xiangtan Urban Agglomeration" of Hunan Province and "Development Plan for Liaoning Coastal Economic Belt" of Liaoning Province are relatively easier to be implemented owing to the promotion under the auspice of the provincial government. However, a cross-provincial plan, such as "The Rise of Central China Plan" and "The Yangtze River Delta Region

Economic Plan," is much more difficult to put into practice and implemented because the coordination of interests may encounter resistance from all provinces due to their conflicting interests. An effective mechanism is called for to address that issue, and the following is an attempt to solve the problem.

7.6.1 Major Barriers in Coordinating Interests

With the rising awareness of the regional main body and of competition comes the local governments' awareness of interest. The interregional conflict of interest has become one of the major factors that impede sustained economic growth. In addressing this issue, the planners need to sort out the following three types of barriers.

First comes the barrier against the free flow of products and production factors. The fragmentation of the regional market and the conflict of interests in market competition stall the formation of an integrated, fair, and normative market of products and production factors.

Second comes the barrier against industrial division of labor. The failure to allow full play of the regional comparative advantage makes it difficult to form a network of trans-regional industrial transfer and division of labor. The coordination of this issue has a great stake in promoting the integration of regional economy.

Associated with the second barrier is the barrier against intergovernmental cooperation. The increasingly fierce competition arising from tax revenue, political promotion, and economic performance appraisal for local officials exacerbate local protectionism, market blockade, and monopoly.

The barriers to be abolished can be shown in the following triangle. The three edges respectively stand for the three barriers facing the coordination of interests, and the three vertices respectively for the three goals of the coordination of interests. From Figure 7.1, we can easily find that the prerequisite for industrial integration is the abolition of the barriers against industrial division of labor and against intergovernmental cooperation; the prerequisite for market integration is the abolition of the barrier against the free flow of products and production factors and against intergovernmental cooperation; the prerequisite for the institutional integration

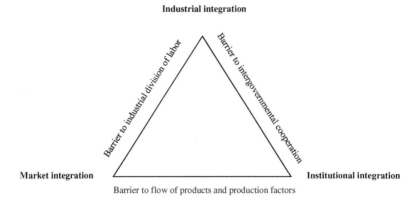

Figure 7.1   Triangle of Regional Conflict of Interest

is the abolition of the barriers against the free flow of products and production factors and against intergovernmental cooperation.

7.6.2 Causes of the Conflict

The conflict of interest is ubiquitous in planning at different administrative levels such as counties, cities, prefectures and provinces (autonomous regions and municipalities). The causes are rooted in five facts as follows.

7.6.2.1 *One-Sided Development Concept*

Because China had been a feudal society for more than 2000 years, remnant feudalism, administrative hierarchy, supremacy of officials, regional fragmentation, and ideology of fiefdom are still very common and inveterate in the current China. Even in the Yangtze River and the Pearl River deltas, where the market economy is most developed, departmentalism is still prevalent. It is the above -isms that increase the difficulty to arrive at a consensus and impede the process of coordination.

Guided by the concept of "development being the overriding objective," people's enthusiasm for development is sparked unprecedentedly high, on the one hand, but local governments often equate development with economic growth and neglect sustainability, on the other hand. In other words, China used to adopt the imbalanced development mode, which features fast but unsustainable economic growth and worsening living environment. In the future, China is supposed to pursue a coordinated, harmonious, and balanced development mode.

7.6.2.2 *Lack of an Interest-Coordinating Mechanism*

Regional planning used to focus only on spatial resources, industries, ecological environment, and facilities, but left aside the conflict of interests among local governments. Although the overall interest of the whole planned region is stressed, the local governments within the region, for the sake of economic performance, tend to have their own arrangements in urbanization, function positioning, industrial division of labor, and infrastructure construction. As a result, the subregional economies are not complementary and cooperative as expected.

It is undeniable that local governments, on behalf of the local stakeholders, play a great role in maximizing economic benefits. The history of market economy shows that economic efficiency is positively correlated to the openness of the market, and local governments will actively seek cooperation if conditions permit. However, it must be noted that cooperation under market economy is based on competition. This implies the local governments will be reluctant to implement the plan if there is no interest-coordinating mechanism.

7.6.2.3 *Rigid Constraints of the Administrative District Economy*

The so-called administrative regional economy, resulting from rigid constraints on regional economy due to the division of administrative regions, is a special regional economy in the transformation of regional economy from vertical operation system to horizontal operation system. The typical operation of an administrative regional economy can be summarized as follows: government intervention in the market competition; hindrance of the cross-regional flow of production factors by local governments; industrial isomorphism in different administrative regions and stable industrial structure; high degree of consistency of political and economic centers; exhausting momentum for economic growth in the outer ring of the administrative region (Liu, 2004). Theoretically, if there is no local political division within a nation, economic operations between different administrative regions will generally not be divided. However, due to the special historical and institutional background, local government is virtually a powerful economic player. The boundary of an administrative district is in fact an "invisible wall" that constraints the district from having effective economic cooperation with another district.

7.6.2.4 *The Effect of Evaluation Mechanism for Officials' Performance*

For a long time, the evaluation of officials' performance has always focused on short-term economic indicators, such as gross local product, tax revenue, and employment, but neglected the fostering of sustainable potentials and indicators related to social, cultural, ecological factors. As the evaluation is closely linked to the political promotion of officials, it is very natural for them to pursue short-term economic success. This evaluation mechanism has certainly contributed to an immediate hike of gross domestic product (GDP), but it has also prompted local protectionism that should be blamed for the deceleration of social and economic development. Meanwhile, local governments scramble for investments, projects, and resources, further contributing to their eagerness for quick success and instant benefits. In addition, overemphasizing short-term economic performance may also eliminate the possibility of repeated game among the administrative regions, instigating officials during their term to pursue economic growth regardless of costs and consequences. Thus, many regions are plagued with excessive exploitation resources, increased loans, and ecological overdraft.

7.6.2.5 *Lack of Cross-Regional Coordination Agency*

It is extremely difficult to achieve coordination and to guarantee the implementation effect only through negotiation without administrative intervention. There is no authoritative agency to deal with the problems arising from the coordination. The so-called cross-regional coordination agency is usually a deliberation council that has no authority to give a verdict to a dispute. In addition, the voluntary coordination organizations are mostly loose, unofficial, and low efficient. The provincial government, an "invisible" coordination agency, can serve as a de facto coordination body for a regional plan that involves several districts within its administrative jurisdiction. However, coordination among authorities at the same level is not easy. It is urgent to establish a cross-provincial agency to deal with the coordination of the relationships involved in a cross-provincial regional plan.

7.6.3 Possible Solutions

With traditional regional planning, the interests of all players are often balanced by central planning and administrative means and rarely by the forces of the market. However, as China's socialist market economic system has undergone significant reform, the government is increasingly shifting its roles, practices, and administrative spheres. Against that backdrop, the traditional coordination mechanism may become ineffective. The establishment of a new type of benefit-sharing and interest compensation mechanism will help rule out the conflicts of interests between regions and promote harmonious cross-regional development.

7.6.3.1 *Establish Regional Interest Coordination Agencies*

In order to maintain an orderly competition between local governments in a nation where a vertical administrative system has long been adopted, it is advisable to set up at different levels a regional comprehensive agency empowered with the authority of planning and regulation so that flattening management system and a common platform can be formed to concentrate the functions of the management departments within the region, abolish the cross-regional barriers, minimize transaction costs, and facilitate the integration of regional economy. Such an agency shall be responsible for arbitration of complaints about cross-regional conflict of interests. This agency can be a standing organization or a consultative body that meets regularly. In addition, attention should also be paid to the role of intergovernment economic cooperative organization such as a government joint conference.

7.6.3.2 *Optimizing Regional Interest Coordination Mechanism*

A rational regional division of labor cannot be achieved by traditional administrative dictation but is promoted by economic development. The cornerstone and incentive of coordinating interregional conflict of interests is a mechanism for common interests whereby an *ex-ante* and *post-ante* coordination mechanism should be established to ensure common prosperity instead of mutually sacrificing the benefits. *Ex-ante* coordination mechanism, namely the combination of regional conventions and protocols that the relevant parties have reached, reflects the principle of equal opportunities and fair competition. *Post-ante* coordination mechanism, namely the compensation given to the party for its losses in industrial division of labor and pro-poor measures provided to economically backward areas, reflects the principle of balanced interests and moderate compensation.

In addition, attention should also be paid to benefit sharing and compensation. It must make sure that differential benefits can be reasonably distributed in different regions through the adjustment of industrial policies. There are two issues worthy of extra attention. Meanwhile, it makes certain that the interests of different industries can be reasonably shared in different regions. As for the compensation system, those parties who give up their short-term benefits for long-term benefits should be compensated. In this case, a regional common development fund can be set up to provide funds for shared public services, environmental protection, and infrastructure.

7.6.3.3 *Exploring Ways to Interest Coordination*

Although the process of coordinating of interests of all parties in an economic region depends largely on the governments' will and behavior, it also depends on the liberalization of the market, the unleashed economic potential of which relies on the enterprises' will, and behavior to allocate capital and resources in a broader geographical space or market and further to facilitate the integration the regional social and economic development by gradually optimizing resource allocation and improving the economic structure (Wang, 2008). Regional conflict of interest can be coordinated through the agreements, conventions, and protocols reached between the relevant parties within the economic region and through bilateral or multilateral consultation or negotiation. Relevant parties should establish a complete coordination and management system that includes the agreements about exploitation of natural resources, common markets, foreign trade, technology development, investment invitation, land lease, and so on. Consultation or negotiation is a complementary means. This includes tax drawbacks or rebates and the decomposition of GDP indicator in transferring investment and industries.

7.7 A CASE STUDY: THE YANGTZE RIVER DELTA INTEGRATION PLAN AND THE INTERESTS COORDINATION PRACTICE

The Yangtze River Delta, the strongest in terms of comprehensive economic strength in China, has always played a strategically leading role in China's economic and social development. To coordinate the economic and social development of the Yangtze River Delta, the State Council reviewed and approved the "Guiding Opinions on Further Promoting Reform, Opening, and Economic and Social Development in the Yangtze River Delta" in August 2008, giving instructions on the Yangtze River Delta regional economy in the form of a central government document for the first time.

In recent years, the Yangtze River Delta has gained powerful development momentum, but with the increase of cooperation between local governments within the region, the conflict of interests among the relevant parties is intensifying. To consolidate the growth pole of the Yangtze River Delta, it is incumbent on the local governments to set up an interest coordination mechanism.

7.7.1 Existing Planning Interest Coordination Mechanism

At present, Shanghai, Jiangsu, and Zhejiang have made many breakthroughs in exploring and innovating interest coordination mechanism. The intergovernmental institutional cooperation has begun to shift from hardware to software, from economy to people's livelihood, from the common construction and sharing of infrastructure to the integration of public services, basically forming the following three levels of coordination.

First, at the decision-making level, there is a consultation mechanism for the top officials of Shanghai, Jiangsu, and Zhejiang to meet regularly to discuss the issues related to regional development. In 2004, the top officials held talks in Shanghai and initiated a regular consultation mechanism. In 2005, the top officials met in Zhejiang and agreed to work together to establish cooperation platforms for transportation, technological innovation, environmental protection, and energy resources. In 2006, the leaders met in Jiangsu, where they discussed the revision and improvement of regional planning for the Yangtze River Delta under the guidance of the scientific development concept as a new starting point.

Second, at the implementation level, there is a "Shanghai–Zhejiang– Jiangsu Economic Cooperation and Development Symposium" chaired by the executive vice-provincial governors or the vice mayor. It was jointly launched by the top officials of Shanghai, Jiangsu, and Zhejiang in 2001. The symposium was held to promote the implementation of the key tasks outlined by the regular consultation meeting of the top officials. Abiding by the principle of "close cooperation, mutual benefit and common development," the symposium aims to optimize the development environment in the Delta and seek to address issues of common concern.

Third, the operational level, the relevant departments of Jiangsu, Zhejiang, and Shanghai have set up a communication and consultation mechanism, and the mayors from 16 cities have started the Urban Economic Coordination Meeting for Cities in the Yangtze River Delta. These liaison mechanisms are designed to address issues related to the implementation of the regional development plan.

Intergovernment cooperation in the Yangtze River Delta has made substantial progress. Great achievements have been made in a series of major research projects, such as social welfare, tourism, transportation, information, science and technology, education, environmental protection, and credit. For example, the two provinces and one municipality have agreed to jointly set up a "Yangtze River Delta Comprehensive Education Reform Experimental Zone." Another example is cooperation in medical insurance reimbursement. On December 1, 2008, the medical insurance agencies of Shanghai and Hangzhou (the capital of Jiangsu) merged their online Medicare reimbursement system. In the Delta region, patients who have received medical service outside their household registration province or municipality need not go back to their own province or municipality. Instead, they can have their medical costs reviewed and reimbursed at the hospital through this online system. After that, Shanghai and Ningbo officially launched a similar system. The Yangtze River Delta is planning to establish a platform for joint response to financial risks and other financial cooperation projects.

The Yangtze River Delta has in succession established cross-provincial information sharing platforms in the fields of freight, information sharing, tourism, environmental protection, human resources, regional planning, social credit system, technological innovation, and energy.

On March 27, 2009, the two provinces and one municipality established financial cooperation, medical insurance, exhibitions, and Expo 2010 as the key fields of cooperation. Soon after the first Pan-Yangtze-Delta joint conference for social security cooperation and development in Nanjing in October 2009, off-site settlement of medical fees was open between Shanghai and Hangzhou, Ningbo, and many other cities.

7.7.2 Interest Conflicts in the Yangtze River Delta

Industrial isomorphism is the major problem besetting the cooperation of the Yangtze River Delta. According to "2008 Yangtze River Delta Development Report: Synergic Innovation and Scientific Development" by Shanghai Contemporary Research Institute, the similarity degree of industrial structure is as high as 70%, mainly concentrating on electronic information, automobile industry and parts, oil refinery, food and beverage, and textile printing. Nearly every city in the lower reaches of the Yangtze takes shipbuilding as their pillar industry. Among the 16 major cities in the Yangtze River Delta, 11 rely on automobile industry as the core industry, 8 on petrochemicals, and 12 on telecommunications (Qi and Jing, 2009: 236).

According to a 2009 survey, disorderly competition and industrial isomorphism plague the Yangtze River Delta. To be specific, the major problems are as follows.

First, vicious competition in attracting investment reduces government revenue. The governments of Shanghai, Jiangsu, and Zhejiang competitively reduce prices to attract foreign investment with policies that are even more preferential than the national policies. They exempt foreign investors from the payable fees demanded by the central government and land transaction fees. In addition, they even pledge to provide investors with infrastructure facilities as required. As for corporate income tax incentives, many local governments in the Yangtze River Delta race to the bottom of preferential tax policies of "exemption for the first two years and half reduction for the third year" and grant preferential policies to enterprises investing in nondevelopment zones.

Second, regional barriers exacerbate the conflict of interests and the integrated market is partitioned by administrative units. For example, many well-known enterprises headquartered in Jiangsu and Zhejiang wished to relocate their quarters to Shanghai so that they could take advantage of the resources of the largest economic hub of China and the officials of Shanghai also expressed their warm invitation, which, however, was condemned as "poaching talents" by the local governments of Jiangsu and Zhejiang. To retain the sources of tax revenue, Jiangsu and Zhejiang dissuaded these enterprises to relocate their headquarters to Shanghai.

Third, repeated construction of ports along the Yangtze squandered a lot of resources. In order to become the shipping hub, Shanghai invested RMB30 billion in building deepwater Yangshan port on December 9, 2005, rendering futile the attempt to integrate the ports in South Jiangsu and upgrade Ningbo to the first-rate port in the East. Ironically, it is difficult for Yangshan and Ningbo, only 76 km apart, to cooperate in port construction.

On January 1, 2006, the Ningbo–Zhoushan Ports Integration Project, headed by Zhejiang Provincial Governor Lu Zushan, was officially launched. As a big component of the project, the Hangzhou Bay Bridge connected Ningbo and Jiaxing, a prefecture-level city 100 km away from the Shanghai proper simply because the Ningbo government hoped that goods would be exported and imported via Port Beilun within its jurisdiction instead via Port Yangshan. The Shanghai International Port Group (SIPG) had even expressed its wish to jointly set up an investment company for potential construction of ports. However, in the 2008 financial crisis, both SIPG and Ningbo were locked in a container rental price war.

Fourth, the rise of South Shanghai dealt a blow to the development of South Jiangsu. When Kunshan, a city in South Jiangsu, billed itself at Hongqiao Airport, Shanghai deemed it as a practice of attracting customers and scrambling for freight transportation. On October 2002, Shanghai transferred all international flights from Hongqiao Airport to Pudong Airport, severely hitting the IT industry in Suzhou, Kunshan, and Wujiang in South Jiangsu because the logistic cost increased greatly with the journey time increased by 2 h. Because IT industry relies heavily on air transportation, the battle for airports reflects the intense scramble for international IT industrial capital. To prevent goods and tourists from flowing into Hongqiao and Pudong airports in Shanghai, South Jiangsu decided to build a new international airport, which in turn triggered another row over the site of the airport between Suzhou and Wuxi.

Fifth, competition in the Internet of Things (IoT) is heated. Many cities including Shanghai, Suzhou, Wuxi, Jiaxing hoped to take the preemptive opportunity to develop IoT. After Ex-Premier Wen's proposal to build Wuxi into a center of "Internet of Things" during his inspection in Wuxi in August 2009, Wuxi grabbed the headline of news media as the most potential candidate for IoT center. In February 2010, China Mobile, a heavyweight operator of telecommunications industry, officially signed a cooperation agreement with Suzhou Municipal Government in the hope to turn Suzhou into a regional IoT application center. In March 2010, Shanghai officially announced its cooperation with Shanghai Institute of Micro-Nano Research of the Chinese Academy of Sciences, hoping to establish Shanghai as a center of IoT R&D, engineering, application, and industrialization of core technology. As a matter of fact, Shanghai has listed the development of IoT as one of the priorities for its information industry. Yet, the Chinese Academy of Sciences had established an IoT center in Jiaxing, a prefecture-level city in Zhejiang Province many years ago. The competition for gaining an upper hand in IoT in the Yangtze River Delta has reached a fever pitch. Unfortunately, the central government has not formulated any planning about the development of IoT. Although IoT has grabbed the attention of many ministries and commission affiliated to the State Council since 2009, it is still very difficult to coordinate regional conflict of interests because six ministries and commissions involve it.

Sixth, Shanghai, Jiangsu, and Zhejiang are deeply split on the approach to the development of Shanghai Metropolitan Region. Shanghai insists on development like "spreading pancake," but Suzhou, Wuxi, Hangzhou, and Ningbo stress the importance of complementary development on their own comparative advantages. Kunshan, a county-level city in South Jiangsu outshining many suburban counties of Shanghai in terms of economic development, finds itself more difficult to benefit from Shanghai's urban planning.

What has been going on in the Yangtze River Delta manifests how difficult it is to avoid conflict of interests among different players in a region.

In 1992, 14 cities in the Yangtze River Delta began their joint conference on urban cooperation. After Taizhou's separation from Yangzhou in 1997, the 15 cities established an economic coordination council and made a substantial progress in urban cooperation. In 2003, Taizhou was accepted into a member of the council. Later, this council evolved into the current cooperation among Shanghai, Jiangsu, and Zhejiang despite more stringent criteria for membership.

The controversy over whether Anhui Province should be accepted into the Yangtze River Delta to form a "3 plus 1" pattern also involves the distribution of interests because Shanghai, Jiangsu, and Zhejiang fear that many of their industries may be transferred to Anhui. Anhui, an important coal base accounting for half of coal production in East China, hopes to be the industrial transfer demonstration region in the Yangtze River Delta with its own advantages in low-cost labor and land labor.

7.7.3 Dilemmas in Coordinating Interests

7.7.3.1 *Rigid Administrative Barriers*

Under the current institutional background, it is difficult to coordinate the interests of many parts relevant to regional planning. As revealed by what is going on in the Yangtze River Delta, the coordination of interests across administrative units is plagued with a lack of internal motivation. The current design of government performance evaluation entices the officials to maximize the interests of their own administrative areas and thus result in the conflict of interests. This parochial attitude toward integration of regional economy handicapped the cooperation at the micro level between enterprises in different administrative areas. It is the absence of an evaluation criterion for official's performance in horizontal intergovernmental cooperation and an incentive mechanism for cooperative platform construction and subject research that resulted in the difficulty to break through the barriers arising from administrative division.

7.7.3.2 *Absence of Authoritative Regional Spatial Coordination Mechanism*

A regional plan is closely tied with urban and rural development, infrastructure construction, exploitation of resources, and ecological environment protection. This fact denotes intertwined conflicts of interests between administrative regions, between departments, between the central government and local governments, and between the individual and the collective. It is obvious that a satisfactory comprehensive coordination scenario is difficult to come into existence. The Yangtze Delta Regional Economic Plan has not yet overcome administrative division even when it has now been elevated to a more authoritative national-level regional plan. The current three-tiered coordination mechanism involves only consultation, communication, and dialogue among the local political elites. Great endeavors should be done to put intergovernmental protocols and agreements into effect. For many regional economic development plans, the reality is that "they are much easier discussed, proposed, and approved than implemented."

Administrative barriers and the absence of an administrative body to undertake the coordination of interests have long been the retardants to the integration of the Yangtze River Delta economy. Hence, the abolition of administrative barriers is the key to the coordination of the interests of all parties concerned.

7.7.3.3 *Slow Progress in Building an Interest Compensation Mechanism*

Local interests are the major concern of local governments. One of the reasons for slow progress in regional cooperation is a spate of demands of interests. However, the local governments in the Yangtze River Delta do not have any idea about establishing a cooperative system of shared responsibility. It is urgent to work out an interest-sharing mechanism involving issues about income distribution, cross-provincial industrial transfer, tax sharing, land quota, water conservation, waste management, and emission reduction. It is also urgent to establish a responsibility-sharing mechanism for major projects, a regional ecological compensation mechanism and innovative fiscal transfer payment methods, and a long-term mechanism for ecological protection.

Due to conflict of interests, the "Regional Planning of Yangtze River Delta," which was originally slated to be issued in 2006, was postponed several times. The compilation of the plan involved 400 economists, officials, and professors from the central ministries to local governments, including a special leading group populated by officials of the National Development and Reform Commission and provincial governors and vice-governors. The Chinese Academy of Sciences the Chinese Academy of Social Sciences, top universities, and district planning institutes in Jiangsu, Zhejiang, and Shanghai were all invited to participate in the planning. It took nearly two years to complete the draft plan, but it failed to receive a positive response at the grassroots level due to their varied demands of interests which the draft plan could not satisfy.

The evolution of economic integration in the Yangtze River Delta makes salient function positioning. However, industrial isomorphism and excessive competition hamper the integration process. Therefore, an effective integration plan must incorporate the function positioning, industrial division of labor, development strategy, and key projects of each city into the plan so as to achieve a more balanced and synergistic economic growth.

REFERENCES

Liu, Junde. "An Analysis of 'Administrative Regional Economy' in the Transformation Period." *Frontier of Economic Theory*, 2004 (10): 75–82.

Qi, Benchao, and Tihua Jing. *Report of China Regional Economy: 2008–2009.* Beijing: Social Sciences Publishing House, 2009.

Wang, Kexiu. "A Reflection on the Construction of the Interest-Coordinating Mechanism in Pan-Pearl River Delta." *Journal of Hunan Administrative Institute*, 2008 (5): 48–53.

Chapter 8

Development Planning Reform at the County Level

The national development plan has always been the guiding platform for all economic work at all levels of the government. However, the plan's effectiveness tends to become weaker at the grassroots level for a variety of reasons, which is not conducive to developing market economy, accelerating urbanization, promoting urban–rural integration, and the transformation of government functions. Therefore, it is imperative to further deepen the reform of the planning system, especially the planning system at the city and county levels. The reform can start with integrating development and urban planning at the county or city level. In October 2003, the Planning Department of the National Development and Reform Commission initiated pilot reforms of this kind in Suzhou, Jiangsu Province, Anxi, Fujian Province, Qinzhou, Guangxi Autonomous Region, Yibin, Sichuan Province, Ningbo, Zhejiang Province, and Zhuanghe, Liaoning Province.

8.1 PROBLEMS IN DEVELOPMENT AND URBAN PLANNING

Affected by market fragmentation under the traditional planning economic system, the compilation years and terms of development planning and urban planning are out of phase (see also Figure 11.4). In addition, they have unequal legal status. What's worse, they are decoupled and incompatible in content design and thus parallel without any coordination.

205

8.1.1 Low Degree of Coordination

The two types of planning are drafted by different administrative departments, which, to a certain extent, led to contradictions in the design of objectives concerning economic development, urbanization, environmental protection, and other issues. For instance, it is difficult for development planning to play a coordinating role in the layout of functions for a city where the cost of optimizing resource allocation and opportunity cost is extremely high and where all factors including social and economic development, population, resources, ecological environment, and urban construction are intertwined. Likewise, urban planners, although having innovated on planning methods and content design, still find it difficult to take into account resource allocation in urban space and the reasonable utilization of urban land. Ironically, development planning is supposed to serve as a guide for making urban planning, but in practice, they are cross-referenced and mutually complementary. National development planning, in particular, seems to have no effect on grassroots urban planning. Urban planning is usually pragmatic and specific, but it is not forward-looking and theory-based as development planning.

8.1.2 Overlap and Contradiction in Content Design

Due to institutional entrenchment, development plans and urban plans are compiled by planning departments in their own administrative systems, which do not have adequate communication and dialogue for major issues concerning planning. A five-year urban development plan is easier to be adjusted than an overall urban plan, the former being relatively subject to change with the will of new mayors who focus more on instant benefits than sustainable development for their potential political promotion, while the latter remaining relatively stable until it is revised as necessary. In this case, the above two plans may diverge on object design about the same issues. After the establishment of market economic system, urban planning should shift from pursuing pure material satisfaction to juxtaposing material and spiritual development. In addition, there are overlapping, repeated, inconsistent, and even contradictory contents in the two types of planning in terms of overall objectives, industrial development, and key projects. Those overlapping or contradictory contents often lead to the waste of manpower, natural, and financial resources. In view of the above-mentioned problems, to fuse urban planning with development planning as one is an unavoidable trend and the most effective way to address the problems.

8.2 THE NECESSITY AND FEASIBILITY OF REFORMING CITY–COUNTY PLANNING SYSTEM

8.2.1 The Necessity of Planning System Reform

8.2.1.1 *Requirement for More Effective Regulatory Function*

Practice has proved that with the development of market economy and the transformation of government functions, it is difficult for the current city–county planning system to be macroscopic, strategic, and policy-oriented as well as practicable and to play a due role as a means of macro regulation. Therefore, it is urgent to carry out comprehensive reforms and innovations to scientifically integrate development planning and urban planning by giving full play to their respective strengths and overcoming their respective shortcomings.

8.2.1.2 *Requirement for New Social Functions*

At the mesoscopic and microscopic levels, development planning and urban planning should be integrated into one planning, which, through land use control and planning, is supposed to demonstrate its following social functions: navigating stable economic growth and reasonable layout of industrial structure, rationally exploiting and reclaiming land resources, providing public facilities, providing special funds for environmental protection, national parks and museums, providing low-income families with public housing and employment training through income redistribution mechanism.

8.2.1.3 *Requirement for the Transformation of Government Functions*

With the establishment and improvement of the socialist market economic system, governments at all levels should free themselves from specific economic operations and pay more attention to the allocation of public welfare services and scarce social resources, and further strengthen its role in macroeconomic regulation and social security. Accordingly, the growth-oriented objective will be replaced by comprehensive social development, such as the creation of a fair social environment, ecological civilization, and the protection of the interests of vulnerable groups. Meanwhile, the government needs to reform itself under the principle of "small government serving a big society." Thus, reformation of the planning system is needed to accommodate the transformation of government functions.

8.2.1.4 *Requirement for Advancing Urbanization*

Urbanization has become an important part of the overall national strategy. In the coming years, quicker urbanization will become the driving force for economic development. With the acceleration of urbanization, it is incumbent on the governments at all levels especially at the city–county level to readjust the urban internal functions and improve the spatial layout of cities and towns so as to prevent a spectrum of concomitant problems, such as urban diseases, excessive exploitation of natural resources, and ecological disasters, that arise from the proliferation of tiny towns. In this sense, it is an imperative development planning and urban planning should be synthesized into an urban–rural development planning.

Since the government management at city–county level — the most basic administrative unit that serves as the middle ground connecting the vast countryside and metropolises or central cities — is relatively independent and complete, the integration of all types of planning at the city–county level is of great implications for future planning reform in China.

8.2.2 Feasibility of Planning System Reform

8.2.2.1 *Interdependence between Development Planning and Urban Planning*

First, the development planning and urban planning, though compiled by different departments, are both aimed at promoting sustainable urban development, the difference being that the former is more concerned about urban development content design and the formulation of policies, while the latter about marking out different functional zones in an urban space. The fact that they are theoretically and practically similar becomes the prerequisite for merging the two into one. As a matter of fact, both have drawn on each other's advantages. An urban plan should be substantiated with the content of development, and in turn, a development plan should be implemented in a particular space.

8.2.2.2 *Converging Trend of City–County Development Planning and Urban Planning*

On the one hand, the geographic scope involved in an urban plan is shifting from urban areas to the whole administrative region. In other words, urban planning system is shifting toward comprehensive urban–rural planning. Planners and development economists are exploring urban–rural integration planning. On the other hand, development planning aimed at macro control and regulation, from the national level to the city–county level, is becoming more workable, adaptive, and special. Meanwhile, the experiment of integrating the city–county development planning and urban planning has proved to be effective, which lays a foundation for the integration of the two in the future.

8.2.2.3 *Urban–Rural Integration*

Urban and rural economies are more closely tied than ever before, and the division between urban and nonurban areas is becoming blurred. The cities and towns within a county have gradually shifted from a relatively self-reliant economy to an economy featuring a specific division of labor and the central city in the county is increasingly interconnected with towns and townships. Meanwhile, the central city is expanding rapidly, and the construction intensity in non-built-up urban areas is increasing. All these facts show that it is necessary for urban planning to shift its focus on built-up area to a larger geographical scope. It is obvious that urban–rural integration demands for the integration of development planning and urban planning. In addition, most of China's land is owned by the state, which also provides a favorable condition for compiling an urban–rural planning centered on land use.

However, the reform of the planning systems should be bolstered by the reform of legal and institutional systems. In other words, legislation on planning should be strengthened to legitimize and justify the integration of planning systems. Besides, the colossal and complicated system of government departments involving planning needs to be streamlined.

8.3 REFORMING THE PLANNING SYSTEM AT THE CITY–COUNTY LEVEL

8.3.1 Overall Objectives

It is necessary to establish a planning mechanism that is compatible with the market economy to ensure effective control over the national economic development by combining China's current conditions with successful experiences of some nations (see also Chapters 7 and 10). The overall objective is to merge, on the basis of planning legislation to meet the requirements of the socialist market economy and in the principle of "small government serving the big society," the development plan and urban plan at the city–county level into a single urban–rural development plan covering the economic, social, cultural, demographic, and environmental issues.

8.3.2 Specific Conception

The new planning system should consist of the five levels of new spatial planning, namely strategic, master, zoning, regulatory, and detailed planning, each of which has its own content design in its own spatial dimensions. Of the five levels, special plans for land use, environmental protection, and infrastructure construction can be formulated for a particular purpose.

8.3.2.1 *Strategic Planning*

The strategic planning for urban–rural integration, the overall blueprint for regional development, determines major strategic issues and spatial arrangements for urban and rural development. The strategic planning, centering on urban development, should include strategic thinking, development objectives, spatial layout, and policies and measures encompassing economic, social, cultural, demographic, environmental issues. The strategic planning should be illustrated with a general arrangement drawing and other relevant flow charts so that it can be easily understood.

8.3.2.2 *Master Planning*

The master planning for integrated rural–urban development focuses on the layout of land use for different functions across all towns and townships within the jurisdiction of the city or county as guided by the strategic planning. The new master planning is designed to realize the integration of urban and rural areas, which had been cleaved for so long through a holistic approach to such issues as population distribution, industrial structure, division of functions, land use layout, infrastructure construction, environment protection, and ecological restoration.

8.3.2.3 *Zoning Planning*

A geographically (not demographically) large city can formulate a zoning plan guided by its master plan for its congruency with other microlevel plans. Such a zoning plan should determine the nature of land use, population distribution, land for buildings, and building capacity; the distribution of public facilities and land use scale; red lines for primary and secondary main roads, major crossroads, plazas, parking lots; the greening system, rivers and lakes, high-voltage cable corridor; boundary of scenic spots and cultural relics; the location of the engineering pipes; and many more.

8.3.2.4 *Regulatory Planning*

Regulatory planning is, on the basis of overall planning or zoning planning, to make detailed arrangements for land use, population distribution, public facilities and infrastructure construction, land development intensity, and environmental protection. It also makes provisions for the functions of the buildings in some special zones.

8.3.2.5 *Detailed Planning*

The detailed planning, guided by a higher level of planning such as regulatory planning, is directed at the floor plan of each plot of planning land and the spatial arrangements of all material factors within the spatial dimensions of the proposed planning zone. The overall control of the whole zone can be achieved through detailed planning, which include construction condition analysis and integrated techno-economic analysis, spatial layout of buildings and green spaces, landscape planning and design, general plan, road system planning, green space planning, engineering pipeline planning, vertical planning, engineering quantity calculation, demolition quantity and total cost, and investment benefits analysis.

8.3.3 Institutional Reform

The institutional reform of urban–rural planning involves the transformation of the functions of government departments as well as the adjustment of organizational structures. It is about time to make institutional readjustments through either of the following options.

One is to reshuffle the local development and reform commission and the planning bureau into a development planning commission composed of many planning affiliates, especially some relatively independent planning institutes or special divisions staffed by registered planners who will be relatively free from the will of the government top officials. To be specific, some of the functions of the planning bureau will be merged with the new development planning commission and others will be delegated to a permanent advisory council populated by planning experts, scholars, representatives from all walks of life, leaders from all concerned government divisions, and technical experts. The advisory council will be responsible to the mayor or county magistrate, and all appointment or removal of the members should be reconsidered by the local People's Congress. The council has no authority to make a decision over a development plan, but has the right to veto it.

The other is to establish an urban development committee headed by the mayor. The committee is a city-level administrative authority. All development plans should be jointly compiled by the local development and reform commission, the construction bureau, the planning bureau, and the land bureau. The local development and reform commission should be responsible for the daily management and coordination of the new committee.

8.3.4 Legal Support

To improve integrated urban and rural development planning, it is necessary to give it more legal and authoritative weight. At present, the laws and regulations concerning urban and rural planning include the "Urban Planning Law," "Measures for the Preparation of Urban Planning," "Measures for the Examination and Approval of Urban System Planning," and "Several Opinions on the Methods and Procedures for the Compilation of the Tenth Five-Year Plan." To carry out the planning reform, it is advised that those legal or official guidelines be fused into Urban and Rural Development Planning Act. This new Act should be binding for all geographical and spatial planning, including cities (towns) and villages. The Act should be the parent law or general law for all departmental laws concerning space use in China. And it is necessary to coordinate the Act with the Land Management Law and the Environmental Protection Law. The implementation of the Act also needs the support of relevant administrative and criminal laws.

Chapter 9

The Planning of the Major Function-Oriented Zones: Initiation and Evolution

---

The 11th Five-Year Plan for National Economy and Social Development of the People's Republic of China initiated the planning of major function-oriented zones (MFOZs), intending for, on the basis of the positioning of the MFOZs, readjusting and improving policies and performance appraisal system, as well as regularizing territorial space development and shaping an orderly spatial structure. The introduction of the MFOZ is a major innovation in the development of Chinese national administration of territorial space development. It rounds out the strategy of coordinated regional development and thus has both theoretical and realistic significances.

9.1 THE MFOZs AND THE MFOZ PLANNING

9.1.1 Initiation of the MFOZs and Its Implications

Rapid economic development since the opening up and reform has reshaped urban and rural economic landscapes, but it has also brought about a widening interregional gap, excessive exploitation, ecological degradation in some regions and uncoordinated interregional development as a result of the lack of correct guiding line in terms of territorial space development. All of these questions add cost to development and pose a formidable challenge to sustainable development. Thus, it is incumbent on development economists to conduct research on the readjustment of space pattern and improvement of utilization efficiency.

Against such a background, the Fifth Plenary Session of the 16th Central Committee and the national 11th Five-Year Plan proposed the strategic task of establishing MFOZs. In October 2005, *Suggestions on the Formulation of "Eleventh Five-Year Plan" by the Central Committee of the CPC* initiated a new program of "determining the functional positioning of different regions, introducing relevant policies and evaluation indicators, and forming distinctive regional development patterns in accordance with requirements of four different levels of optimized, key, restricted and prohibited development." On January 15, 2006, the *Outline of the Eleventh Five-Year Plan for Economic and Social Development* elucidated the issue of the MFOZs: "On the basis of the bearing capacity of resources and environment, existing development density and potentials, [we] should consider, in a unified way, population distribution, geographical distribution of different sectors of economy, territory utilization and urbanization layout, and the division of land space into four major function-oriented zones of optimized, key, restricted and prohibited development." Promoting the formation of MFOZs, so to speak, is a new strategy, guideline, and measure to carry forward the Scientific Outlook on Development (SOD) and boost interregional coordinated development. The implications of MFOZs can be interpreted from the following four factors:

First, an MFOZ is an area assigned a particular major function that specifies development concept, orientation, and model on the basis of its development foundation, bearing capacity of resources and environment, and comparative strategic advantage with a view to highlighting the overall requirements of regional development.

Second, an MFOZ differs from a commonly functional area, such as an agricultural or industrial or commercial area. It is also different from some areas with particular functions such as a nature reserve or flood control and discharge region or development area. The functional positioning of an MFOZ transcends, yet includes its common and particular functions.

Third, MFOZs can be classified, according to different spatial dimensions, into different levels of zones, such as MFOZs with city and county as the basic unit and those with township as the basic unit, which depends on spatial managerial expertise and requirements.

Fourth, the type, boundary, and scope of an MFOZ should remain stable over a long period of time, but readjustments are necessary with the change of development foundation, bearing capacity of resources and environment and comparative strategic advantages.

Fifth, the term "development" in "optimized, key, restricted and prohibited development" refers to large-scale industrialization and urbanization. Optimized development is designed to realize better and faster development by laying more emphasis on the mode, quality, and efficiency of economic growth. Key development concentrates on the projects that most suitably demonstrate the major functions of an MFOZ. Restricted development stresses protective measures such as making restrictions on the scope, scale, and intensity of development in order to preserve ecological functions. Prohibited development is not an indiscriminate ban on all economic activities, but prohibition on those activities unsuitable to the positioning of the major function of an MFOZ.

9.1.2 Positioning and Orientation of the MFOZs

This section is to clarify the basic concepts and the main functions of the four zones of optimized, key, restricted, and prohibited development.

9.1.2.1 *Optimized Development Zones*

Optimized development zones (ODZs) refer to advanced and populous areas with a high level of development density and attendant serious ecological problems. The introduction of this type of zone is not only an urgent call for optimizing development due to the potential risks of over-exploitation of resources in some advanced regions but also a strategic need to consolidate China's comprehensive national strength in the increasingly fierce international competition. ODZs are intended to be the pioneers of promoting national competency by participating in global labor division and global competition, improving originative and innovative abilities, optimizing and updating economic structure, and transforming the economic growth model.

9.1.2.2 *Key Development Zone*

Key development zones (KDZs) are defined as areas with the following conditions: a certain degree of development foundation and bearing capacities of natural resources and environment; comparatively great potentials for sustained growth; favorable economic and demographic conditions and human resources. The initiation of KDZ is not merely a need for the implementation of the overall strategy of regional development, for the expansion of development space and for the facilitation of interregional coordinated development, but also a need for the avoidance of overreliance on a small number of highly developed regions in economic construction, and for the relief of pressure exerted by population, resources, and environment. Not that every inch of land in a KDZ is to be utilized but that the development density should be controlled to a certain degree. In addition to concentrating economic activities in a zone, the government should also encourage a certain number of people to converge on that zone to match that scale of economy. Furthermore, the government should preserve arable land, lower energy consumption, and reduce harm to ecological balance.

As important centers where economic activities are concentrated and people converge, KDZs are encouraged to be a new growth pole that can boost the national economy. In this case, all missions concerning the promotion of KDZs — economic development, urbanization, and industrialization as well as acceptance and absorption of industrial transfer from ODZs and population transfer from restricted and prohibited zones, for instance — should be based on structural optimization, efficiency improvement, and energy conservation. It is important to differentiate the time sequence of short-, medium-, and long-term development. The land that is currently not necessary for development should be reserved for future development.

9.1.2.3 *Restricted Development Zones*

Restricted development zones (RDZs) are areas not suitable for massive and intensive industrialization and urbanization for the purpose of guaranteeing ecological security and the supply of farm produces. The introduction of RDZ is not only an urgent need to curb the deterioration of ecological environment from an overall perspective and prevent continuous shrinkage of arable land but also a foresightful measure to improve the living standards of the local residents. Restriction should be imposed on massive and intensive industrialization and urbanization, but not on industries that are within the affordability of resources and environment. Fiscal subsidies should be granted to these zones to improve public services and living conditions. Meanwhile, the government should also help local residents improve their educational level so that they could be able to transfer to other regions and thus ease the employment pressure in RDZs.

RDZs are marked out as the important base for ecological security and agricultural products. Such zones are usually divided into agricultural areas and ecological areas, the primary task in the former being the conservation of arable land with a view to improving agricultural comprehensive production capacity, the major task in the latter being ecological restoration and environment protection through water and soil conservancy, windbreak and sand fixation with a view to maintaining biological diversity. Moderate exploitation, if necessary, of mineral resources, tourism, processing of agricultural and forest products or other ecological industries, should be based on the precondition that agricultural development and ecological security are prioritized over other economic activities. It is necessary to stress punctiform layout of development, strictly control the intensity of development and strengthen the public service of townships. Emphasis should be laid on bettering public services in townships and transferring rural population and overloaded population in ecological areas to other places in an orderly way. Natural vegetations should be strictly protected, and overgrazing, disorderly mining and reclamation of timberland, wetland, and grassland for farming should be strictly forbidden.

9.1.2.4 *Prohibited Development Zone*

Prohibited development zone (PDZ) refers to all kinds of natural and cultural protection areas established according to law, including natural reserves, cultural and natural heritage, scenic spots, forest parks, geoparks, and so on.

Prohibited development area should be marketed out for the protection of natural and cultural heritage, including some representative protection areas for natural ecosystems, naturally concentrated areas of rare and endangered species of wild animals and plants, and natural and cultural relics with special values. Existing laws, regulations, and related plans should be enforced to mandatorily protect PDZ to maintain its authenticity and integrity. Sabotage and vandalism of natural and cultural reserves and relics should be severely punished, and any commercial and industrial activities not suitable to the positioning of the PDZ should be strictly forbidden.

9.1.3 The Significance of the MFOZ Planning

The MFOZ planning is a major move of the implementing the SOD and of maintaining the "Five Balances" — balancing urban and rural development, interregional development, social and economic development, human and nature development, and domestic development and opening to the outside world. It will be of great significance to the development of the Chinese nation in the long run.

9.1.3.1 *The Promotion of the MFOZ Planning*

The MFOZ planning is a spatial regulatory planning, which determines the spatial distribution and quantitative features of optimized, key, restricted, and PDZs and enacts laws and regulations to govern the intensity and orientation of development on the basis of a comprehensive and quantitative evaluation of the affordability of natural resources, existing development density, and potentials. This planning is a work-in-progress demonstration of pushing forward the division and formation of the MFOZs. In October 2006, the *Circular of the General Office of the State Council on the Compilation of the National MFOZ Planning* (State Council, [2006], No. 85) defined clearly that the compilation was a new complicated move, which should take into consideration a spectrum of elements such as geographic conditions, natural resources and environment, social development level of different regions, population distribution, land utilization, and urbanization pattern of the whole country. The circular also prescribed that basic principles and instructions and a protocol of the MFOZ planning should be worked out to guide mainland provincial administrative regions (all provinces, municipalities, and autonomous regions except Hong Kong, Macau, and Taiwan), all of which specifically formulated in a separate chapter in their 11th Five-Year Plan Compendium and some of which made a further tentative yet constructive exploration in determining the development orientation and differentiated regional policies.

9.1.3.2 *The Significance of the MFOZ Planning*

The MFOZ planning is a major move intended for the full implementation of the SOD and the construction of a harmonious socialist society. This people-centered strategic action is conducive to bridging the interregional gap in public services, expediting interregional coordinated development, steering economic layout, population distribution toward compatibility with the affordability of natural resources and environment, that is, the attainment of spatial equilibrium in terms of population, economy, and resources. It also helps reverse the deterioration of ecological balance, alleviate extreme climate and weather changes, and conserve natural resources. Meanwhile, differentiated rather than uniform policies and performance assessment systems could be targeted toward different types of MFOZs and thus interregional regulation could be easily fulfilled.

First, the division of the national territory into four types of MFOZs is a basic requirement for people-centered development. A conspicuous fact in China's current regional development is that some regions attract investment and quickly boost economic growth, but other regions not suitable to economic development blindly follow suit and regard the increase of economic aggregate as the sole starting point for bridging regional gap. However, some rich regions have not yet been able to absorb a large population to match their economic aggregate and high growth rate, perceivably widening the gap in living standards and public services between regions. As a people-centered move aimed at the substantial improvement of each individual's felicity, the MFOZ planning is confronted with multiple objectives of underpinning underdeveloped regions to develop the economy by virtue of preferential policies, transferring dwellers in ecologically vulnerable and economically hardscrabble areas to rich regions. In a word, through the promotion of MFOZ planning, all people, wherever they are from, will be the beneficiaries of national economic prosperity.

Second, it is an effective means to achieve a rational spatial layout. Modernization does not in any circumstance mean that all land will be industrialized and urbanized. As previously mentioned, there is a tendency for each region to indiscriminately promote industrialization and urbanization, which will over time inevitably result in excessive competition and redundant projects. In this case, it will be difficult to materialize coordination and complementary advantages among regions.

Third, it is an urgent requirement for resource conservation and environment protection. Due to shortage of water and land resources and vulnerability to natural calamities, such as earthquakes, mudslides, and sand storm, many parts of the territory are not suitable for large-scale urbanization and industrialization. However, some local governments disregard ecological situations and appropriate hectares of land for development, and thus exacerbate ecological degradation. The MFOZ planning is designed to economize on limited natural resources and improve the utilization rate of them containing and eventually reversing this worsening trend.

Fourth, it is an important measure to enhance and improve macroeconomic regulation and control. Indiscriminately adopting uniform policies concerning tax revenue and investment in a vast country with varieties of natural conditions and differentiated development status quo will inevitably make it difficult to effectively tackle the unique yet urgent problems confronting a particular region. Likewise, a uniform evaluation system is unable to make an objective appraisal of a local government's achievements in social and economic development. In other words, differentiated regional policies and performance appraisal system should be issued so that different regions can decide their investment and development priorities in accordance with their own comparative advantages.

9.1.3.3 *The Strategic Objective of the MFOZ Planning*

The overall strategic objective of the MFOZs is to create a harmonious homeland to sustain economic growth, narrow urban–rural gap and enhance sustainability and competitiveness. To be specific, the strategic objective can be subdivided into the following four mutually-supporting tasks.

- *To form a clearly defined territorial spatial layout*
Optimized and KDZs should be positioned as an urbanized center of population and industrial conglomeration, while restricted and PDZs as an

agricultural and ecological base to ensure foodstuff safety and avoid natural calamities.

- *To match population distribution well with the layout of its economic space*

It is recommended that the government adopts a balanced development model in larger zones and a concentrated development model in smaller regions. The main urbanization space should concentrate about 60% of its national population and 70% of its national economy. While increasing national economic aggregate, the government should methodically help reduce the population living in agricultural and ecological zones.

- *To coordinate population and economic distribution with ecological environment*

Specifically, the government should establish a rational spatial layout of living, production, and ecological spaces while sustaining the stability of the ecosystem in nature reserves after restoring and enhancing the ecological function.

- *To equalize public services*

By helping people in ecologically vulnerable and economically hardscrabble regions migrate to more livable regions, adopting a substantial measure of financial transfer payment and moderately developing industries within the affordability of environment, the government should improve the public services and living conditions in restricted and PDZs and bridge the gap between regions and between urban and rural areas.

9.2 COMPILATION OF THE MFOZ PLANNING

Compiling a feasible MFOZ plan is indeed an ambitious yet daunting mission that requires the compilers to straighten out various forms of relationships and determine primary tasks and steps.

9.2.1 Guiding Line

9.2.1.1 *Basic Principles*

The basic principles of compiling the MFOZ planning are as follows:

1. Insistence on people-centered ideas, directing toward a rational and well-balanced distribution of population and economic activities within the space of the national territory, and making public services equally accessible to both urban and rural people.
2. Intensive development, forming an urbanization pattern characterized with agglomerations of central cities with a network of satellite townships; improvement on the utilization efficiency of land, water, and other resources; and enhancement of sustainability.
3. Ecological and environmental awareness, ensuring ecological security, reversing environmental pollution, and materializing harmonious coexistence of human and nature in the process of economic development.
4. Overall planning of urban and rural areas, preventing excessive encroachment of rural areas in the process of urbanization, and providing necessary living space for migrants from the countryside to cities.
5. Overall planning of land and sea, strengthening the awareness to exploit marine resources, taking into consideration the affordability of marine resources, and materializing the compatibility of marine and land development.

For the MFOZ planning to be reasonable, it is necessary to balance the following pairs of relationships.

1. Exploitation versus development. Development is of overriding importance, but it must be based on scientific, rational, and methodical exploitation of natural resources. Now that industrialization and urbanization are on full swing, the MFOZ planning is supposed to aim at coordinating resources of different types of MFOZs and hence at realizing quicker and healthier development.
2. Government versus market. As an overall layout of territorial space development, the MFOZ planning reflects a national strategic intent. The government should rationally base the allocation of public resources on the positioning of different MFOZs, bring into full play the primary role of market-based resource allocation system, enact laws, regulations and regional policies, adopt every possible means to

direct the behaviors of the market subjects to meet the demands of the positioning of each MFOZ.

3. Overall interests versus local interests. Basically, the MFOZ planning is launched for the maximization of the long-term interests of the country and its people as a whole. Local interests should be subordinated to overall interests and the two should be reconciled.

4. Primary functions versus secondary functions. Great importance must be attached to the primary and leading role of an MFOZ, and due attention should also be paid to its auxiliary role. For instance, optimized and KDZs are supposed to be population and economic centers, but it does not necessarily mean that no space will be granted for the sake of ecological protection or agricultural production.

5. Administrative regions versus MFOZs. It is essential to abolish those policies and performance evaluation systems that have been promulgated by the government of an administrative region but that run afoul of the guiding principle of the MFOZ planning. Nevertheless, it is also important to depend on a certain administrative level (such as county or township) for the effective implementation of the MFOZ planning.

6. Four different types of MFOZs. It is important for different types of MFOZs to cooperate for mutual promotion. For instance, in order to reduce the pressure on the massive cross-regional flow of population and resources and on the ecological environment, some industries in the ODZs should be transferred to KDZs.

7. Static stability versus dynamic readjustment. Once determined, the primary function of an MFOZ cannot be arbitrarily changed unless the transformation from one type to another is justifiable under some specific conditions. Stability is helpful for the continuity of relevant policies, and dynamic readjustment reflects flexibility. For instance, a KDZ can be transformed to an optimized one with the changes of social and economic development and the affordability of resources.

9.2.1.2 *Compilation Procedures*

The compilation procedures are shown as follows.

1. Determining evaluation indices. It is desirable to choose representative indicators such as affordability of environment and resources, existing development density, and development potential. Much attention should be paid to the indicators as to environment and resources.
2. Evaluating the territorial space. A comprehensive evaluation of the territorial space should be based on the value of each indicator and the geographic information obtainable from remote sensing (RS) and other space analytic technology.
3. Delimiting the MFOZs. With the help of the evaluation results, the compilers should determine the number and geographical demarcations of different MFOZs.
4. Positioning the functions. Orientation, basic targets, principles, and development sequence should also be determined.
5. Enacting policies. Policies should be enacted in accordance with the specific conditions of an MFOZ.

9.2.1.3 *Planning Levels*

The MFOZs include national and provincial functional zones, so the planning should be conducted at the national and provincial levels.

As for the MFOZ planning at the national level, the main task is to address the overall and decisive issues such as the guiding ideology, strategic objectives, and development principles of national territorial space development and some supporting measures such as performance evaluation system and fiscal transfer payment.

On the one hand, the provincial-level governments make sure that the national MFOZs under their jurisdiction are identical to the national overall planning in terms of type, number, location, and range. On the other hand, these local governments should determine the functions of the territorial space not specifically incorporated within the national overall planning and divide them into different types of provincial-level MFOZs by combining the national guiding line and regional specific conditions.

Because the spatial scope of the two-level administrative districts of cities and counties is relatively small and territorial space development and management are relatively specific, it is not necessary to subdivide the MFOZs. The local governments at the levels of city and county are responsible for implementing the national and provincial-level MFOZ planning, demarcating the "red line" between different types of MFOZs, determining the orientation according to the overall planning of social and economic development, and regulating development density and standardize development order.

9.2.2 Main Tasks of the Compilation of the MFOZ Planning

As mentioned above, the compilation of the MFOZ planning is to be conducted at the national and provincial levels. The national MFOZ plan shall be jointly prepared by a national leading group and the provincial governments. It is slated to be completed by 2020 and subject to rolling readjustment through interim evaluations. The provincial-level MFOZ plan, also scheduled to be completed by 2020, is prepared by the concerted efforts of the provincial governments and their subordinate city and county governments. National MFOZ planning should start up earlier than the provincial-level planning to form a national comprehensive spatial planning framework whereby the local governments at the provincial and county levels can formulate a more specific and feasible planning.

Basically, the main task of compiling the national MFOZ planning is to determine the number, location, and scope of various types of MFOZs at all administrative levels on the basis of an all-inclusive analysis and evaluation of the national territorial space, and to specify the positioning, target, regulatory principles, and regional policies.

9.2.2.1 *Analysis and Evaluation*

The MFOZ planning begins with a comprehensive evaluation of all the national territorial space based on a preset and scientific index system under the help of RS and geographic information system (GIS) and other means of spatial analysis (or spatial statistics). It is noted that the evaluation should be based on a uniform index system and the following factors should also be taken into consideration:

1. Carrying capacity of resources and environment, that is, the capacity of a particular region to bear a certain scale of economic activities and a

certain size of population on the condition that the natural environment sustains a sound ecosystem, including the abundance degree of water and land, environmental capacity of water and atmosphere, the ecological sensitivity in desertification and soil loss by water erosion, biological diversity, water conservation, and the frequency of occurrences of calamities such as earthquakes, sandstorms, floods, and droughts.
2. Existing development density, that is, the level of industrialization and urbanization and the exploitation of land and water resources.
3. Development potentials, including social and economic development, science and education, geographical conditions, historical and cultural elements, and regional strategic orientations.

9.2.2.2 *Determining the Division of the MFOZs*

The number, geographic location, and scope of each of the national- and provincial-level MFOZs should be determined according to the analysis of the changing trend of territorial spatial pattern in the future. Furthermore, elaborate efforts are needed to do more clearly defined tasks including the development sequence and regulation principle of each MFOZ so as to make its development well matched with the affordability of resources and environment, existing development density, and development potentials.

The four types of MFOZs at the national level do not necessarily cover all the land area of the whole country. In principle, optimized, key, and RDZs are generally marked out with the administrative level of county as the basic unit and PDZs are marked out with natural or legally defined boundary. In addition, it is also important to clearly define the primary responsibilities of the administrative regions at the provincial and county levels, respectively, in the process of promoting the formation of the MFOZs in accordance with the overall requirements, guiding lines, and primary objectives.

The provincial governments, when compiling their planning, must make sure that their plans are not conflicting with the national master plan in terms of the number and demarcations of the MFOZs. To be specific, the territorial space is planned as follows:

1. The land not specifically incorporated within the national overall planning should be, in principle, arranged with the administrative level of

county as the basic unit by combining the national guiding line and regional specific conditions.

2. The regions where agriculture is predominant should be basically defined as RDZs.
3. The regions with relatively strong homogeneity at the borders between provincial administrative regions should be identified as the same type of MFOZs.
4. Land and marine MFOZs in the coastal provinces should be interlinked and coordinated.
5. KDZs should be planned according to the time sequence of short, medium, and long terms.
6. The regions abundant in minerals but vulnerable to ecological calamities should be principally identified as RDZs though moderate exploitation of minerals is permissible.
7. The legally established provincial-level natural and cultural heritage zones shall be determined as PDZs.

9.2.2.3 *Improving Regional Policies*

The Circular of Compiling the MFOZs Planning issued by the State Council has clearly defined the main direction of improving the regional policy and formulated various regional policies including: implementing the fiscal policy that is aimed at equalizing basic public services; adopting the investment policy that is based on the combination of the MFOZs and neighboring regions; enacting industrial policies according to the overall requirements to promote MFOZs; adopting differentiated policies of land utilization; guiding population migration in an orderly way; and proposing environment classification management policy according to environmental affordability in different MFOZs.

Performance appraisal and evaluation system should also be differentiated in different types of MFOZs. As for the evaluation indicators and methods for ODZs, attention should be focused on economic structure, resource consumption, and independent innovation instead of economic growth. In KDZs, the government should adopt a comprehensive appraisal system that takes into account economic growth, quality and efficiency, industrialization and urbanization level, and other related fields. In RDZs, some evaluation indicators such as ecological construction and environmental protection should be highlighted and others such as economic growth, industrialization, and urbanization should be downplayed. In PDZs, the evaluation indices are only ecological construction and environmental protection.

9.2.3 Main Problems in the Compilation of the MFOZ Planning

The planning of MFOZs is confronted with a protracted and arduous task because China is so vast a country with drastic spatial differences, a large population and relatively small amount of resources per capita that a full-fledged and sound market system has not yet been established.

9.2.3.1 *Poor Understanding of the MFOZ Planning*

Since the MFOZ planning was initiated for the first time in the 11th Five-Year Plan, there are neither ready models to be reproduced nor available research results or work foundations in this realm. To a certain extent, it is a pioneering and exploratory mission through trial and error. It is for this reason that the governments at different administrative levels have an inconsistent and even a vague understanding of the MFOZ planning in some specific aspects. At present, the majority of local governments and departments can understand the necessity and urgency of promoting this great mission and believe that this is of great significance to sustainable development. However, a lot of problems still exist.

First, local governments and departments fear the obstacles and difficulties in data collection, departmental coordination, and technical means, claiming that the conditions are not ripe enough for promoting MFOZ planning. Second, because some important issues such as norms, units, and levels to categorize MFOZs have not yet been clearly defined, many local governments and departments take a wait-and-see attitude toward this work and lack initiative to make an exploratory attempt. Third, many local governments have unrealistic ideas about classification policies, blindly demanding that their administrative regions be counted within KDZs and unwilling to have their regions included in restricted and PDZs. All these problems need to be solved promptly so that MFOZ planning will strike in the right direction.

9.2.3.2 *Interrelated and Miscellaneous Fundamental Tasks*

MFOZ planning, which requires efforts from relevant governmental departments, enterprises, and nongovernmental organizations (NGOs) due to its inclusiveness of natural, social, and economic factors, is now faced with a wide range of interrelated and miscellaneous fundamental tasks.

First, a lot of basic data need to be collected, screened out, and processed. MFOZ planning needs to be supported by basic data about natural resources, environment, population, economic, and social development conditions in the MFOZs of different levels, so it is extremely difficult to vouch with certainty for the accuracy, continuity, and comparability of all sorts of data ranging from natural resources to social development. Second, it requires advanced and complicated technological means and methods. Technologically, a comprehensive survey of the national territory necessitates satellite remote sensing (SRS) and GIS, which provide a wide range of detailed and reliable data that help to make a scientific decision on the choice of evaluation indicators and criteria, the demarcations of different MFOZs, and the partition of a certain MFOZ into smaller functional areas. However, in many regions and departments, the hemorrhage and lack of such talents in SRS and GIS are a big problem. Third, the lack of inter-department consultation and communication stalls the process of MFOZ planning, which unavoidably involves division of labor and cooperation among different departments, some of which hold a wait-and-see and evasive attitude due to their poor understanding of the mammoth undertaking. Obviously, it is important to expedite the paperwork and communication between departments. Fourth, a specialized institution populated by experts from different disciplinary subjects concerned should be established whose responsibility is to guarantee the efficient operation of funds earmarked for the MFOZ planning. This is the prerequisite for a sure promotion of this planning.

9.2.3.3 *Difficulties in the Formulation and Implementation of Supporting Policies*

Whether MFOZ planning can be methodically promoted depends to a large extent on the formulation and implementation of supporting policies. MFOZ planning, however scientific and systematic it is, is doomed to failure in the case of no complementary or auxiliary policies. At present, popular skepticism still prevails among some local governments due to their insufficiency of understanding. In the context of economic globalization and domestic integration of regional economies, the formulation of the MFOZ plan indeed faces formidable challenges. To begin with, the classified policy design of an MFOZ cannot run afoul of the basic requirements of the World Trade Organization (WTO) because generalized system of preferences (GSP) has become a fundamental precondition after China's entry into the WTO. Moreover, the classified policy design of an MFOZ must match the trend and orientation of the market economic system, but the allocation of resources in planning economy and regional policy still exists in this fledgling socialist market economy. Finally, the classified policy design is more difficult particularly in the case of a big difference concerning the target orientation between central and local governments, together with the degree of enforcement of the differentiated policies that are in close association with such factors as economic strength and governmental management capabilities. If not handled properly, the MFOZ planning will be in a dilemma: failure to be put into effect in the case of no enforceable supporting policies and overdependence on government's financial means and governance in the case of more differentiated classified policies being granted to local governments. This is the crux of the MFOZ planning to which deliberate consideration should be given when designing differentiated policies.

9.2.3.4 *Insufficiency in Legal Protection*

In China, a subject plan that is targeted at a particular field such as environment protection, forestry, water conservancy, and others, can be effectively carried out due to the fact that it is guaranteed by a relevant law — such as *Land Administration Law* and *City Planning Law* which respectively support land utilization and urban overall planning — and by the supervision of a regulatory body, which is responsible for the concrete implementation of rules and regulations. Internationally, a typical example is West Germany's spatial policy where under the federal system, the authorities at both the federal and state level stipulated not only laws concerning spatial planning but also set forth detailed provisions on intergovernmental exchange of information, participation, consent, collaboration, and obligation. Chinese national MFOZ planning is supposed to play the role as a pilot for all subject plans; however, due to the lack of supporting laws and regulations, it is difficult to work out an overall and cohesive planning that takes into account the interests of other types of subject plans on the one hand and to organize and mobilize departments concerned on the other. It is necessary to formulate laws and regulations as soon as possible, clarifying the status, nature, compilation procedures, examination and approval departments, management, and evaluation criteria so as to provide legal guarantee for the implementation of the MFOZ plan. In the short run, priority is preferably given to the issuance of technical regulations and compilation methods, which will be followed up by the formulation of special regulations to ensure the furtherance and readjustment if necessary.

9.3 POLICY GUARANTEE OF THE MFOZ PLANNING

As mentioned earlier, one of the important tasks of the MFOZ planning is to formulate and implement a series of supporting policies concerning finance, investment, industry, land, population, and environment protection. It is demanded that different policies should be targeted at different types of MFOZ.

In addition, it is necessary to conduct research on other feasible measures that could promote the MFOZ planning, including the advancement of the planning system reform that is supposed to establish the strategic implications and constraint conditions of the MFOZ planning and clarify its kinship with the master plan of national economic and social development and other plans associated with rural and urban layouts, land utilization, environment protection, and transportation.

9.3.1 Guaranteeing Measures for the MFOZ Planning

The heart and soul of the MFOZ planning are the betterment of relevant policies, laws, regulations, and performance evaluation system to form benefit-oriented mechanism and delicacy management.

9.3.1.1 *Fiscal Policy*

It is essential to establish a public finance system that aims at equalizing basic public services and meets the requirements of the MFOZs.

It is important to improve the financial transfer payment system of the central government and the provincial (city and district) governments with particular emphasis on the financial transfer payment for the public services and ecological environment compensation in the restricted and PDZs. Specific tasks include: (1) to determine the scope, level, and expenditure standard of the basic public services; (2) to add to the current transfer payment the spending on the MFOZs, especially ensuring that the per capita expenditure on the restricted and PDZs is equal to the national average level; (3) to set up and then institutionalize a more comprehensive transfer payment system for ecological restoration on the basis of the current system that targets at "Grain for Green" and "Protection of Natural Forests"; (4) to add special transfer payment for eco-migration, providing due financial support to migrant families and areas that accept migrants; (5) to increase the expenditure standard for management and protection of natural reserves.

9.3.1.2 *Investment Policy*

The investment policy should take into consideration the arrangements for different fields such as public services, environment protection, industry, and urban infrastructure and for different MFOZs such as optimized, key, restricted, and PDZs. Government capital should be mainly invested on the improvement of public services and environmental protection in restricted and PDZs. Meanwhile, investment on agriculture and environment protection should be mainly directed toward RDZs, urban infrastructure construction toward KDZs and self-dependent innovation, and high-tech industrialization toward ODZs.

9.3.1.3 *Industrial Policy*

For a classified management-based industrial policy to be worked out *in accordance with* the positioning of different types of MFOZs, it is necessary to amend the current *Catalogue for Guiding Industry Restructuring and promulgate a new Catalogue for Guidance of Industries.*

Such a policy is intended to guide key, restricted, and PDZs to develop what is most suitable to their own model of development. It also aims at adjusting fixed asset investment regulation tax, adopting differential tax rates, and specifying standards of land use, energy and water consumption, and emission of pollutants for investment projects in different types of the MFOZs.

9.3.1.4 *Land Policy*

The land policy is to ensure that the minimal quantity of cultivated land reserve is by no means less than 180 million *mu* (approximately 12 million hectares). Differentiated policies should be adopted for land utilization. Intensive and economical utilization of land should be encouraged.

Specifically, the land policy should: strictly reduce the acreage of the construction land in the ODZs but moderately increase the acreage in the KDZs; strictly control the increase of industrial land and properly increase urban residential land; and to regulate land use and protect lakes, wetlands, and timberlands in restricted and PDZs from being utilized for other purposes.

9.3.1.5 *Population Policy*

The population policy is designed to ensure orderly flow and residence of population: to urge the ODZs to localize the population with stable jobs and permanent residences and encourage the KDZs to accept more migrants from restricted and PDZs; to help people in nature reserves migrate to other regions and entrust some of them with preserving parklands; to reform household registration system and education, medical care, social security, housing therewith; and to support vocational education and training in restricted and PDZs so as to improve migrants' opportunities to seek employment in optimized and KDZs.

9.3.1.6 *Environment Policy*

It is supposed to adopt a classified management-based environment policy in accordance with the environment affordability of different MFOZs.

In the ODZs, it is essential to adopt a more stringent environment standard for industry access, strictly control pollution permits and pollution right trading to effectively reduce the emission of pollutants. In the KDZs, a moderate relaxation of pollution permits and reasonably higher pricing for the paid use of pollution rights are necessary to ensure output increase amid emission reduction. In the RDZs, ecological restoration is the priority and pollution permits should not be issued in general. In the PDZ, all enterprises that discharge pollutants should be closed for zero emission and pollution permits are strictly forbidden.

9.3.1.7 *Laws and Regulations*

Laws and regulations are the code of conduct for space development. The legislative process should be sped up to improve the legal system that is conducive to promoting the formation of the MFOZs and strictly enforce the law. Specific tasks include to enact and define the legal status of *Act of Territorial Space Development* and *Act of Regional Planning*; to revise the current regulations on nature reserves, scenic, and historical areas into Act of Nature Reserves; to revise the regulations on the protection of arable lands into *Act of the Protection of Basic Farmlands*; to strengthen law enforcement and strictly control the space development intensity; and standardize development order.

9.3.1.8 *Planning System*

The planning system serves as a guarantor for space development. It is necessary to promote the reform of the planning system and form an MFOZ-based planning system, which clearly defines accurate positioning, complementary functions, and the unified goal of different MFOZs.

It is necessary to enhance the role of MFOZ planning as a guide and regulator in the overall planning of national economic and social development prescribed in the 12th Five-Year Plan. A lot of work to be done includes to reassess the existing regional planning before approving a new plan; to formulate regional planning for optimized and KDZs so as to clearly define the boundary of urbanized, rural, and ecological zones and the layout of major infrastructure construction and industrial parks; to readjust and improve relevant varied planning of urban development, land use, population, environment protection, and transportation in the MFOZs of each of the provinces, autonomous regions, and municipalities.

9.3.2 Performance Assessment for the Implementation of the MFOZ Planning

The performance assessment is a guide to the evaluation of territorial space development. It must be a classified appraisal-based system that can fully reflect the implementation of the SOD and satisfy the basic requirements of promoting the formation of the MFOZs.

For the ODZs, the performance assessment should be mainly focused on the degree of optimization of economic structure and the transformation modes of development. It should increase the weight of appraisal on such indicators as modern service industry, resource consumption, environmental protection, innovation, and the public service for migrants but decrease the weight of appraisal on growth rate and attraction of foreign direct investment. For the KDZs, the assessment indicators should cover growth rate, quality and efficiency, industrial structure, resource consumption, and so on. For the RDZs, the principal assessment indicators should be environment protection and agricultural development, mainly including ecological factors such as water and soil conservancy and forest acreage, agricultural comprehensive productivity, and public service. Other indicators, including gross regional domestic product, fiscal revenue, and urbanization rate, should be excluded. For the PDZs, the principal indicators should be the preservation of natural and cultural heritage and public service (Table 9.1).

Table 9.1   Policy Mix of the MFOZ Planning

	ODZs	KDZs	RDZs	PDZs
Fiscal policy	Encourage hi-tech, high value-added industries; Restrict industries with high consumption and pollution; Encourage resource conservation, environment protection, and technological innovation	Support infrastructure construction, auxiliary, and labor-intensive industries	Improve infrastructure and ecological environment; Provide more and better public service; Support specialty industry	Improve ecological environment; Support development suitable for local resources
Investment policy	Strictly control the projects not suitable to the positioning of the ODZs	Provide more potentials for the investment in fixed assets; Create economic growth poles	Strictly control the projects not suitable to the positioning of the RDZs; Support the projects related to ecological environment protection	Strictly forbid the projects not suitable to the positioning of the PDZs; Invest in projects of ecological environment protection
Industrial policy	Congruent with the fiscal policy	Guide the development of relevant auxiliary labor-intensive industries	Guide the development of specialty industries; Relocate the industries not suitable for the positioning of RDZs	Moderately develop green industries
Land policy	Strictly control land use, especially the land use of high-energy consumption and pollution	Provide more space for industrial development; Create better conditions for urbanization	Strictly forbid land use for projects not suitable to the positioning of RDZs; Provide more living space for residents	Strictly forbid land use for projects not suitable to the positioning of FDZs

Population policy	Encourage immigration; Facilitate an open labor market	Encourage immigration; Facilitate an open labor market	Encourage emigration; Strengthen labor training	Encourage emigration; Strengthen labor training
Environment policy	Restrict industries with high consumption and pollution; Input more materials, human and financial resources in environment protection	Forewarn to follow the way of "pollution preceding governance"	Encourage more ecological projects; Strictly control emissions of effluents and other pollutants	Encourage more ecological projects; Strictly forbid any activity that could harm ecological environment
Planning policy	Strictly control the land use for development projects; Develop hi-tech and high value-added industries	Guide the formation of more economic growth poles; Develop labor-intensive industries	Guide the development of specialty industries; Strictly control the industries not suitable to the positioning of RDZs	Strictly forbid any activity not suitable to the positioning of RDZs; Moderately develop green industries
Performance assessment	Introduce hi-tech, high value-added industries; Improve ecological environment; Transform development mode	Promote economic growth, industrialization, and urbanization; Stress the quality of economic growth	Introduce specialty industries; Improve ecological environment	Moderately develop industries suitable for local ecological conditions; Improve ecological environment

MFOZ: major function-oriented zone; KDZ: key development zone; ODZ: optimized development zones; PDZ: prohibited development zone; RDZ: restricted development zones.

9.4 SOME SUGGESTIONS ON MFOZ PLANNING

MFOZ planning, as a new concept of territorial space development, is of great importance to a scientific and orderly space development structure. However, many problems and controversies exist about how to classify them and how to make a classified management. In this section, some suggestions are provided below.

9.4.1 Policy Priorities: Prohibited and Key Development Zones

The PDZs, namely the various nature reserves legally established in the 11th Five-Year Plan, should be prioritized against the background of market economy due to their strong externality and commonweal. The policy design in connection with this type of functional zone is relatively workable because of its small acreage and clearly defined boundary. KDZs should also be propped by policies. Since reform and opening up, it has been an important development strategy to choose a number of areas with more favorable conditions as the development zone supported by national preferential policies, funds, and social resources so as to facilitate their own development and stimulate neighboring and backward areas. History shows that this strategy is effective and feasible. The numbers and scope of the KDZs should also be limited and clearly defined in accordance with the national strategic requirements and possibility of support policies and therefore the regions with good development conditions are not necessarily identified as the KDZs. In the realm of classified management policy, the PDZs should be given more financial support and the KDZs should be given greater autonomy and flexibility in institutional and policy innovation.

9.4.2 Dynamically Readjusting MFOZ Planning

The affordability of resources and environment in a region is not static but dynamic with the changes in technological level and economic structure. It is difficult to make an accurate prediction about the development potential that in the long run does not depend totally on the affordability of resources and environment but mainly on the ability to mobilize and utilize social resources in a wider sphere. In other words, the initially designed functional position and orientation may not be well suited to the possible changes. However, the requirement for harmony between human and nature necessitates the MFOZ-based territorial spatial planning and classified management on the one hand but the role of the government and planning cannot be unduly emphasized lest the local enthusiasm for development might be thwarted on the other. In view of this, the initial planning and classified management should be readjusted accordingly to make for effective and scientific promotion of the MFOZ plan.

9.4.3 Guiding Optimized and Stimulating Prohibited Development Zones

For ODZs that are mainly concentrated in economically developed areas, emphasis should be laid on the full play of the governmental role as a guide and instructor because these zones can effectively cope with the affordability of resources and environment by drawing on technological progress and market means. Meanwhile, their awareness of sustainable development is constantly being heightened after they have enjoyed economic prosperity and established a relatively perfect market system.

By contrast, RDZs mainly scatter in sparsely populated and economically backward hinterlands where natural conditions are abominable. Poverty alleviation is still a sizable mission due to large population, insufficient financial resources, and impracticality of relocating local residents for reducing environmental pressure. Moreover, vast geographical distribution, complex subdivisions, multiple functions, and obscure boundaries render it difficult to pinpoint the orientation for RDZs. Thus, the problems involving resources and environment have to be progressively resolved in the process of development. The plans designed for RDZs should be preferably flexible and instructional rather than detailed and straitjacketed with focus on the coupled force of government support policies and market mechanism so as to promote development of RDZs.

9.4.4   Setting an Overseeing Institution for the MFOZ Planning

The methodical promotion of the MFOZs should be guaranteed by a planning commission under the auspices of the State Council. This commission should be primarily responsible for the establishment of an efficient interdepartmental cooperation mechanism to integrate departments and organizations participating in regional planning and policy formulation. Meanwhile, it is necessary to set up a fund guarantee system aiming at supporting sustainable development alongside special funds for ecological compensation in restricted and PDZs and for development in KDZs. The funds are mainly from the Special Appropriation of the Central Finance. In addition, the merger of currently existing special funds is important, such as funds for development in underdeveloped regions, for relieving the problems of insufficient food and clothing in poor regions where ethnic minorities inhabit, for development in old revolutionary areas, and for poverty alleviation. Local governmental funds, fines, and confiscations from ecological compensation and private capital are also an important source of funds.

9.4.5   Coordinating the MFOZ Planning and the Current Regional Policies

The existing regional policies are complementary in many aspects too but occasionally inconsistent with the supporting policies for the MFOZ planning. This explains why it is necessary to make currently disparate regional policies compatible with the national strategic MFOZ planning from a systematic perspective.

First, the policy objectives should be consistent with each other. As inseparable components of coordinated development, existing regional policies and the MFOZ planning should be kept consistent and complementary rather than conflicting and contradictory. Consistency will go a long way toward reducing the friction of disparate policies and smoothly promoting the MFOZ planning.

Second, the policy system should be the same. Existing regional policies and the MFOZ-supporting policies are both issued by the central government for the same particular purpose, but they are usually overlapping in some aspects and both are tinged with the intent of the state organs that draw up the policies. This is not only unhelpful to the formation of a coupled force but also wastes policy resources and therefore a unified state organ is needed that is responsible for the formulation of a unified regional policy system.

Third, priority should be given to the MFOZ-supporting policies. Existing regional policies and the MFOZ-supporting policies were issued in different historical periods that called for different overall strategies and guidelines for economic growth. According to conventional wisdom, new regional policies are better suited to national basic conditions and to socioeconomic sustainable development. Therefore, in the case of incompatibility of the MFOZ-supporting policies with regional policies, the latter should be replaced.

Fourth, the existing regional policies should be progressively readjusted. The existing regional policies are a complex system and its readjustment involves changes in the pattern of interests between the central, local, corporate, and even individual levels; therefore, a slight move may affect the situation as a whole. In addition, the formation of the MFOZs is a long-term and difficult process, and it can never be achieved at one stroke. Due to historical limitations, the MFOZ-supporting policies can by no means solve all the problems in regional development and need to follow the historical trend accordingly. The readjustment of existing regional policies should be based on the principle of "advancing gradually in due order" lest the cost of readjustment might be too burdensome and that unwarranted policy changes might occur.

Coordination of regional policies and the MFOZ-supporting policies is to be achieved from the following aspects:

- *Planning formulation*: All regions (provinces, counties, and townships) should reexamine or revise the economic and social development plan by referencing the "The National Major Function-Oriented Zone Planning" and readjust the economic growth mode and the choice of the industrial development to the requirements of the MFOZs.
- *Tax and fiscal policy*: The current regional fiscal and tax policies, mainly propped by the four plates of East China, Central China, West

China, and Northeast China must be revised in light of the principle of "MFOZ-supporting policies first."

- *Industrial policy*: At present, the national industrial policies are carried out mainly through a review of whether a single project is up to the requirement of the Industrial Directory. This is not helpful to have a notion of the impact of industrial development on resources and environment. In the future, industrial policies should be carried out by creating a database of the MFOZ industrial development and then having a comprehensive review of the existing industrial scale, affordability of resources and environment, and technical and economical data of the proposed projects.

- *Land policy*: In terms of land use, the central government checks and ratifies construction land quota for a province, municipality, or autonomous region which then in turn does so for cities or counties and the process continues to the smallest administrative unit. In the future, the central government can directly ratify land use quota for the MFOZs.

- *Environment policy*: The implementation of environmental protection policy is currently propped by the environmental regulatory agencies below the provincial level. These agencies, affiliated to local governments, often put a high priority on local interests but neglect overall general interests. In the future, an environmental supervision system under the vertical leadership of the central government should be created to eliminate the local governments' intervention in environment protection and weaken the impact of short-term behavior on long-term development.

9.5 A CASE STUDY: EXPERIENCES OF COMPILING MFOZ PLANNING IN HENAN PROVINCE

9.5.1 Work Arrangements

The Henan provincial government established the Office of the Leading Group for the Compilation of MFOZ planning (hereinafter referred to as the Office). It also set up the MFOZ planning Drafting Panel and the

MFOZ planning Expert Advisory Committee. The compilation work is divided into four phases.

9.5.1.1 *First Phase*

- **Basic Research and Analytical Appraisal**
The Office commissioned research institutes to verify technical criteria for the classification of the MFOZs, reviewed classified policies and positioning of key, restricted, and PDZs. It also organized all provincial cities and some provincial government departments to make a special research and comprehensive evaluation on the territorial space within its boundary.

- **Investigative Work**
The Office sent working groups to emulate other pilot provinces or municipalities, organized the cities and counties under its jurisdiction to make basic research so as to provide detailed data for the compilation of the MFOZ planning, and held seminars to exchange ideas about the furtherance of the compilation work.

- **Pilot Program**
The Office determined Zhengzhou (capital city of Henan) alongside other five provincial cities and four counties as the pilot administrative units, which guaranteed efficient operation of inputted manpower and funds and cooperated well with the Office for future all-round promotion.

- **Trial Plan**
The Office determines the technical outline for the MFOZ planning by combining national standards and index system with the specific conditions of Henan province and then proceeds with its trial plan.

9.5.1.2 *Second Phase*

- Special Research Report
After the promulgation of "The National Major Function-Oriented Zone planning," the previous research results were revised and improved pursuant to the overall guideline of the state planning. The research units

completed relevant research reports on the classification of the MFOZs, including technical standards and functional positioning, and submitted them to the Office.

• Precise Positioning of MFOZs in Pilot Cities and Counties

The pilot cities and counties, in the light of the national planning and the provincial expected result of the trial plan, completed the classification of the territorial space within their own administrative boundary and proposed territorial space control, development time sequence, and approval procedures.

• Issuance of Classified Management Policy

All relevant departments, in the light of the regional policies issued by the central government and the first-hand research results and the specific local conditions, formulated supporting policies, providing policy guarantees for the smooth furtherance of the MFOZ planning.

• Drafting

Based on the experiment work, the MFOZ planning Drafting Panel populated by backbones, alongside with the relevant departments of the pilot cities and counties, worked out an MFOZ planning Draft and also started the compilation of the special planning for KDZs. The Draft was submitted to the Office of the National MFOZ planning Compilation Leading Group.

9.5.1.3 *Third Phase*

After the initial completion of the first draft, the Panel sought advice from other departments for revision, scrutinized the draft for fear that it might counter the national overall planning, expressed the hope that the central government should take the realities of Henan into consideration when categorizing the MFOZs, and then reported it to the Office of the National MFOZ planning Compilation Leading Group for review.

The Office (Henan) integrated and utilized the research results and demanded some relevant departments to take Henan MFOZ planning into consideration in their compilation of land use planning, urban system planning, and environment protection planning, respectively.

Bearing in mind the neighboring provinces' MFOZ planning, the Office (Henan) also concerned itself with the integrity of the whole ecological system and other communal interests.

9.5.1.4 *Fourth Phase*

Further revision was made on the draft according to the feedback of the Office of the National MFOZ planning Compilation Leading Group. The Expert Advisory Committee conducted a feasibility demonstration, which, alongside with the Henan MFOZ planning (Draft) was submitted to the provincial government for deliberation, and then to the Provincial People's Congress Standing Committee for approval and implementation.

9.5.2 Technology Roadmap

On the basis of the criterion of classifying the MFOZs, Henan adopted space analysis technologies such as GIS and RS to quantify various indicators and construct relevant computational models. Relying on the initial analysis of each individual factor and a subsequent comprehensive review of multiple factors including affordability of resources and environment, current developing density and potentials, Henan determined the major function of each geographic unit which usually overlaps the boundary of a county and made a planning map. Two major steps are as follows:

- *Pilot implementation and fitting verification*
Representative administrative units — some prefectures (an administrative unit between a province and a county) and counties or cities (Yongcheng, Gongyi, and Xichuan) under the jurisdiction of prefectures — are chosen for the experiment model. The major function of each of the chosen pilots is to be determined in accordance with the chosen indicators and evaluation methods. Experts are recruited to evaluate the MFOZ classification of the pilots and readjust the indicators and their weights if necessary to ensure a scientific, reasonable, and feasible system of indicators.

- *Stratifying different types of MFOZs*
Stratification goes this way: to identify PDZs (with emphasis on ecologically functional areas) by means of the single index, and then to determine optimized, key, restricted, and prohibited zones by the multi-index model; to single out restricted and prohibited zones within the preset bounds of the KDZs and single out prohibited zones within the bounds of the restricted ones. The flow chart is presented in Figure 9.1.

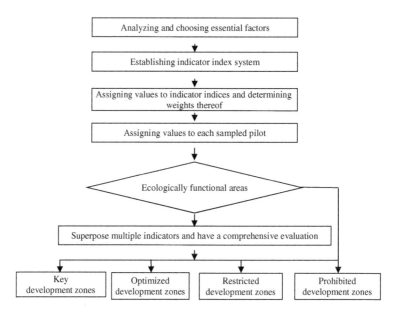

Figure 9.1   A Flowchart of Henan's MFOZ Planning Compilation

In the process of the classification of the MFOZs, spatial analysis methods such as RS and GIS are adopted. In addition, analytic hierarchy process (AHP) and Delphi method are used to determine the weight of each of the indicators and the elements that constitute it. The value of each indicator and the analytic results are displayed on visualized maps so that the information can be well matched with geographical units. A combination of quantitative and qualitative methods is used to make a comprehensive evaluation about the indicator analysis so that the division of the MFOZs can be visualized. The framework of technical roadmap is shown in Figure 9.2.

9.5.3 Indicator Design

In the process of determining the indicator system of the MFOZs in Henan Province, it is necessary to link it with the national indicator system so as to reflect the guiding principle of "combining development and protection," and meanwhile to ensure availability and comparability of data. The initial indicator design is shown in Table 9.2.

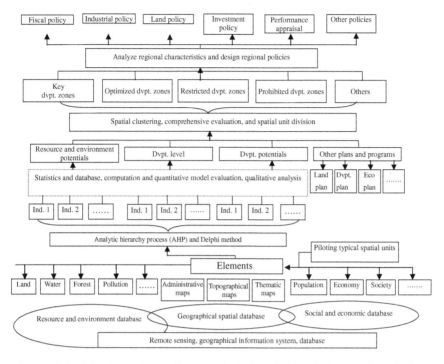

Figure 9.2 A Technique Route Framework of Henan's MFOZ Planning Compilation

As a result of the limitation of data, we chose only 25 indicators (see Table 9.3) and made a research on 138 evaluation units (including counties, townships, and districts) in Henan Province.

9.5.4 Problems to Be Settled

9.5.4.1 *The Size of the Evaluation Unit*

In the trial planning, indicators easily obtainable were assigned with the latest statistical data collected and computed within a county-based evaluation unit. Some composite or comprehensive indicators hard to be expressed by statistical data, such as climatic potential productivity, traffic accessibility, central city impact, and so on were obtained through graphic method based on RS and GIS. The spatial and attribute data are characterized with a continuous distribution of varied sizes of kilometer-grid–based

Table 9.2   The Indicator System of the MFOZs in Henan Province (Initial Design)

Category	Elements	Indicator	Nota Bene
Affordability of resources and environment	Abundance of natural resources	Water resource per capita	Including local water resources, passing-by water, and drinking water
		Arable land per capita	
		Climatic potential Productivity	Output of biomass (including sunlight, heat, and water) per square kilometer
		Forest acreage	
		Area of forest per capita	
		Potential values of mineral resources	
	Environment capacity	Treatment rate of industrial effluents	
		Treatment rate of industrial waste residues	
		Ratio of fund for environment protection to GDP	
		Number of days of air quality index levels I and II (AQI ≤ 100)	
	Vulnerability of eco-logical environment	Annual losses caused by natural catastrophes	Including all sorts of disasters
	Importance of ecology	Ratio of the acreage of ecological function area to the territorial space	Including nature reserves, wetland, waterhead reserves, bird sanctuaries

Current development density	Land use intensity	Population density	
		Urbanization level	
		Ratio of built-up land to territorial space	
		Ratio of construction land to territorial space	
		Ratio of Land for Transportation to Territorial Space	
	Water resource development intensity	Multiple-cropping index	
	Environment pressure	Water use intensity	
		Water consumption per RMB10000	
		Air pollution index (API)	$\text{API} = \max(I_1, I_2, I_3, \ldots, I_i, \ldots I_n)$
		Pollutant discharge level	
Development potentials	Geographic condition	Geomorphic types	Ratio of mountainous regions and hills to the area of the administrative unit
		Influence of central cities	
		Traffic accessibility	

(Continued)

Table 9.2 (*Continued*)

Category	Elements	Indicator	Nota Bene
	Development foundation	Ratio of the output value of second industry to GDP	
		Economic density	
		Tourism revenue (OR: number of tourists per year)	Number of tourists or occupancy rate
		Ratio of cultural industry input to GDP	
		GDP per capita	
		Urban per capita disposable income	
		Rural per capita net income	
		Fiscal revenue	
		Engel coefficient	
		Ratio of three items of expenditure on S&T to GDP	Expenditure on trial production of new products, fund for intermediate test and allowance on major scientific projects
		Concentration degree of key cities	
		Road network density	National, provincial, and inter-township highways and roads
	Development trend	Preferential policies	The number of pilots and honors
		Deviation coefficient	Deviation coefficient between the regional dominant industrial structure and the provincial medium- and long-term guiding industrial structure

GDP: gross domestic product; MFOZs: major function-oriented zones.

Table 9.3   Indicators and Weights of Henan MFOZ Classification

Category	Elements	Indicator
Affordability of resources and environment (0.3)	Abundance of natural resources (0.6)	Water resource per capita (0.35)
		Arable land per capita (0.35)
		Climatic potential productivity (0.15)
		Area of forest per capita (*mu: 1/15 hectare*) (0.15)
	Environment capacity (0.4)	Modulus of runoff (0.3)
		Number of days of wind scale over VIII (*speed over 17.2 m/s*) (0.1)
		Number of days of torrential rain (*rainfall 16 mm/h*) (0.2)
		Total volume of COD/total volume of water (0.25)
		Ratio of discharging volume of SO_2 to the area of a region (0.15)
Current development density (0.35)	Land use intensity (1.0)	Population density (0.2)
		Urbanization level (0.2)
		Ratio of built-up land to territorial space (0.2)
		Ratio of construction land to territorial space (0.2)
		Ratio of land for transportation to territorial space (0.1)
		Multiple-cropping index (0.1)
Development potentials (0.35)	Geographic condition (0.3)	Geomorphic types (0.4)
		Influence of central cities (0.4)
		Traffic accessibility (0.2)
	Development foundation (0.7)	Ratio of the output value of second industry to GDP (0.2)
		Economic density (0.2)
		GDP per capita (0.15)
		Urban per capita disposable income (0.1)
		Rural per capita net income (0.1)
		Fiscal revenue (0.15)
		Ratio of three items of expenditure on S&T to GDP (0.1)

GDP: gross domestic product; MFOZ: major function-oriented zone.

evaluation unit. This accords with the current situation and vouches to a certain extent for the authenticity of data.

It is noted that we did not take into consideration natural geographical demarcations, such as between mountains and plains, between south and north landscapes, and between different climates, when dividing provincial-level MFOZs. The next procedure of heightening conception of natural demarcations and transition regions is very important to the division of MFOZs in Henan.

9.5.4.2 *Indicator System*

Despite the necessity of an inclusive analysis of every socioeconomic aspect when dividing the MFOZs in Henan, 25 indicators were selected from all possible candidates, some of which are inherently difficult to be accessed, obtained, or computed. These selected indicators, though validated as reliable and effective from the result of the trial planning, are still a little far from the original indicator system. All indicators should be scientifically defined in the aspects of implications, constituent elements, and functions. Future improvements will be focused on such indicators as population mobility and regional innovation capability, and future supplements will be given to regional policy and strategic choice.

9.5.4.3 *Computational Methods*

After a preliminary analysis, indicators were processed by various methods such as extremum standardization, min–max standardization, and scoring method. Indices with little difference, such as per capita arable land area and per capita net income of peasants were processed with extremum standardization. Indices with large difference were processed with min–max standardization. Indices with optimal value were analyzed with scoring method. For diffusion indices, such as influence degree of central cities, traffic accessibility, we first obtained the factor action scores and influence radiuses, then used distance attenuation formula to deal with them before finally getting the interaction index of the evaluation unit. The application of these methods and other new methods in the division of provincial MFOZs is still in the exploratory stage and will be discussed further.

9.5.4.4 *Weighted Assignment*

Weight assignment was conducted by Delphi method, which relies on a panel of experts for more accurate judgments and assessments. The experts had varied opinions as to the weights of those indicators with multiple implications such as affordability of resources and environment, current development density and development potentials. After several rounds of expert appraisal, the relatively average value was assigned to the indicator in question. It needs further discussion as to whether this method is reasonable or not. Since a provincial-level MFOZ involves all aspects including natural resources, social–economic development, and environmental protection, emphasis in the future should be laid on more rigorous requirements for the expert group and their scoring criteria to guarantee the accuracy of the weight assigned to each indicator.

9.5.4.5 *Determination of Thresholds*

We drew frequency histograms or exponential curves to determine the thresholds of influencing factors. According to the distribution, we chose the valley points with the most drastic changes or the most significant turning points as the cutoff (demarcation) point of different types of MFOZs. The geographic scope of key, optimized, restricted, and forbidden development zones need further verifications and modifications.

9.5.4.6 *Definitive Description and Quantitative Assignment*

The influencing factors did not show a unidirectional change (increase or decrease) in each section but assumed a relatively complex curvy undulation. Whether the threshold of each section and their respective index value can reflect the actual situation of each MFOZ remains to be further discussed.

9.5.4.7 *Governmental Regional Development Policy*

The trial planning did not take into consideration the indicators that are hard to be quantified, such as policy orientation and strategic choice, which, however, need an in-depth analysis in the future because they are essentially important to the MFOZ planning.

Chapter 10

Institutionalization of National Development Planning

With the continuous advancement of economic reform over the past six decades, China has made much progress in compiling and implementing the national development plan and formed relatively habitual or customary working methods and procedures. However, its institutionalization obviously lags behind the practice of planning. In the new historical era, it is an important task to institutionalize development planning in accordance with the requirements of law-based administration.

10.1 NECESSITY OF INSTITUTIONALIZING NATIONAL DEVELOPMENT PLANNING

Institutionalization is not only merely a key link to solve the existing problems in the practice of national development planning but also the only pathway to make it more standardized and scientific.

10.1.1 Implications of Institutionalization of Planning

Institutionalization of national development planning has two layers of implications.

First, there must be a strict code and a relatively stable set of rules for compiling and formulating national development plans. The purpose of establishing such a set of rules is to avoid arbitrariness and randomness of planning that must otherwise be rule-based. This implies that not only the scope, contents, and indicator system of planning but also the procedures, methods, and steps of planning should be standardized to avoid excessive external intervention and reduce the influence of the will from the authority. In this way, the compilation of plans will be more transparent, foreseeable, scientific, and democratic, and thus guarantee the purpose of improving the effectiveness of planning.

Second, there must be a relatively stable set of rules for implementing and evaluating planning lest the planning might be an armchair strategy or an idle theory. It is not only necessary to publicize all information about planning so that a solid foundation can be laid among the public but also to form an inspection and evaluation system so that it can be effectively put into practice.

10.1.2 Planning and Law of Planning

For a long time, especially in the pre-Reform product economy, a misconception was prevalent that development plans were equivalent to laws. As a matter of fact, they fall within different categories and the differences mainly manifest in the following three aspects.

As for the subjects and procedures of making laws and programs, the Constitution of China specifies that governments at all levels are the statutory subjects of compiling national economic and social development plans. In other words, only governments at all levels are authorized to compile plans, and the power to review and approve plans belongs to people's congresses at all levels. As for the formulation of the law of planning, only the National People's Congress and its Standing Committee have the authority. Generally, the compilation of China's national economic and social development plan is a "top-down" process, and the formulation of the law of planning should be carried out in accordance with the procedures prescribed in the Legislation Law.

As for the nature of law and planning, China has never formulated a law to regulate the formulation and implementation of planning although it has never stopped to issue national development plans or programs involving every aspect of national economy every 5 or 10 years since it began its First Five-Year plan in 1953. In 1982, the Constitution replaced "National Economic and Social Development Plan" for "National Economic Plan," empowering the National People's Congress to review and approve plans or programs. The approved plans or programs, though validated by the supreme legislative organ, is in essence not a law but only a legal document with the nature of planning work. However, a Law of Planning is a law enacted by the top legislature and has the denominators of general law.

Third, planning establishes in a particular period of time the development strategies and objectives that guide the behaviors of the governments at all levels and the market subject, while a Law of Planning is the code of conducts that the planning subjects must abide by in their planning activities. In addition, when confronted with uncertain factors, such as national policy adjustments or especially serious natural disasters, planning agencies can make timely adjustments according to legal procedures. By contrast, planning rules are relatively stable, subject to no change without major decisions from the authorities.

A Law of Planning is undoubtedly law-binding on planning. Faced with the passivity and hysteresis of market mechanism, China has formulated and implemented various economic plans and policies, guiding and promoting economic development through economic leverages such as tax, interest and exchange rates, and other policy tools. In this case, China has promulgated relevant laws and regulations to ensure rational and scientific compilation and effective implementation of the programs.

10.1.3 Necessity of Legislating Planning

10.1.3.1 *Inevitable Requirement of Socialist Market Economy*

First, legislating planning is the necessary requirement to guide the behaviors of market subjects. As an action program to methodically guide social and economic activities, national development planning should be regulated by law to ensure that it is scientific, authoritative, and continuous. A market economy necessitates a planning law, a law that protects the legitimate behaviors of the market subjects and promotes a sound development of market subjects and objects.

Second, legislating planning is an inevitable requirement to enter into the World Trade Organization (WTO) and to observe international conventions or standards. The WTO requires that the administrative behaviors of the government must be institutionalized. Legislating planning determines not only whether a development program will be scientifically compiled or effectively implemented but also whether its contents are in conformity with the WTO rules, thus ultimately deciding whether China's economy can be integrated into the wave of the global economy.

Third, legislating planning is necessary to coordinate social and economic development. The frequent conflict between economic and social development in the current market economy can only be removed through institutionalizing planning to correctly reflect the inherent link and common goal of social progress and economic development.

10.1.3.2 *Inevitable Choice of Law-Based Administration*

Law-based administration is the main link and core content of building socialist rule of law, while legislating planning is a concrete embodiment of law-based administration. To begin with, planning is the "constitution" that guides national social and economic development. To be specific, the "constitution" confirms the legal status of the planning authorities, vesting them with macro-planning power and guaranteeing their statutory entity. In addition, only by legislating planning can the administrative measures of the governments at all levels, such as promulgating, implementing, modifying and revising programs, and even supervising the execution of the plans, be ensured by law. Plans, as the outcome of the joint participation of the government departments, planning agencies, and other social sectors concerned, are compiled on the basis of national social and economic development goals in a particular historical period of time. Therefore, all plans, once ratified by the people's congress at all levels, should be legally validated. The administrative acts, particularly those involving planning, of the government departments at all levels, should be strictly implemented to the letter, subject to no change or revision without legal proceedings. The supervision and inspection departments should also strictly fulfill their responsibility of overseeing the implementation or progression of these plans in accordance with the planning "constitution."

10.1.3.3 *Requirement to Establish a New System for Planning*

A sound set of regulations can vouch for the formulation, implementation, evaluation, and revision of programs. In this case, legislating planning is a prerequisite for better planning and guaranteeing its formulation. First, legislating planning is the need to ensure that planning is scientific and authoritative. A scientific planning is based on democracy, while democracy is guaranteed by law. In the context of market economy, especially in the transitional period of system, many conflicting issues will inevitably arise in the course of planning, the most outstanding issue being the conflict between the basic role of the market in resource allocation and the governmental function in macro control. Such being the case, the governmental authoritativeness in planning can only be ensured by incorporating formulation, implementation, supervision, and inspection into a law to vouch for its legal enforcement. Second, legislating planning is the requirement to ensure its stability and continuity. Without sanction from market subjects or participants, planning can hardly allow full play to guide the market. To judge the degree of acceptance of planning by market participants mainly depends on whether the planning satisfies the interests of all parties. Precisely, the stability and continuity of planning are an important basis to make such a judgment. The formulation and implementation of planning should be conducted in accordance with the inherent law of national socioeconomic development instead of being changed easily with the will of top officials.

10.2 A HISTORICAL SURVEY OF CHINA'S LEGISLATION OF PLANNING

The planning mechanism under market economy has undergone drastic changes. Only by means of legislation can planning play its due role. As an important part of legal system construction, a Law of Planning has been put on the legislation agenda by the seventh and eighth NPCs and the State Council. Entrusted by the Standing Committee of the NPC and the State Council, the National Planning Commission began drawing up the Law of Planning in the early 1980s and submitted a draft to the State Council for a review in June 1995. The draft prescribed a spectrum of issues about planning, including its nature and principle, planning management functions, its formulation and implementation, the balance between aggregate demand and supply and comprehensive coordination, industrial policies, structural optimization, local planning, social participation in planning, legal responsibility, and so on. The planning draft is still on the table because law makers have not arrived at a consensus over the relationship between planning and the market, the nature and status of planning, and democratic and scientific planning.

Here is a brief historical retrospective of China's legislation of planning. In 1952, the Finance and Economics Committee of the State Council issued the *Interim Measures for the Compilation of National Economic Plans*, the first regulation specially designed to adjust planning. In the following 10 years or so, a set of rules prescribing principles, methods, and procedures related to planning as well as the authority of planning agencies followed up, culminating in the promulgation of the *Regulations on the Planning Work (Draft)* in 1963 and the *Regulations on Reforming the National Economic Planning Work (Draft)* in 1964. Stalled by the tumultuous Great Cultural Revolution, legislation resumed in 1984 with the issuance of the *Interim Provisions for Improving Planning System*. In the 1980s and 1990s, the State Planning Commission conceived of drawing up *Act of Planning* and *Act of Stabilizing National Economic Growth*, attempting to normalize all procedures related to planning, such as compilation, approval, revision, supervision, and so on. However, the two acts have not come into being. In 1999, the General Office of the State Council forwarded "Several Opinions on Planning Methods and Procedures of the Eleventh Five-Year Plan" by the State Planning Commission. In 2005, the State Council proposed "Several Opinions on Strengthening the Compilation of Planning for National Economic and Social Development," a historic document that accumulates experiences for legislating planning in that it provides specific normative suggestions on a spectrum of issues ranging from planning system, coordination, social participation, and demonstration to examination, supervision, and readjustment.

Since the founding of New China in 1949, especially after the Third Plenum of the 11th Central Committee of the CPC in 1978, legislative and executive organs from the National Congress and its standing committee, the State Council to local governments, for the sake of readjusting planning, have issued a series of regulations and decisions and opinions, such as the *Interim Measures for the Compilation of National Economic Plans* (1952), the *Decision on Strengthening the Fiscal Planning* (1960), the *Interim Provisions on Improving Planning System* (1984), and the *Interim Measures on Specifically Designating Industrial Conglomerates in the State Planning*. These normative documents played a positive role in quickening legislation planning. However, due to rapid social development and economic growth, many provisions and regulations do not abide by the new requirements, some have been pigeonholed indefinitely, and others abolished. It is necessary to resume the task of legislating planning in the new era when national macro control should be more effectively carried out to better promote the socialist market economy.

10.3 PROBLEMS AND DIFFICULTIES IN PLANNING LEGISLATION

In current decisions, measures and provisions related to planning, there are many problems ranging from problematic provisions that fail to keep up with rapid economic development to omission and vacancy, which result in no legal provisions to abide by.

10.3.1 Problems in Legislating Planning

10.3.1.1 *Haphazard and Fragmentary Legal Construction*

There has not yet been a basic law on planning in China. Provisions related with state planning are scattered in various laws and regulations and opinions. Moreover, there are no uniform normative prescriptions to guide or restrict various plans. Many laws and regulations only stress the necessity to draw up a plan, but fail to propose specific feasible and operational provisions. The main problems are as follows:

First, there is a quite obscure relationship between different types of planning at all levels. Land planning and urban planning are supposed to be systematically combined and coordinated, but are actually quite self-contained. They should be both subordinates to economic and social development planning, but are actually often overlapping or even conflicting to the latter. Second, with a few exceptions, the compilation of most plans, including the outline for national economic and social development plan, do not follow a law-based procedure but a customary practice. Third, the articles of the existing regulations are not normatively expressed and many of them are heavily tinted with planning economy. Fourth, many laws and regulations clarify the legal status of plans, but lack due articles and clauses to protect the implementation of these plans.

10.3.1.2 *Inconsistent Requirements*

The current planning laws and regulations are mostly drafted by various departments. However, these departments, which have no basic law to abide by when drafting a law, are susceptible to the influence of authorities at different levels and make the requirements for different laws vary greatly. For instance, according to the *Occupational Disease Prevention and Control Law*, it is the State Council and the local people's governments at or above the county level that are authorized to formulate plans for occupational disease prevention and control; the *Education Law* stipulates that the State shall formulate plans for educational development; the plans related to the highways and waterways shall be submitted to the State Council for approval, but it is not clear that who shall be responsible for the final decision of railway construction; the general plans for land use at different levels are prepared by different subjects at the national and provincial level, but all should be submitted to the State Council for examination and approval.

10.3.1.3 *Outdated Contents*

With the establishment of the social market economic system, the external environment of the compilation and implementation of planning has changed drastically, and the specific contents of plans and the function of planning have also been adjusted accordingly. Some contents of existing laws and regulations are unsuitable to the ever-changing situation. Take the fields that need planning as an example. Many fields that have been incorporated into some of the current plans actually no longer require direct government planning, but other fields in dire need of planning cannot be legally protected because the planning of a certain field mainly depends on the legislation progress of the departments in charge. For example, the layout planning of coastal ports had not come to its own until the promulgation of the Law of Ports.

10.3.2 Difficulties and Principles

The establishment and improvement of the market economic system provide a relatively stable macro-environment for planning legislation. The long-term practice of planning, especially the aggressive exploration and audacious innovation in recent years, has laid a solid theoretical foundation and accumulated experiences for planning legislation. It is the high time for planning legislation, but many tough difficulties remain outstanding.

First, the innovation of planning system has long been closely related to the reform of government management system; therefore, it is difficult to straighten out the long-term division of functions and interests of departments within a short period of time. In light of the orientation of government management reform, it is certainly a task of no small dimensions to establish a set of proper planning laws in the context of dynamic socioeconomic change. Second, associated with the dynamic change is that of planning work in the transitional period: the change of the nature, function, and content of the national development planning with the continuous improvement of the market economic system; incongruity between national and local planning, between temporal and spatial sequence planning; and lack of foresight in rulemaking. Third, many characteristics of planning — complexity of the planning object, the unpredictability of the planning content, the uncertainty of the development environment, and the multilevel of the planning system — also pose a formidable challenge to a unified planning legislation.

Unlike civil law or criminal law, planning legislation is the norm of government behavior in the process of development. It should fine-tune the relationship between inheritance and development, principle and flexibility, aggressive innovation and steady progress: encouraging exploration and innovation in practice while proposing principled requirements;

renewing ideas and guiding the future orientation while standardizing the planning work.

10.4   LEGISLATION PRACTICE OF PLANNING IN SOME MARKET ECONOMIES

In this section, a historical retrospective is given about the evolution and characteristics of planning legislation in some market economies, such as France, Japan, and South Korea.

10.4.1   Planning Legislation in France

France, the first advanced country that boasted the most time-honored legislation in economic planning after WWII and the most distinctive and complete planning theory, has formulated and implemented 10 medium- and long-term plans since 1947. The first three plans were termed as "modernization and equipment plans," the fourth to the eighth plans as economic and social development plans, and the ninth plan as an economic, social, and cultural development plan, indicating that planning legislation has changed from absolute macroeconomic management to the promotion of balanced social and economic development. From the point of view of constraints of plans, the French planning legislation underwent semi-compulsory, indicative, and strategic stages.

10.4.1.1   *Semi-Compulsory Planning (the First and Second Plans, 1947–1957)*

WWII wreaked havoc on the French economy and the French Fourth Republic (1945–1957) was beset with political disturbance and economic plight. The dominant idea of the Republic's planning legislation was to develop economy in a comprehensive manner and attach importance to the improvement of product quality, labor productivity, structural change of national economic sectors on the basis of recovery from the wartime rubble. From 1947 to 1953, the Republic implemented its first modernization and equipment plan, with its gross national product (GNP) growing rapidly by 43.2% and industrial output value hitting a new record high. In its second modernization and equipment plan from 1954 to 1957, its GNP increased by 30% (Huang, 1990: 112). In general, the plans in this stage went off smoothly, some targets being achieved in advance.

The war-torn France was sorely in need of economic recovery and revival through planning means that could invest limited national wealth in reconstruction. Its plans were to a certain extent mandatory, especially in terms of investment control and government control. In this stage, the government-controlled investment accounted for half of the total and in the late-1950s, half of the enterprise investment funds came from loans granted by government agencies at all levels. Consequently, enterprises became increasingly dependent on the government and their behaviors were also accordingly restrained by government regulations. In the early years of post-WWII France, the government limited the prices of industrial products and main consumer goods. Meanwhile, it had the authority to freeze prices and wages, a case in point being the government orders to freeze prices respectively in 1946 and 1949. In addition, the government intervened in international trade by means of currency arrangements and import licensing. Moreover, the government exerted stringent planning constraints on state enterprises.

10.4.1.2 *Indicative Planning (the Third to Fifth Plans, 1958–1970)*

During the heyday of the French economic planning from 1958 to 1970 when the indicative characteristics were most prominent, the government stressed the importance to form complementary advantages between planning and market regulation. The thread running through planning legislation in this state was to improve France's international competitiveness, with the third plan campaigning for international competition, the fourth focusing on boosting national economic growth by balancing domestic finance and international balance of payments, the fifth specifying the goal of improving international competitiveness of industries. All these plans diagnosed main symptoms in economic development and prescribed corresponding economic policy tools to cure them, and thus facilitated the fulfillment of the specific development objectives. These plans basically discarded the mandatory measures and introduced indicative income prices and price contracts to replace frozen prices. Nevertheless, the French government still maintained strict planning control over state enterprises. In general, the French planning legislation in this stage began to put a premium on the role of market mechanism and the reasonable division of labor between planning and market regulation. With the weakening of mandatory planning and strengthening of indicative planning, the plans achieved more satisfactory results than expected. It is at this stage that France created a remarkable "economic miracle."

10.4.1.3 *Strategic Planning (the 6th and 10th Plans, 1971–1990s)*

In the early 1970s, a worldwide economic crisis ignited by energy crisis dealt an unprecedented telling blow to France's economy, marking the ascent of liberalism and the descent of planning and the shift from indicative planning to strategic planning in its history of planning legislation. Strategic planning, as its name suggests, is referred to as a blueprint for economic outlook and development orientation in a long or short term in which some sectors with strategic significance should be prioritized to ensure a sustained and balanced national economic development. One of the outstanding achievements of in planning legislation at this stage was the issue of the Reform Act of Planning (*Réforme de la Planification*) in 1982, which aimed to democratize, contract, and decentralize planning legislation. This act made the following four stipulations:

1. Democratization of planning legislation, with emphasis on democratic compilation and supervision, alternating the practice of planning wholly arranged by the central government to the practice involving the joint participation by representatives from administrative organs, public and private enterprises, academics, trade unions, and some professional groups; strict discipline of the National Assembly's approval; and supervision of plans, including drafts and final plans.
2. Sole responsibility for drafting plans undertaken by the French National Planning Commission, populated by representatives from administrative regions, trade unions, employer organizations, and public and private enterprises and headed by Director of the General

Commission of Planning whose job was by no means meddled with by anyone from any governmental agency.

3. Decentralization of planning legislation, with each administrative region having authority to draw up its own plans and determine the priority of development projects and necessary funds; decentralization of fiscal power, allowing local governments to control their own share of fiscal revenue.

4. Contracting planning, with plan contracts (including the objectives to be attained by a firm and measures to achieve the objective and the obligations to be undertaken by the firms and the government) being the main means to implement plans or rather to fulfill contracts between the central government as one party and administrative regions, public and private enterprises, or other legal persons as the other; coordination of the relationship between national planning and corporate planning by combining government intervention and enterprise self-management.

In the Western developed countries, France's planning legislation system has its own characteristics. A draft plan can be promulgated as a final plan in the *French Gazette* only after going through the following procedures in succession: internal negotiation within the nongovernmental Modernization Commission, approval of the plan by the General Commission of Planning, decision by a special committee of the French government, and approval by the National Assembly (*Assemblée Nationale*). The planning legislation involved the following five organizations or commissions:

1. *Decision maker: The Central Government*
The French Prime Minister issued an executive order to formulate plans to the Director of the General Commission of Planning. The French government had the authority to examine and approve the guidelines and draft plans. There were two main decision makers: the interministerial Economic and Social Planning Commission established in May 1953 and the French Central Planning Commission founded in October 1974. The former, convened by the Prime Minister, was responsible for coordinating the actions of various departments, guiding and supervising the

formulation of plans while the latter, chaired by the Prime Minister monthly and met by the Minister of Economy and Finance, the Director of the General Commission of Planning, the Minister of Labor, and the chief executives of other ministries and commissions, was responsible for setting the orientation of planning and determining major policies and principles for medium-term development.

2. *Planner: The General Commission of Planning*

This Commission, a permanent administrative body directly answerable to the Prime Minister, was responsible for planning, specifically, guiding the research work about economic and social development, organizing the preparation of drafts, supervising the implementation of the plan, and revising the plan if necessary. As a core body in the French planning legislation system, it had three horizontal ministries of economy, finance, and region under which there were 10 bureaus, including agriculture, energy, water conservancy, transportation, and so on.

3. *Coordinator: The Modernization Commission*

This Commission, in cooperation with other planning agencies, was responsible for drafting various proposals and plans for selection by the General Commission of Planning. Its members, including scholars and representatives from administrative organs, academic institutions, and trade unions, were recommended by the General Commission of Planning and then appointed by the Minister of Finance. It had five horizontal committees to regulate the overall economic plan and 23 vertical agencies to link economic activities of various sectors. In addition, regional development committees were responsible for researching regional public investment.

4. *Advisor: The Economic and Social Commission*

This Commission became the advisor in 1958 when the French Constitution stipulated that it shall participate in planning and consultation from the fourth plan. It was populated by 200 people from all walks of life, including the government personnel, entrepreneurs, workers, peasants, overseas returnees, and so on.

5. *Approval authority: The National Assembly*

From the third plan, the National Assembly and the French Senate (*Sénat*) were responsible for examining the preliminary report and the final plan.

Once examined and approved by the National Assembly, a draft plan became a law and would be put into effect immediately.

10.4.2 Planning Legislation in Japan

Since the commencement of its Five-Year Plan for Economic Independence in 1956, Japan has issued over 40 medium- and long-term plans on the basis of surveys and appraisals of the long-term trend in terms of its population, employment, production, consumption, labor productivity, and natural resources. These plans not only put forward the guiding ideology for the development of its national economy but also showed the general trend of the government's regulation and control of the market economy. Therefore, economic planning plays an important role in Japan's macro-adjustment legal system. Basically, Japan's plans can be divided into three categories.

1. *National comprehensive land development plan*
This sort of plan, a comprehensive plan concerning the direction, keynote, layout, and scale of economic infrastructure construction, was designed to realize the comprehensive utilization of land and the rational distribution of productivity. All told, Japan formulated and revised such plans in 1962, 1969, 1977, and 1989. These plans were intended to achieve the optimal comprehensive benefits from an overall viewpoint of national economic development rather than focusing on the economic efficiency of individual public utilities. In addition, these plans rationally prioritized the construction of individual projects and allocated resources to those sectors that were decisive to national economic development. As outlined in long-term visionary outlook, these law-ensured plans had weak legal binding force and failed to achieve desired results (Zhang and Zheng, 1997).

2. *National economic development plan*
From the *Five-Year Plan for Economic Independence* in 1955 to the *Economic Operational Plan for Coexistence with the World* in 1988, Japan has formulated 11 national economic development plans. The national economic development plan was the most important type of plan in Japan's macro-control system. In contrast with the comprehensive land development plan, it was a typical structural plan, which stipulated a

medium-term development framework and objective and prescribed the process to realize the objective. In addition, as a guiding plan without no compulsory effect on private enterprises, it incorporated the economic activities of private enterprises into planning through economic means such as private credit and price and soft measures such as "window guidance" or moral persuasion. Moreover, its implementation was sufficiently guaranteed by relevant laws or decrees promulgated by the legislature, backed by financial allocation or bank-lending funds pursuant to the priorities, and supported by government departments responsible for the management and implementation of each project. Finally, except a few long-term plans, most of them were five-year medium-term plans.

3. *Plan for public utilities*

A plan for public utilities guaranteed and concretized the above two sorts of plan, which involve all fields of the national economy. It held an important position in Japan's planning system and it covered all fields including housing, environmental protection, transportation, ports, mines, and so on, and the investment in these fields accounted for more than half of the total. It should be submitted to the cabinet for approval before the ministries and departments in charge implement it into effect in accordance with the relevant laws. Because this heavily invested plan was central to the improvement of public well-being, it was mandatory and its goal was more likely to be secured.

Japan's macroeconomic planning began with the Prime Minister's consultation with the Economic Deliberation Council, which was based on the compilation of the Economic Planning Agency and on the investigation and deliberation of temporarily organized special commissions, branches, and the Council itself. The Council presented to the Prime Minister a plan that was to be discussed by the Cabinet before it became an official plan.

There were two main planning organs: the Economic Planning Agency and its affiliate Economic Deliberation Council. The Agency was responsible for the formulation of plans and comprehensive adjustment in the implementation of policies and programs related to the plans. The drafting and revision of plans were undertaken by the Comprehensive Planning Bureau affiliated to the Economic Planning Agency, populated by members from the internal staff of itself as well as outsiders from the Ministry of Industry and Industry (the predecessor of the METI, Ministry of Economy, Trade and Industry), the Ministry of Finance, financial institutions, companies, and other economic organizations. The Council, composed of representatives from the financial community, trade unions, academics, journalism, and consumer groups, was responsible for investigation and deliberation. It had the authority to present opinions to the Prime Minister, but no power to revise plans, much similar to the function of the French Modernization Commission.

Japan's planning legislation procedure seemed to be lengthy: decision making, drafting, consultation, and final adoption. The Prime Minister advised the Economic Deliberation Council on the formulation of a new plan and then the Comprehensive Planning Bureau made an analysis and prediction on his opinions and proposed a draft plan. Later, the draft plan was submitted to special commissions and branches and the Council itself for discreet investigation and deliberation on macroeconomic objectives and policy tools. In the case of revision, the draft plan would be submitted to the Comprehensive Planning Bureau and then to the Economic Deliberation Council for repeated deliberation. This stage normally took six months to even one year before a report on the plan was presented to the Prime Minister, who then convened the Cabinet for examination and approval. The draft plan, once approved by the Cabinet, could be ratified as a formal plan without parliamentary approval.

When implementing an economic plan, the Japanese government usually utilized financial leverage to regulate the economy and maintain a moderate and relatively stable economic growth rate according to changes in the economic situation. In addition, it formulated and revised relevant regulations to create favorable conditions for the implementation of policies and plans. Moreover, it persuaded, encouraged, supported, or restrained private enterprises through "administrative guidance" and well-directed taxation and loan policies to keep corporate behaviors consistent with the objectives of the plan.

10.4.3 Planning Legislation in South Korea

South Korea, after implementing seven five-year economic development plans from 1962, grew rapidly from an "absolutely poor" country in the early 1960s to a wealthy industrialized country, creating the term "Miracle on the Han River."

The South Korean government intervened in its economy via planning. Planning played in its economic takeoff a role that could never be replaced by financial and other economic leverages. South Korea welded development plans and the budget plan, with the latter supporting the former. Once a plan was formulated, the governments at all levels had to resolutely execute it; otherwise, they would be prosecuted for legal responsibility. Therefore, although not binding on enterprises, the plan still had a great influence on enterprises through the mandatory implementation.

To ensure the effectiveness and feasibility of a plan, the Korean government seriously considered the opinions of various departments and experts and made the plan more rational through repeated consultations and verifications. The government adjusted and revised the plan in time according to the actual changes in social and economic development to make the various indicators of the plan more realistic and feasible.

Planning in South Korea was continuous and pertinent. Its economic and social development planning system was dominated by five-year plans, complemented by departmental development plans (promulgated in the form of laws and giving preferential policies to key industries), annual economic plans (analyzing and predicting annual economic performance and environment), and special plans (focusing on a particular problem in economic development). The government strove to ensure the continuity and pertinence of planning and meanwhile readjusted policies based on the changes in external and internal situations to reduce risks that might be caused by a scattershot approach to the implementation of the plan.

The plans were nonmandatory. Like other market economies, Korea's economic plans were not legally binding on enterprises and individuals who could readjust their economic objectives and operating modes with reference to the plans. These plans were termed as "incentive plans" because the Korean government motivated corporate behaviors to smoothly put the plans into effect.

The Economic Planning Board, established in 1962, was the most important planning management department in South Korea. Its main functions were to formulate and implement the national economic and comprehensive development plan, readjust industrial policies, prepare budgets, formulate policies to stabilize prices, and fair trade and readjust its economic relationship with other nations. The Board sought advice from citizens from all walks of life as it did in the Seventh Five-Year Plan from 1992 to 1996 in order to reach a consensus on medium- and long-term plans (Jin, 1999: 238).

Besides the Economic Planning Board, involved in planning were many ministries, including the Ministries of Science and Technology, of Finance, of Rural Fisheries, of Industry, of Commerce, and of Construction. To ensure interministerial cooperation, the government provided institutional guarantee mechanism where a Deputy Prime Minister chaired a meeting of Chief Economic Officers to quickly reconcile the disputes between departments. In the case of readjusting internal economic plan to adapt to international economic climate, the Economic Planning Board consulted with many departments concerned to make countermeasures and report them to the Foreign Cooperation Committee led by the Deputy Prime Minister for consideration and approval.

10.5 PLANNING INSTITUTIONALIZATION IN CHINA

Though having not issued a Planning Law so far, China has issued some administrative normative documents in recent years to strengthen planning management. The enhancement of planning legislation in terms of institutionalization can to a large extent ensure that planning can play an effective and positive role under the context of socialist market economy.

10.5.1 Models of Planning Institutionalization

There are three models of planning legislation: codified, distributed, and mixed. The codified model refers to the enactment of planning laws to regulate all planning relationships, such as the *Planning Law for Economic and Social Development of Romania* and the *Law of Planning* of Hungary in 1972. In the distributed model where there is no complete planning code, planning relationship is regulated and readjusted by administrative laws and economic laws. The mixed model refers to the enactment of a separate planning law to prescribe general issues such as the basic principle of planning as well as specific issues in administrative and economic laws. Considering the planning practice, the mixed model is applicable to China. However, the condition for enacting a planning code is still not mature and China gained its experiences in the context of planning economy instead of the market economy whose planning management has not been pertinently understood. The codification of planning will be effective only if the nature, position, and function of planning are clearly defined on the firm basis of summing up experience and the establishment of market economy.

Currently, the main task is to promulgate relevant laws and regulations for compiling a specific plan and legislate planning procedures, including various codes of conduct in proposing a project; drafting a plan; interlinking departments; and justifying, evaluating, revising, and abolishing a plan. The compilation of a plan should be preceded by a comprehensive analysis and a scientific prediction of statistical data from different channels. Attention should also be paid to seeking suggestions and requirements from different walks of life and forming a panel of experts whose responsibility is to evaluate and review the plan outline. In addition, after the implementation of the plan, feedback should be collected to make timely adjustments within the statutory authority.

10.5.2 Main Contents of Planning Institutionalization

An important means of macro control, national development planning should be incorporated into the category of legal readjustment to accelerate the process of legislation. The government's strategic intention and core of work should be clearly articulated in the form of law to ensure the continuity and stability of national social and economic development. Greater importance should be attached to the implementation of the *Administrative Licensing Law*, the *Regulations on the Compilation of National Economic and Social Development Planning* and the promotion of planning legislation, and gradually establish a legal and regulatory guarantee system. In general, the following aspects of planning should be legislated.

10.5.2.1 *Nature*

Once approved by the NPC, a plan becomes the government's program of action for economic construction in the following years. Its smooth formulation is guaranteed by the affirmation of its nature in a legal sense: esteeming it as a key to the overall arrangement of reform and modernization, a programmatic document to observe in the formulation of other economic plans and policies, and a blueprint for economic and social development. In other words, a plan is a strategic and macroeconomic policy, a notion that should be deeply rooted in the public so that a powerful engine formed by all social forces can speed up the process of economic and social development.

10.5.2.2 *Content*

The legislation of planning aims to maintain the basic balance between total social supply and total demand; coordinate important macroeconomic indicators such as economic growth rate, inflation rate, and balance of payments; and determine the objectives, tasks, and priorities of macro control and provide a legal basis for formulating macroeconomic policies and measures in all aspects. As far as the main contents are concerned, four factors should be considered. First comes the determination of index system, of which economic development and social progress, especially the rigid indices such as public well-being and ecological environment are indicators that should be clearly defined. Second comes the implementation of major projects that are directly related to regional distribution of productivity and industrial development. Major projects in a plan are generally proposed after overall consideration and made known to the public in the form of law and thus subject to no government's intervention and adjustment. Associated with this is the assurance of continuous implementation of these major policies to avoid potential losses incurred by possible flip-flops. Major policies, often spelling out the government's orientation and resolution in macro control, will by no means work like magic unless they are put into effect for a certain period of time. Therefore, it is necessary to maintain the continuity of implanting these major policies through legislation; otherwise, too much time and capital will be squandered, and opportunities will slip away. Fourth and finally, top priority should be given to the development of key industries through legislation. Apart from considering an all-round development, planning legislation should determine the industries that need to be supported and invested. Obviously, a plan without statutorily binding force would breed the risk of leading economic development astray and abdicating the responsibility to support some enterprises that are currently weak but have a promising prospect.

10.5.2.3 *Procedure*

Only through a rational and effective operation procedure can a legal provision assume a realistic form of justice. The legislation of the planning procedure is the precondition for the whole planning work. First, departments involving planning at all levels should strengthen the presence of staff to conduct a preliminary study on the basic idea about planning, particularly on hot and difficult issues that have a significant impact on local development, and then report the results to the government. Second, coordination and interlinkage between departments at different levels should be improved as requested by the development strategy specified in the planning outline. Third, planning departments should make a diligent study on the contents of the draft plan and then submit it for review by the State Council before it is ratified as a statutory programmatic document by the NPC.

10.5.2.4 *Interlinkage*

Interlinkage aims to consummate the integral systematic project of planning legislation by linking many factors related to planning to form a centripetal force. Key indicators must be well matched to form a unified index system, and economic indicators at the national, provincial, and municipal levels must be mutually consistent and compatible. Moreover, special planning should pass muster with the requirements of the overall plan, planning for particular trades must be consistent with special planning, and local planning must highlight its key points and embodies its own features. Finally, major projects and policies should be interlinked up to ensure the continuity of economic construction. The construction of major projects that are arranged on the basis of scientific justification, social requirements, and financial resources is a key plank in the strategy to shore up economic and social development and structural readjustment.

10.5.2.5 *Time Span*

A national development plan, which is designed as a programmatic document that determines the focus of the government's task and the behavior of the market participants, may unwittingly impede social and economic development in case it becomes unsuitable to the new situation over time. Therefore, it is vital that time span be set for different categories of plans according to actual situations, for instance, a five-year span for national and provincial overall plans. A plan with a long time span is usually impractical and hard to implement and a plan with too short a time span cannot reflect the strategic intent of the government. It is advisable that one-year general plans be designed at the municipal and county levels. In addition, too many specialized plans will not only waste social resources but also weigh on local governments, let alone play a virtually marginal role in economic development.

10.5.2.6 *Implementation*

The national development plan, a program of action reviewed by the government and submitted to the people's congress for approval, is highly enforceable by law and therefore it should be issued in the form of law. The government should take the initiative in implementing the plan and delegate specific tasks to various specialized departments. It must be stipulated through legislation that a medium- and long-term plan is the main basis for the implementation of annual plans, which are in effect step-by-step plans worked out by various specialized departments to guarantee the integrity and continuity of the overall planning. The means of implementing a plan should be, by degrees, shifted from market regulation to comprehensive and full use of interest rates, tax rates, exchange rates, and prices. It is necessary that economic and legal means be introduced to regulate the market, change the economic environment, affect the interests of behavior subjects, and thus guide them to act as required in the plan. When implementing a plan, governmental departments or agencies should ensure the unity of authority and responsibility. In other words, the plan, once approved, should be deemed by governmental departments as a statutory duty to allow it full play in regulation and guidance.

10.5.2.7 *Evaluation and Revision*

Evaluation and revision, a procedure designed for the governmental departments and agencies to listen to public opinion, improve management techniques and efficiency, and minimize mistakes, is also an important guarantor of allowing a plan full play in guidance and macroeconomic control. Therefore, it is necessary for the organ of power to supervise the implementation of a plan through legislation. In the mid-term of implementing a plan, an objective and impartial appraisal should be conducted to find and attack possible problems. Departments in charge of specific objectives of the plan should diligently analyze and examine those parts which need revision, monitor the progression of key major projects, and report without delay to the People's Congress major changes in economic operation or readjustments in planning. After the termination of a plan, reevaluation is necessary for providing experience or reference for the next round of planning. In addition, rulemaking in this respect should ensure that the news media and public are informed of the progression of planning and that they have the democratic right to take comments on planning so that they can actively participate in national economic and social development.

10.5.3 Accountability for Violation and Nonperformance in Planning

In the case of no provision for legal liability in the planning legislation, any state organ, enterprise, institution, nongovernmental organization, or individual may escape punishment when they infringe laws or regulations on planning at will and cause damage to development, thus rendering planning legislation futile. Therefore, a strict system of accountability should be established to defend the legitimacy of a plan by enforcing a law on the right and duty to be fulfilled by various subjects involving the planning.

In the process of making a plan or a decision, the following behaviors or acts will be deemed as illegal: falsification in planning, prediction, decision making, and readjustment that incur major errors and losses to economic and social development; violation of planning procedures to decide planning tasks; impingement on the purview of other departments, commissions, or agencies and arbitrary formulation, review, issuance, revision of plans, and arbitrary decision on constructing key projects or setting other targets; defiance of the coordination by the authorities; refusal to or delay in reporting to the authorities data and information concerning the formulation of planning; and divulging any secret about national planning.

In the process of implementing a plan, the following behaviors or acts will be deemed as illegal: negligence of duty that results in the failure to duly fulfill a plan; incompetence or indolence in meeting obligatory targets required in a national plan; refusal to meet the standards and conditions required for national strategic material reserves, or profiteer by selling strategic materials in short supply; obstruction of the planning staff's exercise of their authority; and other misconducts that thwart the implementation of a plan.

In the process of monitoring planning, the following behaviors or acts will be deemed as illegal: transgression of provisions for monitoring procedures that incur serious mistakes; neglect of main tasks and failure to differentiate major points from minor details, resulting in the default of the formulation and supervision of a major planning; disclosure of confidential information or deliberate concealment of information, resulting in serious mistakes in formulating and revising a plan; dereliction of duty or failure to conduct of a diligent monitoring that result in serious consequences; and ignorance of the basic law of social and economic development and the actual laws related to local natural resources and environment and falsification of information concerning the formulation and implementation.

In the process of planning evaluation and revision by planning agencies, the following behaviors or acts are deemed as illegal: defiance of any provision concerning evaluation and revision, rendering evaluation and revision futile and incurring great damage to national development or loss of natural resources; failure to analyze accurate data channeled from various sources and make a timely correction on mistakes caused in planning work, or disregard of the mistakes in formulating and/or implementing a plan, or refusal to attempt any revision in the case of mistakes; failure to evaluate and revise a plan in accordance with the basic law of social and economic development and the actual situations related to natural resources and environment.

The above behaviors or acts of which a government is believed to be guilty should be investigated by the people's congress or its standing committee at the same level. The behaviors or acts of which a governmental department or agency or commission is believed to be guilty of should be investigated by the people's government or the planning department responsible for the overall planning. The behaviors or acts of which an state-owned enterprise (SOE) is believed to be guilty of should be investigated by the department in charge at the same level. The behaviors or acts of which an individual is believed to be guilty of should be investigated by the working unit to which he or she is affiliated. Any crime should be sued to judicial organs for legal action. Planning legislation should also consider a reconsideration system and time limit and purview thereof. A planning law should prescribe the administrative sanctions (including warning, record of demerits, record major faults, demotion, dismissal, retention for inspection, and dismissal from office), and economic and criminal responsibilities a subject involving planning work shall bear when found guilty. Those who cause damage or loss due to dereliction of duty shall make economic compensation.

REFERENCES

Huang, Wenjie. *Macroeconomic Management in France*. Shanghai: Fudan University Press, 1990.

Jin, Xiaoli. *An Introduction to Foreign Macroeconomic Management*. Beijing: China Wujia Publishing House, 1999.

Jin, Xiaoli, Zhang, Jie, and Xin Zheng. *Japan: A Market Economy Integrating West and East*. Wuhan: Wuhan University Press, 1997.

Chapter 11

Improvement and Innovation of National Development Planning System

11.1 PLANNING SYSTEM UNDER SOCIALIST MARKET ECONOMY

Planning system, as its name suggests, is a synthesis of myriads of inter-linked, interactive and mutually complementary plans articulated from different perspectives. Since a national development planning system involves the realization of many objectives in economic, scientific, tech-nological and social aspects and some of them, particularly macroscopic and mesoscopic objectives can only be realized by degrees and across regions, it is so complex that no single plan can incorporate so many inter-linked contents and intricate relations thus far formed. Therefore, the coordination between specific objectives, processes and means in a plan must be based on its specific contents to achieve a comprehensive balance under the guidance of the overall objective and hence form a unified plan-ning system.

As an integral mix, a planning system can be understood from the fol-lowing perspectives.

(1) *Integrity*
A planning system is by no means the total of individual plans. Though inconsistent or even conflicting with the overall objective of the whole planning system if viewed individually, the primary objective of each individual plan is essentially compatible with the overall objective.

Plainly, the planning system can only play its role when each individual plan is well coordinated.

(2) *Hierarchy*

In different phases of development, each individual plan in the planning system is not equally important but plays a minor or major role. For instance, medium- and long-term plans dominate the planning system, but annual plans (short-term plans) are in the subordinate position.

(3) *Openness*

Planning system interact with actual economic and social development. On the one hand, since the reality of economic and social development on which planning is based is dynamic and mutable over time, planning system should keep pace with the requirements of economic and social development and constantly absorb new contents and adopt new forms while eliminating those out of date with the reality. On the other hand, various types of individual plans are the barometer of economic and social development, but the history of market economy has revealed the consequences arising from the lack of macro control means such as planning. Planning and socioeconomic development is an interactive process, in which the planning is constantly being improved.

According to the system theory, the subsets that constitute a whole system are not equally important. Likewise, planning, if viewed as a system, consists of constituents (individual plans) and each of them has its own distinct features that accordingly determine its function and status in the planning system.

Plans, in the sense of the spheres they are concerned about, can be categorized into economic, scientific and social development plans. Economic development plans, which aim to blueprint futuristic national economic development, hold a dominant position insofar as material production is the basis of social existence and development. Scientific development plans that aim to provide powerful momentum for economic development through innovating and transforming science and technology into productivity. Social development plans, designed to arrange every aspect of social life and development of social causes, are not only the outcome of but also the condition for economic and scientific development. Social development plans, separated from national economic development plans since the Sixth Five-Year Plan, aim to provide guidance for the social coordination and sustainable development. With the shift of the function of national planning management and the introduction of people-centered concept, social development plans are becoming increasingly prominent in the planning system.

So far as contents are concerned, plans can be categorized into overall, specialized and sectoral plans. Overall plans, all-round plans for major economic activities, scientific progress and social development, aim to set on the basis of analyzing the trend of social and economic development the main goal and basic principle of macro-control policies. Specialized plans are flexible plans well-directed at the solution to specific problems in economic and social development. Sectoral plans, relatively narrower in contents, are designed to set goals and formulate policies for specific sectors of industry. Unlike western developed countries, China laid emphasis on comprehensive plans due to its immature market economy. It is aware that an extremely comprehensive plan is susceptible to scattershot approach and thus has shifted its attention to the formulation of specialized and sectoral plans intended to solve specific problems.

From the spatial distribution, plans can be divided into national, local and regional plans. National plans are programmatic and uniform, whereas local and regional plans, consistent as they are with the guideline incorporated in the national plans, are distinct from national plans in varying degrees and highly workable. Unlike western federal countries where each state issues its own plans under its relatively independent legislative and executive systems and the federal government participates in planning through indirect financial means such as federal grants, China, a traditionally centralized country where the central government grips decision making, formulates a dominant national master plan that theoretically can by no means be challenged by local and regional plans.

From the time span, plans can be divided into long-, medium-, and short-term plans. Medium- and long-term plans have increasingly become the main form because national planning is mainly responsible for the coordination of major issues concerning development orientation, aggregate demand and structural readjustment. Highly strategic long-term plans, proposing the scenario for social and economic development in a long period, are the basis for formulating medium-term plans that define clearly the specific goals of economic, scientific and social development and estimate the conditions for realizing these goals. Short-term plans are usually highly feasible annual plans which aim to ensure the equilibrium of the macroeconomic aggregate. With the improvement of market economy, this type of plan is no longer a main form of planning.

11.2 THE CONCEPTION OF PLANNING REFORM

The problems in the current planning are closely related to the ill-managed compilation procedure and jumbled management system and poor competence in compiling plans. Most planning management departments compile plans from their own interests and occasionally result in serious conflicts with other groups of interests. A council of regular and expert professionals is urgently needed to reshape the current situation where the plans are still short-sighted, nondescript, indefinite, incomplete, and inflexible. To allow planning system full play in guiding and readjusting national economic and social development and ensure authority, consistence, and operability of planning, China needs to establish a well-structured planning system that features clearly divided functions and clarifies a series of matters including the nature, duties, compilers, executors, means, and approvers of planning.

11.2.1 Planning System

The current planning system consists of plan outlines and other types of plans concerning key special projects, sectors of industry, urban development, land utilization, and urban system. Plan outlines, usually regarded as the general plan for economic and social development, have a high legal status. Other types of plans, if viewed in the sense of spatial–temporal sequence, can be classified into regional plans and specialized plans. Therefore, planning can be designed as a "triangular structure" of overall, regional and special planning. Regional planning covers plans of urban development, land use, economic zones, other functional zones, and urban agglomeration and specialized planning covers plans of economy, society, policies and projects.

In the levels of planning, it is essential to lay emphasis on a highly efficient system in which the functional orientations and mutual relationships of the plans at different levels should be clearly defined to avoid excessive workload at each level in the case of uni- or double-layered design and confusing and overlapping division of labor in the case of multilayered design. Based on administrative levels, the current planning is managed at the national, provincial, city, and county levels. Planning at the city level is quite similar to that at the county level and therefore can be merged into one. Thus, China can form a triple-level planning at the national, provincial and city–county levels. In terms of development trends, planning is facing a movement from rigidity to flexibility, from the separation of temporal and spatial planning to the combination of them. To sum up, the planning framework with a triple-layered, triangular structure is sketched as shown in Figure 11.1.

Different sorts of planning are interlinked. Subordinate to overall planning, regional planning is designed to concretize or localize overall planning in accordance with local actual situations. Specialized planning is highly flexible and subject to readjustment as actual situations change.

The conception of planning system reform aims at an establishment of the foremost position and authority of the overall plan by addressing the messy and tangled relationship between different categories of planning;

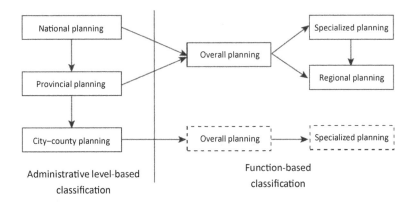

Figure 11.1   The Conception of Planning System Reform

Note: The overall planning at the city–county level is different from that at the national and provincial levels. Dotted lines indicate that the planning in the box is not absolutely necessary.

acclimatization of development trend to coordinate regional economic development by optimizing spatial sequential planning; incorporation of temporal and spatial sequence planning for overall consideration so as to solve the outstanding problem of disunity between the administrative level-based and function-based divisions of planning.

National planning, as an overall general plan which has a great stake in long-term interests of national economic and social development, mainly focuses on the primary orientation, strategic objectives, and priorities in a certain period of time. It is required that provincial and city–county planning shall be formulated by the local governments at or above the county level in accordance with the principles and policies of the national planning and specific conditions of the local regions, or with a particular sector of industry.

Overall planning includes national, provincial and the city–county (if necessary) overall planning. National planning should be submitted by the State Council to the NPC for consideration and approval, and implemented through national specialized planning, national regional planning, provincial overall planning, annual planning and financial budget. The time span for overall planning is generally 5 years or can be extended to 10 years if necessary. Provincial planning should be submitted by the provincial government to the people's congress at the provincial level for consideration and approval, and implemented through provincial specialized planning, provincial regional planning, city–county overall planning, annual planning and financial budget. Its time span should tally with that of national overall planning. City–county planning should be submitted by the city or county people's congress for consideration and approval and implemented by organizing relevant departments and mobilizing social forces. The time span for such planning can be altered with the change of actual situations.

Specialized planning includes national and provincial planning. The major projects related to infrastructure, strategic resources, ecological environment, public services and any other project with large investment and long construction cycle for which the central and provincial governments hold responsible should be incorporated into national and provincial specialized planning which then should be respectively submitted by the National and Provincial Development and Reform Commissions to the

State Council and to the provincial government for approval. In principle, the state and provinces (municipalities and autonomous regions) no longer make special plans respecting other fields except the major projects mentioned above. The fields where market mechanism has played a fundamental role in resource allocation nullify specialized plans therein, so only market analysis and forecast reports prepared by trade associations are necessary. The term of specialized planning is subject to change with the objective of the overall planning.

Regional planning includes regional planning at the national and provincial levels. National regional planning should be considered by the State Council before it is submitted to the Standing Committee of the NPC for approval; provincial planning should be considered by the provincial government before it is submitted to the Standing Committee of the Provincial People's Congress for approval. The term of regional planning, both at the national and provincial levels, is usually not less than 10 years. City–county regional planning is unnecessary and can be merged into one in that the two sorts of planning are likely to overlap with each other in a small administrative region.

11.2.2 Nature, Function and Relationship of Each Type of Planning

(1) *National Overall Planning*
The national overall plan, aka. the outline for national economic and social development of the PRC, is a strategic, macro- and policy-oriented plan based on the recommendations of the Central Committee of the CPC on the formulation of the five-year plan. The plan prepared by the departments of state development and reform is the basis on which national specialized and regional plans and provincial overall plan are worked out.

(2) *National Specialized Planning*
This is a generic term for all sorts of plans such as sectoral plans, specialized plans, key specialized plans and project plans compiled by the central agencies and commissions. As an action plan, a national specialized planning is directed at a specific field of economic and social development, in other words, it is an extension and refinement of the national overall plan.

(3) *National Regional Planning*

National regional planning is made by the central government for specific economic regions across provinces (autonomous regions or municipalities). The relevant plans are compiled for areas closely related to economic and social development, urban agglomerations based on mega cities whose influence can radiate to its surrounding regions, and key development zones or preserves determined in the national overall plan. These plans, as the implementation plans of the national overall plan and national specialized plans in different regions of the country, are a guide and a straitjacket, that is, the basis for the formulation of various types of plans in administrative regions at the national, provincial and county levels.

(4) *Provincial Overall Planning*

Provincial overall planning refers to outlining the five-year plan for the national economic and social development at the level of provinces, municipalities or autonomous regions. Based on the national overall plan, a provincial overall plan is a strategic, macro- and policy-oriented plan for social and economic development and the basis for formulating provincial special and regional plans and city–county overall plans (if necessary). Provincial overall planning horizontally links the national overall planning at the top and city–county planning at the bottom.

(5) *Provincial Specialized Planning*

This is a generic term for all sorts of plans such as sectoral plans, specialized plans, key specialized plans and project plans compiled by provincial departments, agencies or commissions. As an implementation plan, a provincial specialized plan is targeted at a specific field of economic and social development, in other words, it is an extension and refinement of the provincial overall plan. The central government shall make no compulsory administrative orders to demand provincial departments to compile a provincial specialized plan.

(6) *Provincial Regional Planning*

Provincial regional planning is made by provincial governments for specific economic regions across cities and counties. As the implementation of the provincial overall plan and relevant provincial specialized plans in the territorial spaces within the jurisdiction of a city or a county, it is a guide and a straitjacket, that is, the basis for the formulation of various types of plans to be compiled by administrative units within the jurisdiction of the said city and county.

(7) *City–County Overall Planning*

City–county overall planning refers to the planning outline for the national economic and social development at the level of city and county. Based on a provincial overall plan, a city–county overall plan is a strategic and policy-oriented plan for social and economic development and the basis for formulating city–county specialized plans.

(8) *City–County Specialized Planning*

This is a generic term for all sorts of plans such as sectoral plans, specialized plans, key specialized plans and project plans compiled by departments and agencies at the city and county levels. As an implementation plan, a city–county specialized plan is targeted at a specific field of economic and social development, in other words, it is an extension and refinement of the city–county overall plan in a particular field. The city and county governments may, at their own option, formulate a specialized plan because it is, like a city–county overall plan, an implementation plan. The provincial government shall make no compulsory administrative orders to demand city–county departments to compile a specialized plan.

11.3 INNOVATIONS OF NATIONAL DEVELOPMENT PLANNING

Despite obvious achievements in innovating national development planning since reform and opening up, an array of problems still exist. In the new era, planning must keep pace with historical trends and make innovations to allow it full play in guiding and promoting economic and social development.

11.3.1 Progress in Planning Reform

In a planning economy where the government, as the core of all economic activities, not only managed the macroeconomy but also intervened directly in the microeconomy, government planning played a decisive role in resource allocation and thus created an acute shortage of supplies. Under such an institutional context, the national development plan had the following characteristics. First, due to the shortage of supplies, many contents of the national development plan dealt with production, distribution, circulation and consumption of various materials mainly through fixing indicators and projects and diversifying investments. Second, the national development plan took economic growth as its starting point, highlighting industrial and agricultural development and infrastructure construction but disregarding social development such as comprehensive utilization of resources and environment protection. Third, it was more concerned about physical indicators than value indicators that were only put in a subordinate position. Fourth, it mainly considered the balance of domestic supply and demand.

With the waves of economic system reform since the late-1970s and early-1980s, China's planning management system has undergone a series of reforms accordingly in different historical periods: the guideline of "planning economy supplemented by market regulation" proposed at the 12th National Congress of the CPC in 1982; the objective of developing planned commodity economy put forward at the Third Plenum of the 12th Central Committee of the CPC in 1984; the establishment of a socialist market economic system clearly defined at the 14th National Congress of the CPC in 1992. Since 1992, China's planning management system has undergone the following profound changes.

(1) *Highlighting macro control, strategic and policy orientation*
Basically, planning is but guiding. Its focus is no longer on directly arranging the economic activities of all sectors but on navigating national economic and social development by rationally determining the objectives of macro control and strategies for economic and social development, working out policies related to macro control and industrial development, redressing economic structures and productivity distribution, and ensuring key national construction.

(2) *Stressing government-motivated domains and weakening*
   market-motivated domains
The national and provincial planning outlines prescribe the development direction and path in the domains where the market mechanism plays a

role and set clear objectives and measures in the domains where the government plays a role. Planning indicators, especially mandatory ones, have been greatly reduced, and the scope of guiding planning and market regulation has been enlarged. For the first time, the "Eleventh Five-Year Plan" divided development indicators into two categories: anticipatory and mandatory (binding), which further clarifies the responsibilities of the government and the market.

(3) *Emphasizing the economic overall performance and the improvement of competency*

Planning emphasizes the overall economic performance and core competency in all aspects of economic development. Besides, it shifts from the promotion of economic growth through expanding production capacity to the improvement of economic efficiency through optimizing and upgrading the industrial structure and changing the mode of economic growth.

(4) *Showing solicitude for people's living standards*

Planning in the past laid too much emphasis on industrial production but now it has begun to show solicitude for the welfare of the public. Both the central government and local governments at provincial and county levels have taken the improvement of people's material and cultural living standards as the basic starting point in their planning, substantially increasing the indicators that reflect the enhancement of people's living standards, and making relevant policies and specialized plans to guarantee the realization of this objective.

(5) *Emphasizing the integration of economic development with social development and protection of resources and environment*

Enlarged as the Sixth Five-Year (Economic) Plan was into an economic and social development plan, importance was still attached to economic growth. Not until the 10th and 11th Five-Year Plans did the coordination of economic and social development, environment protection and sustainable development receive due regard. This reflected not only people-centeredness but also the desire to build a resource-saving and environment-friendly society and make continuous progress in the process of building a harmonious society. Since then, both the central government and governments at different levels have incorporated ecological construction, environmental protection, employment, and social security into specialized plans.

(6) *Putting premium on the innovation of planning implementation mechanism*

Since the new millennium, much attention has been paid to the innovation of implementation mechanism in planning. The implementation of planning is guaranteed not only by ensuring the success of key projects, but also by strengthening macro control, propelling system reform, formulating supporting policies, improving development environment, and establishing a tracking and monitoring system.

11.3.2 Major Problems in the Design of Planning Content

Despite some progress made in innovating the design on of planning content, some problems still manifest in the following aspects.

(1) *Greater importance being attached to economic development than to social development*

Until the 11th Five-Year Plan, priority was always being given to economic growth, and the contents involving industrial development in planning had been particularly detailed. Since the incorporation of the Scientific Outlook on Development into the 11th Five-Year Plan, the governments at different levels have highlighted the people-centered concept, redirecting more attention toward education, hygiene and health, human resource development, job creation and social security that are closely related to the improvement of people's living standards. As for economic growth and structure, politically mandatory or binding indicators have been replaced by anticipatory or guiding indicators. Meanwhile, the indicators concerning population, resources, environment, public services and people's lives have become binding indicators. This redirection is conducive to separating governmental responsibilities from market functions. However, the implementation measures concerning the government-motivated fields are not detailed and specific enough. Besides, less attention is paid to fund arrangement for some livelihood projects, much less the still prevalent idea of evaluating political performances solely by economic growth in some regions.

(2) *All-inclusive and out-of-focus planning*

In the aspect of contents, any sort of plan, from planning outline to key specialized and sectoral plans, stresses a uniform framework of contents but disregards the actual situations of a certain region and industry. For instance, the national five-year planning outline is inclusive of the whole gamut of spheres from socioeconomic development and sustainable development to the building of spiritual civilization, democracy, rule by law and national defense, some of which should be undertaken by the CPC Committee, the NPC, CPPCC, and the Central Military Commission. Each province (municipality and autonomous region) follows suit and so does each prefecture, city, and county without taking local situations into consideration. As a result, the planning outline model from the central government down to the county government is basically the same without a special focus on the fields in which the government is required to play a role in resource allocation. Some provinces (municipalities and autonomous regions), though having specified in their planning outline the market-motivated spheres, fail to focus on the areas in which the government is believed to play a role in resource allocation, such as science and technology, education, hygiene and health, employment, social security, and so on. Key specialized plans, originally intended to direct at the major issues having a great deal stake in overall development but seriously obstructing economic development and at some industrial fields that require government intervention, are actually overladen with as many as more than 20 key specialized projects, crammed with the spheres that should be regulated by market mechanism rather than the government planning, and thus blurred with out-of-focus objectives and missions and impractical measures.

(3) *Irrelevance and indistinctiveness in strategic choices*
The 11th Five-Year planning outline of each province (municipality and autonomous region), to a large extent, seems to be a replica and its plan is impertinent to its local characteristics and thus featureless.

On the choice of strategic industries, local authorities lay too much emphasis on the selection of key development industries according to the resources and existing industrial patterns in a small local area rather than making a synergic effort to form a functionally complementary layout of local industries based on a diligent analysis of comparative advantages in natural and economic resources and on a good understanding of information and market. Besides, local planning, without taking into consideration local conditions and needs, follows suit with the central planning in the development planning of high-tech industries and services. The same problem exists in the setting of index system. Due to lack of innovation on index system in the plans at the administrative levels from provinces (municipalities, autonomous regions) to prefectures, cities, and counties, the core competence of a local region cannot be truly reflected in the plans, and what's worse, indicators or rather quotas become increasingly burdensome when assigned to a lower level.

(4) *Mismatch between industry development and spatial distribution*
The self-evident fact that the national planning outline puts more emphasis on development trends than on the spatial distribution of light industries inevitably results in an unsystematic and separated arrangement of division of regional industries. In addition, policies for regional economic coordinated development are too simplistic and there is no specific synergic development mechanism. Furthermore, industrial development is not well combined with land utilization and urban construction.

Similar problems exist in the planning outlines at the provincial level. First, the outlines fail to combine national industrial development with regional development and give full play to the comparative advantages of local regions and the rational division of labor in the region. In consequence, industrial structure is almost the same in regions with different conditions and resources. Second, the outlines fail to base the industrial development on industrial zones and bases intended to stoke up local development. Third, industrial development is not well combined with urban development and the construction of urban system construction. The current provincial planning outlines at hand suggest that they neither put premium on industrial spatial layout centered on cities nor stress the cultivation and division of urban industries and the improvement of the urban functions. As a result, industrial development cannot effectively proceed due to weak spatial basis.

(5) *Lack of efficient implementation mechanism*
For planning, it is essential not only to propose development goals but also to formulate a set of feasible and effective economic policies to guarantee the realization of these goals. Hence, the outline of the 11th Five-Year Plan from the central government to local levels stresses planning implementation and makes some innovations on implementation mechanisms.

As far as the national planning outline is concerned, its economic policy system fails to incorporate the economic policies formulated by some ministries, departments, and agencies affiliated to the State Council or to the National Development and Reform Commission. Nevertheless, these policies are not mutually complementary.

The key specialized plans in some provinces, municipalities and autonomous regions seem to be difficult to be implemented simply for the following reasons: no description of specific tasks in different phases of development despite an overall objective; no clear definition of government responsibilities and obligations; no annual investment plan despite an overall scenario for capital injection into a proposed project; no absolute guarantee of the sources of investment funds.

(6) *Disparity and loose linkage between plans*
Vertically, the contents in the plans at different levels should be well linked. However, due to conflict of interests, disparity still exists in such issues as industrial development and the construction of key projects.

Horizontally, all forms of plans are not well linked. First, different regions are in dire need of synergic efforts. For instance, a local government, when making a five-year planning outline, seems to isolate itself from neighboring counties and cities or other regions with similar resources instead of proposing a regional development strategy from the perspectives of regional division of labor and lateral economic ties. Second, there is a loose linkage between key specialized planning and other forms of planning. In planning work, a department responsible for a comprehensive plan finds itself difficult to balance key specialized plans and sectoral plans that have been or are to be respectively compiled by different panels of experts with different professional backgrounds.

11.3.3 Orientation of Planning Content Reform and Innovation

Considering the problems existing in planning and the basic requirements that must be abided by in the compilation of planning under the socialist market economy, this section attempts to make suggestions for the reform and innovation of the content of China's national economic and social development planning in the future.

11.3.3.1 *Reform and Innovation of Overall Planning*

The national planning outline, a programmatic document suitable to the requirements of the market economy, should basically contain the following aspects: an analysis and prediction of the development environment; the phased development goals; the readjustment of the economic structure; social development; spatial development and structural optimization; development environment and institutional construction; and specific implementation measures and policy system. In addition, it is advisable to add supplementary explanatory materials on strategic choice, target selection, and policy trend so that the outline can be widely accepted.

In view of the maladies that have been diagnosed in the current planning work, prescriptions should be well directed at the following issues. First, there is a "market-oriented" tendency which understands planning outline merely as a market guidance or information publication. It is advised not to give equal but discriminatory weight to different contents in the planning outline.

Second, it behooves the national planning outline, which embodies a concept and a way of thinking by combining development strategy with the phased development goals, to determine the focus of work instead of repeating development strategies and vacuous and verbose interpretations. Third, it is necessary to combine the objectives of economic and social development with the requirements of optimizing of spatial structure and determine the principled requirements of spatial development order to lay a good foundation for the formulation of regional planning and specialized planning. Fourth, it is a realistic option to articulate possible risks and uncertainties that might result from the forecast of long term yet fundamental issues to avoid ambiguous wording and further increase the credibility. Fifth, it is important to make planning more reasonable by wedding long-term and short-term measures and to avoid the tendency to make short-term measures longer than expected. Sixth, it is necessary for a government at a higher level, when making a plan from a holistic approach to national interest, have a leeway for all kinds of planning at a lower level so as to form a complete planning system.

Basically, a provincial planning outline is the localized praxis of the national planning outline and can make flexible readjustments in the content framework according to its actual situations. Likewise, a city–county planning outline is supposed to fulfill the objectives prescribed in the provincial planning outline and attach great importance to infrastructure, ecological environment, public service, land use, job creation, and spatial layout as well as place on the agenda the issues that the government is resolved to tackle.

11.3.3.2 *Reform and Innovation of Specialized Planning*

An array of specialized plans involves a wide range of subjects. Each of these plans is well targeted at the arrangement of a production activity in a certain period of time. A specialized plan, which is supposed to make salient its focal points and clear objectives and contents, should prescribe pragmatic policy measures, define government responsibilities, conceive the layout of a major project, and manage ring-fenced funds.

In the actual planning work, specialized plans can be subdivided into specialized economic, social, institutional, and project (engineering) plans.

Specialized economic plans are mainly directed at industrial development and resource exploitation and such engineering projects as water conservancy, transportation, and energy that are closely related to economic development.

With the gradual improvement of the market economy, the planning of competitive areas is gradually being downplayed, and more efforts are shifted toward public services, basic industries, infant industries and declining industries that need government support. The contents of specialized economic plans usually include environment analysis and prediction, government orientation and objectives, and guiding measures.

Specialized social plans are designed to deal with social development such as scientific, educational, and cultural undertakings and other people's livelihood projects including public hygiene, job creation, social security, and ecological environment. The contents should include an analysis of the current situation and existing problems, the proposal of the main tasks and phased objectives, and the definition of the government responsibilities and formulating corresponding measures.

Specialized institutional plans mainly involve institutional reform, construction and improvement, and enforcement of rule by law. The main

Table 11.1   Type Design of Specialized Planning

Specialized Planning	Economic	Social	Institutional	Project (Engineering)
Scope	Industrial development; Resource exploitation; Water conservancy; Transportation; Energy	Educational, scientific, cultural undertakings; Public hygiene; Job creation; Social security; Environment	Institutional reform; Institutional improvement; Enhancement of legal system; Urbanization	Megaprojects; Project complexes
Content requirements	Analysis and prediction of environment; Government orientation; Guiding measures	Current situation and existing problems; Major objectives; Major measures	Situation analysis and significance Orientation and phased objectives Institutional arrangement Support measures	Necessity; Feasibility; Specific implementation plan; Economic and environment appraisal; Support measures

contents include situation analysis and significance of institutional construction, determination of phased objectives, specific institutional arrangement, and support measures guaranteeing the smooth implementation of the plans.

Specialized project plans are technically compiled for medium- and long-term megaprojects and engineering complexes that entail social resources and have great social and political implications. The main contents of these plans include the necessity, feasibility, specific implementation plans, economic and environmental appraisal, and support measures (Table 11.1).

In addition, the subdivision of specialized plans into government-intervening plans and government-oriented plans is also of great importance to the reform of specialized planning.

The government-intervening plans refer to those concerning the issues with a great impact on overall development that is hard to be resolved without governmental supporting policies and ring-fenced funds. The industries or fields in these plans tinted with mandatory and guiding characteristics often involve allocation of resources by both the government and the market, such as planning about educational and scientific development. Government-intervening plans should live up to the requirements in the following aspects: the linkage of the overall development objective with specific goals in those areas in which the government should play a role in resource allocation; the combination of the development strategy of a particular field with the construction and layout of a major construction; the combination of investment plan; and fund allocation scenario with government support policies.

Government-oriented specialized plans are designed to tackle the outstanding and tough problems that can only be solved by government guidance, instruction, and participation. These plans set concrete goals for major strategic projects in the national planning outline such as West–East Gas Pipeline Project and the South–North Water Diversion Project. The contents of these plans include the following aspects: the overall objective based on the planning outline and phased goals; focal points of development; the detailed plan for a number of key infrastructure projects of nationwide significance, especially the construction scale and layout of these projects; investment plans and fund-raising programs; well-directed strong support policies.

For the provincial specialized plans, the content framework can be flexible. The main problem is to differentiate the government's guiding role in the market from the government's responsibilities and priorities so as to make the plans more workable and feasible. The city–county specialized plans, if necessary, should be issued in accordance with the actual problems existing in the region lest they should be misunderstood as the continuation of the national and provincial specialized plans.

11.3.3.3 *Reform and Innovation of Regional Planning*

Absolute location advantage has a positive impact on production location. The same is true for comparative location advantage on regional division of labor and distribution of productivity on the formation and development of economic zones. The plans for economic zones, ecological environment and central cities (megalopolises) should have their own focal points. The contents of the planning for economic zones are as follows: prediction and analysis of regional economic development; positioning of the region within a larger regional scope; survey of basic resources such as minerals, water, land, and population in the region; the basic pattern of growth pole (development axis) or development network of regional development; development scale and function positioning of cities and towns; distribution of rural residential areas; the spatial structure of land use (planning of construction area, agricultural area, ecological area, and other special areas); the layout of infrastructure such as transportation, electricity, and communication in the region; the layout of construction projects that have a significant impact on local economic development and ecological environment; special provisions in special areas; cooperation with neighboring areas, and so on.

The plans for ecological environment are mainly aimed at ecologically vulnerable areas, natural disaster-prone areas and natural and cultural tourism resorts, and so on. The main contents are to define the scope of the planned areas, put forward clear requirements for conservancy, restoration, and development and other activities, and formulate corresponding safeguard measures.

The plans for megalopolis are mainly aimed at big cities which have great economic radiation effect on an economic circle. The main contents are as follows: prediction of economic development of central cities; development objectives (economic aggregate, population size, urban construction, land use) and urban positioning; network layout and construction of transportation, communications, supply system, and satellite cities; industrial clusters and functional partition; and relevant policies.

As an outcome of economic and social development, the optimization of spatial structure can also have a precursory effect on the economic trend and thus form a feedback loop with economic development. In this sense, spatial planning is proposed to keep up with the socioeconomic trend and rationally allocate resources in the region. The optimization of spatial structure can be reflected in different aspects, such as larger urban scale, greater efficiency, stronger agglomerative and radiation effects as well as the integration of land resources, conservation of ecological areas and improvement of humanistic environment. It can further be reflected in more comfortable living environment, convenient transportation and the formation of a new humanistic environment. It is essential that regional planning emphasize spatiality, especially dynamic spatial layout and dynamic structural optimization and upgrading rather than simple integration of regional planning. Leeway or a certain degree of freedom should be given to a particular region in a spatial plan. Provincial regional planning, compared with national regional planning, is more controllable and practicable as the information for the former is relatively accessible and the geographical scope is comparatively small.

11.4 LINKAGE AND INTEGRATION OF DIFFERENT TYPES OF PLANNING

Different subjects are responsible for different types of plans at different administrative levels. Some plans are jointly drafted by multiple subjects, so coordination becomes an indispensable and inevitable link that runs through the whole process of planning research, formulation, and implementation in the proposal of guidelines, objectives, priorities, policies, and guaranteeing measures. This is aimed to ensure the formation of a scientific, systematic and consistent planning system.

11.4.1 The Actualization of Planning Linkage

A coordinated relationship of a scientific, systematic and consistent planning system is the inherent requirement of the sound socioeconomic development. It is also the objective requirement of realizing national economic management to make the planning system more effective under the context of socialist market economy. Establishing a coordination system among different departments and regions is the organizational guarantee. It is necessary to be serious about the linkup and coordination between different types of plans, end fragmentation of separate plans, avoid overlapping projects, refrain from blindness and thus eventually achieve a sustainable development, that is social and economic development, human and natural resources, ecological environment and population size are harmoniously coordinated.

11.4.1.1 *Identification of Planning Linkage*

It is essential to identify what kind of relationship lies between the objects of different types of planning so that they could be properly linked up for greater efficiency. Three basic relationships can be determined. The first is the holistic and local relationship where some objects are only append-ages to or a subdivision of others, such as the relationship between branch plans and stem plans in regional plans and specialized plans. The second is the overlapping relationship between planning objects in terms of content and spatial dimension, such as the relationship between regional plans of geographically adjacent regions, and between provincial-level and national-level regional plans. The third is the relationship of upstream and downstream, or of substitution and complementation, such as the relationship between electric power and coal industry.

11.4.1.2 *Linkage Path and Principle*

It is essential that the plan-making authorities at different administrative levels follow the principle that specialized plans and regional plans should accord the overall plans at the same and higher levels and that no conflicting interests exist between different specialized plans. In addition, plans respecting land use and urban spatial layout should also be taken into account when compiling regional plans.

From the perspective of administrative levels, the plans at a higher level are a guidebook for the plans at a lower level. In other words, the plans at a lower level are supposed to reflect the intents and requirements of the planning at a higher level.

From the perspective of functions, overall planning serves as a guide for specialized planning and regional planning. To be specific, specialized planning is the extension and concretization of the overall planning in a specific field, and the regional planning is the actualization of the overall planning and specialized planning within a chosen space. Therefore, specialized planning must be linked up with overall planning, so must regional planning.

In addition, a set of rules should be issued to guarantee a methodical implementation of plans and push forward the institutionalization process of planning instead of always balking at the stage of interpreting plans. The key to institutionalizing planning depends on democratizing decision-making power and improving the operational mechanism of the close integration of technical standards and executive authority, compilation and administrative management.

11.4.1.3 *Focal Points of Planning Linkage*

Planning linkage is targeted at its important elements (policies, development objectives, measures, and major construction projects). Different plans should at least be kept in agreement with each other in terms of basic guideline, expectation of development trend, determination of planning indicators, choice of policies, arrangement of major projects and allocation of public resources. As for regional planning, its branch planning should be consistent with its stem planning in terms of functional positioning, layout of infrastructure, and construction of urban–rural system.

The following points should be borne in mind in the actualization of planning linkage. First, the planning authorities should have a comprehensive view and align administrative guidance with democratic consultation and encourage innovation in accordance with the hallmark of each plan while emphasizing the convergence of basic concepts, methods and guiding ideology. Second, it is necessary to make salient the guiding role of the planning outline, the requirements of which is the basis to link up other plans. Third, it is important to stress the comprehensive balancing role of planning authorities, who are responsible for organizing, coordinating and guiding the process of linkup and bridging planning preparation and approval. Fourth, consultation is necessary in this interactive process so that the role of planning linkage can be maximized. Fifth, it is also necessary to emphasize "real time" lest a delayed opportunity cause a lot of damage.

11.4.1.4 *Basic Process of Planning Linkage*

Planning linkage mainly transmits information via informal channels. The linkage between three-layered planning is completed through researches, speeches, reports, seminars, and office meetings. Special attention should be paid to development concept and obligatory indicators and other special requirements in some domains. The linkage in other aspects can be tentatively put at the disposal of the market or via the resultant of the government top–down and market bottom–up forces.

In the early stage of planning research, the main task is to arrive at a consensus through diligently analyzing and evaluating how the previous plans have been implemented and make a research on the major issues concerning economic and social development in the future plans and put forward preliminary ideas on future work.

In the intermediate stage, transparency and openness should be stressed so that all walks of life can be mobilized into the formulation of planning. It is advisable to emulate Germany, where a nongovernmental, neutral and broadly representative planning consultation and review conference is convened. A combination of administrative review and public resource allocation is used to lubricate the linkage between different plans. In other words, the planning authorities at different administrative levels should channel information for formulating the national overall plan, which in turn clarifies the guiding ideology, major policies, main development goals and priorities to provide guidance for different plans.

In the late stage, the focus is on tracking and monitoring the implementation of plans so that deviations and problems in macroeconomics can be detected in time and thus adjust the macroeconomic regulation to sustain a steady and sound national economic development. An institutionalized information detection network should be established to monitor the national overall plan and local plans.

11.4.2 Specific Measures for Planning Linkage

11.4.2.1 *Linkage between Overall Plans*

At the research stage, the National Development and Reform Commission shall organize seminars at an appropriate time to announce to planning departments at all levels the major topics to be studied in the plan. The Commission is responsible for arranging the compilation of the national overall plan, clarifying the guiding ideology, time schedule and main strategic conception involved in the national overall plan. The planning departments at the provincial, prefectural and county levels should proactively contact the higher authority for linkage.

The Commission is responsible for organizing a meeting for linking up the national and provincial overall plans three months before the completion of the national overall plan. The provincial planning department shall be responsible for such a meeting two months before the completion of the provincial overall plan. The department at city–county level shall be responsible for such a meeting one month before the completion of the city–county overall plan. A draft plan should be submitted in advance to a higher planning authority, which gives opinions for revision.

The government at each administrative level should recruit a consultative council which is responsible for giving expert opinions for the draft plan two months before it has been submitted to the people's congress at the same administrative level for approval. Before the draft plan below the provincial level is submitted to the people's congress at the same level, the higher authority should sign for approval or disapproval of the draft plan.

Although the concepts of planning linkage in the 10th Five-Year Plan were still obscure, the 11th Five-Year Plan stressed the importance of planning linkage between national planning and provincial planning in terms of guideline, obligatory indicators (such as emission reduction targets) and specific requirements of national planning for regional development.

11.4.2.2 *Linkage between Specialized and Overall Plans*

The department responsible for specialized planning determines the names and necessary descriptions of the specialized plans and analyzes the importance of these plans in national economic development and then submit them to the authorities in charge, which sift these specialized plans according to their degrees of importance hand them over to the people's congress at the same level for consideration and approval.

After approving these plans according to their names and descriptions, the people's congress should classify them into three categories: those key specialized plans requiring the government approval, those requiring the approval by an agency or commission affiliated to the government and those voluntarily compiled by market subjects organized by associations of special industries.

The plan-compiling units of all categories of plans are required to contact the planning authorities in charge for guidelines and suggestions.

Key specialized plans requiring the government approval should be verified by the planning authorities at the same administrative level and then submitted to the government for approval. Specialized plans requiring approval by an agency or commission should be confirmed by the competent authorities responsible for the industry and then reported to the authorities for the record. Specialized plans that do not require government approval should be ensured to be consistent with the overall plan and then reported to the planning authorities for the record.

11.4.3 Linkage of Regional Planning with Overall Planning and Specialized Planning

Regional planning can be divided into national and provincial regional planning. Since regional planning across the country involves different planning subjects and objects, the linkup processes vary accordingly.

11.4.3.1 *Linkage of National Regional Planning with Overall Planning and Special Planning*

The units responsible for compiling national regional plans are required to report to the National Development and Reform Commission their work programs related to the linkages of regional plans with national overall plan, specialized plans, and the various plans at the provincial level. The Commission shall organize the planning authorities at the national and provincial levels for opinions and suggestions which will be subsequently sent to the plan-compiling units for revising the plans according to specific requirements. The planning authorities at the provincial level are held responsible for revision according to the principle that the plans at lower authorities should be consistent with the plans at higher authorities. The revised plans shall be entrusted to a national consultative council or an expert panel for advice and further revision. The plans shall finally be forwarded by the Commission to the State Council for approval.

11.4.3.2 *Linkage of Provincial Regional Planning with Overall Planning and Special Planning*

The units responsible for compiling provincial regional plans are required to report to the planning authorities their work programs related to the linkages of regional plans with national overall plan, specialized plans, and the various plans at the city–county level. The planning authorities at the provincial level shall be held responsible for organizing specialized planning departments for opinions and suggestions which will be subsequently sent to the plan-compiling units for revising the plans according to specific requirements. The revised plans shall be entrusted to a provincial consultative council or an expert panel for advice and further revision. The plans shall finally be forwarded by the planning authorities to the provincial governments for approval.

11.4.4 Linkage between Long, Medium and Short-Term Plans

It is necessary to realize the linkage between long, medium and short-term plans for the following three purposes: to ensure the continuity and stability of planning, to make planning more scientific and systematic, and to sustain a harmonious and comprehensive development. As the infinity of social development is conflicting to the limitation of the planning term, a good linkup between plans with different terms can reflect the situation as actual as possible. In addition, short, medium and long-term plans are closely related: a short-term plan being most specific, a five-year plan serving a guide for an annual plan, and a 10-year plan envisaging a long prospect of economic development and guiding a five-year plan. In the process of implementing a plan, a series of problems will arise, such as serious emergencies and advancing or delaying or stalling an exceedingly influential major project. Therefore, it is necessary to make timely readjustments of planning according to the changes in international and domestic economic and social environments. What is more, different factors in a society, such as population, social causes, environment protection and reversal of ecological imbalances should be guided by plans with different terms. Only in this way can China sustain a stable and harmonious development.

As for the linkage of short-term and medium-term plans, the former Soviet Union and China tried to draw up a five-year plan with sub-annual indicators in the early stage of socialist construction and matched it with an annual plan. However, it turned out to be unsuccessful and inefficient, as there were too many uncertainties and too much workload.

In the early 1990s, China attempted to simultaneously compile two annual plans. The idea was to compile the 1992 and 1993 annual plans and one year later make necessary readjustment about the 1993 annual plan and simultaneously compile the 1994 annual plan. However, this idea ceased with a new round of governance and rectification sweeping across China in 1993.

Since the 1990s, China has been exploring rolling plan, a practice to actualize the linkage between long and medium-term plans. For instance, the Eighth Five-Year plan (1991–1995) was prepared in conjunction with the 10-Year Development Plan (1991–2000). As the *10-Year Plan for National Economic and Social Development and the Outline of the Eighth Five-Year Plan* put it, "This outline combines the long-term ten-year plan and the medium-term five-year arrangements and constructs the Eighth Five-Year Plan according to the requirements of realizing the strategic objectives at the end of the 20th century."

The Ninth Five-Year Plan (1996–2000) set out the 2010 long-term goal, as put in the preamble to the *Ninth Five-Year Plan for National Economic and Social Development and Outline of Long-term Goals for 2010*: "The 15 years between 1996 and 2010 is an important period that inherits the historical legacies and opens the future prospects in the course of China's reform and opening up and socialist modernization drive. With a brand-new stance, China will usher in the 21st century to establish a relatively perfect socialist market economic system, fully realize the strategic objectives of the second step, and take a great leap toward the strategic objectives of the third step, laying a solid foundation for the realization of modernization by the middle of the 21st century."

When drawing up the 10th Five-Year Plan (2001–2005), the central government was to have drafted simultaneously a long-term plan for 2015, but the wish did not come true. It is advisable to adopt in the combination of long and medium-term plans the "five-year rolling" approach, which is designed to combine long-term plans and five-year plans and make periodic modifications every five years so that the long-term plan can infinitely extend to form a continuity.

The advantages of this approach are as follows. First, a five-year plan links up annual plans and a long-term plan and prescribes the goals, tasks, guidelines and action plans for a strategic period. It generally meets the time limit required for many construction projects and for the promotion or marketing of many major technological renovations and scientific researches. This approach can also periodically review the whole long-term plan and make apposite modifications by comparing the actual situations and planned activities. Second, this approach is conducive to the linkage between medium-term plans. Meantime, the factors proven to be reliable and feasible over a long period of time can be injected into the coming five-year plan to ensure the continuity of planning. Third, the planners have more time and freedom to make a research on the new situations in the real economic life.

The usual practice is to renew the long-term plan for another five years in the fourth year of the five-year plan. This approach is conducive to giving full play to the strategic guiding role of the five-year plan, enabling China to organize economic activities steadily in accordance with the requirements of the five-year plan. Meanwhile, it gives researchers ample time to make a study on the new problems arising during the five-year plan so as to guarantee the quality of the long-term plan.

11.5 LINKAGE BETWEEN PLANS MADE BY DIFFERENT DEPARTMENTS AND SYNERGIC RESEARCH

In the current Chinese planning system, the five-year comprehensive development plan (hereinafter simplified as development plan) compiled by the development and reform departments, the urban–rural master plan (hereinafter simplified as the urban–rural plan) compiled by the construction departments, and the land use master plan (hereinafter simplified as the land plan) compiled by the land departments occupy an important position. For a long time, due to various reasons, the lack of necessary coordination among the above plans compiled by different government departments has resulted in conflicts in economic planning and construction.

11.5.1 Functional Positioning of Three Major Types of Planning

11.5.1.1 *Development Planning*

In light of the division of labor in the current national economic management system, the five-year development planning focuses on the important development goals of national economy, social development, major construction projects and the layout of productive forces. The elaboration of the government's strategic intention and policy orientation and main tasks of economic and social development is an important basis for the government to fulfill its role in economic regulation, public service, market supervision, and social management.

11.5.1.2 *Urban–Rural Planning*

The Urban Planning Law was put into effect in April 1990. The Law stipulated that urban system planning was an integral part of the overall national planning and had no independent legal status. On January 1, 2008, it was replaced by the *Urban and Rural Planning Act,* which separated the urban system planning from the national overall planning and constituted the urban–rural planning system with urban overall planning, township overall planning, and village planning.

Urban–rural planning aims at coordinating the layout of various urban and rural construction activities in territorial space and rationally allocating resources within the space to safeguard the overall interests of social development and promote sustainable development.

Urban overall planning is directed at overall development of cities with the tangible forms of the urban space as the object and the economic and social development goals as the guidance. Based on the definition of the nature, scale, direction, and goal of urban development, the urban overall planning deals with the spatial layout of cities, industrial development and layout, public facilities, social undertakings, and resource conservation. To be more specific, these planning objects include the layout of residential settlements, infrastructure, land use, and significant facilities related to safety, transportation system, disaster prevention, and mitigation as well as the protection of ecological environment, and natural and historical heritage. The most important is land use control, which aims at methodical urban development by rationalizing the use of limited urban land resources.

Urban overall planning is the basis for urban construction and management, the precondition for effective allocation of urban spatial resources and the rational use of land. For instance, the Beijing urban spatial layout of "two axes, two belts and multiple centers" highlights new satellite towns, transportation upgrade, ecological environment and the protection of historical and cultural heritage.

According to the *Urban–Rural Planning Act*, the urban overall planning is in the charge of the city government, and the national and provincial urban system plans are compiled respectively by the administrative department of urban planning under the State Council and the provincial government.

The *Urban and Rural Planning Act* extends the spatial scope of planning from the city proper to the regional spatial level. Article 12 of the Act requires that the national urban system planning be applicable to guiding the formulation of provincial urban system planning and urban overall planning, with the aim of avoiding the disorderly expansion of cities and loss of arable land. In its traditional sense, urban overall planning was to actualize all kinds of urban functions in the corresponding plot of land and from a layout plan but failed to take the balanced urban–rural development into consideration. It is because of the lack of a holistic approach to regional development that the urban system planning focusing on the relationship between various types of cities and towns within the region came into being. Meanwhile, the regional characteristics of urban overall planning stand out. The shift from an atomistic approach to urban overall planning toward a holistic approach to the balanced urban–rural planning is an inevitable requirement for urban development and for the realization of the urban–rural integration under the guidance of the scientific outlook on development.

11.5.1.3 *Land Planning*

Land plans, compiled under the guidance of *Land Management Law* and development planning, are aimed at strengthening the management of land, safeguarding socialist public ownership of land, conserving land resources, rationally using arable land so as to maximize economic, social and ecological benefits.

In 1986, China promulgated the *Land Management Law*, which articulated for the first time that "the people's governments at all levels shall formulate the overall land use plan." The 1999 revised edition stipulates that the central government and local governments at all levels shall formulate the general planning for land use as required by national development planning, land management, and environmental protection, land supply and the demand for land for various construction projects.

The purpose of compiling land plans is to coordinate the demand for land use among various departments pursuant to the overall arrangement of various types of land use, rationally use limited land resources and provide land security for economic and social development.

In October 1997, the State Land Administration promulgated the *Provisions for the Examination and Approval of the Compilation of General Planning for Land Use*, which specifies the tasks of land planning as follows: (1) determining the number and distribution of decomposed indicators of aggregate balance of land use (annual plan management); (2) grading land productivity potential, zoning land quality, and cartography; (3) regulating land use; (4) land exploitation, management, and rehabilitation; and (5) information feedback of dynamic change in land use.

Land plans, based on the *Land Management Law*, are compiled by the people's governments at all levels according to administrative division. The Law also formulates a complete approval procedure for land planning at different administrative levels. Land planning is mainly concerned about land use control and the conservation of cultivated land. Due to the increasingly formidable shrinkage of cultivated land, land plans in recent years make more stringent control of cultivated land.

11.5.1.4 *Relationship between Three Major Types of Planning*

The three major types of planning are mutually complementary (Figure 11.2). Development planning mainly concentrates on a holistic time-sequential arrangement and strategic guidance for development objectives, aggregate amount, industrial structure and industrial policies. Land planning concentrates on the spatial allocation and distribution of resources.

Urban–rural planning, which is often made under the guidance of land planning, makes a comprehensive arrangement of various constructions in particular regions on the basis of determining long-term orientation and target of national economic development. So to speak, land planning

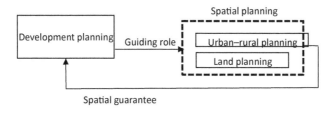

Figure 11.2   Relationship Between the Three Major Types of Planning

provides an important basis for urban–rural planning in terms of urban development direction and productivity distribution. From the perspective of spatial dimensions, both urban–rural and land planning mainly provide a basic framework for urban development in terms of land use, spatial layout, and infrastructure (often decomposed as many mandatory indicators). Development planning guides the compilation of spatial planning, which is usually deemed as the realization of five-year development plans. Spatial planning helps to make strategic decisions in economic and social development as it makes arrangements in spatial development, utilization, management and conservation in different regions. The three types of planning are inextricably inseparable and therefore attention should be paid to the coordination of them.

11.5.2 Problems Arising from the Separation of Three Major Types of Planning

Many problems arise from the fact that, under the current institutional structure, development planning, urban–rural planning and land planning are separately compiled within their own relatively closed administrative system in which planning departments seldom exchange opinions between them.

First, land planning is difficult to put into practice. Although land planning is compiled by the governments at and above the county level, it is still of indicator-controlled planning. The real situation that no other land use except the basic farmland protection is fully implemented within the required territorial space, to a certain extent, brews the local governments' connivance at land abuse. Second, many urban–rural plans lack a clear objective positioning. In the case of no clear functional positioning of an urban area, the urban system plans are merely mechanically compiled from a higher administrative level to a lower one. What's worse, some areas not qualified as a candidate for urbanization blindly follow suit and some cities encroach on neighboring regions willfully. Due to lack of foresight and scientific governance, the positioning of an urban area is often obscure and the phenomenon of "building, demolishing, and rebuilding" in urban construction is quite common in every city. Third, regional integrity is far from being satisfactory in the distribution of infrastructure construction that serves economic activities and facilitates people's lives. Infrastructure construction may be excessive in some regions but insufficient in others. Fourth, terrible wastage besets the planning process. All types of planning are passed down from the central departments (such as Bureau of Land Resources and National Development and Reform Commission) down to the local departments but the central departments responsible for different types of planning do not arrive at a consensus on some issues. Thus, a local government may simultaneously compile a five-year development plan as usual and a land plan according to some statutes. Consequently, a so-called "conceptual plan" is demonstrated again and again when the local government department (such as a local bureau of land and resources and a local national development and reform commission) compiles the urban–rural plan and the land plan respectively. Ironically, both the Bureau and the Commission recruit the same panel of experts to demonstrate the conceptual plan.

Due to many repetitive parts in the three major types of planning, how to make them compatible has become a thorny problem. Both the intellectual circle and government departments call for coordination and even for synthesis of the three into one. However, the progress of the reform of the integration remains sluggish for the following reasons:

(1) *Lack of relevant statutes*

At present, no statute regulates the relationship between various types of planning and defines the behaviors of various planning subjects and objects. In the meantime, no law regulates development planning, and the *National Planning Law* has not been issued despite many years of discussion and deliberation. Article 5 of *Urban and Rural Planning Law* stipulates: "The establishment of the overall planning of a city or town, a township planning or a village planning shall be based on the national and economic development planning as well as the overall planning on land use." Article 17 of *Law of Land Administration* stipulates: "People's governments at all levels shall manage to compile general plans for land uses in accordance with the national economic and social development program, requirements of national land consolidation and resources and environmental protection, land supply capacity and the requirements of various construction projects." Article 32 stipulates: "Urban general (overall) plans and the plans for villages and market towns should be in line with the general plans for land use." Obviously, there is no procedure law for the formulation and implementation of development plans which are statutorily deemed as the guiding plans for urban and rural plans and land plans.

(2) Overlap in planning space and contents
There are overlaps or even contradictions between the three major types of planning in terms of urban development positioning, environmental protection and land use for infrastructure, although their respective emphases are somewhat different. This problem has become increasingly prominent since the 11th Five-Year Plan emphasized spatial constraints. Urban and rural plans overlap in many parts but ludicrously cannot be well linked up with each other simply because they are compiled by different administrative departments. Urban general plans mainly specify the nature, scale, and objective of a city but seldom deals with the spatial layout. By contrast, land plans clearly designate the spatial scope of five types of agricultural land, construction land, and unused land. Nevertheless, the spatial distribution of various urban functions within the scope of urban construction land is determined by the urban overall plan.

According to *Urban and Rural Planning Law*, the spatial scope involved in an urban overall plan should be within the planned area, of which, however, the Law prescribes a flexible provision. In practice, when compiling and revising urban and rural planning, nearly all cities tend to expand the scope of planned areas for urbanization as much as possible. For example, the planned area involved in Beijing's urban overall plan has been expanded from Beijing proper to the whole area under the jurisdiction of the Beijing Municipality. As a result, urban and rural plans and land plans based on different concepts of planning have been concurrently compiled within the same planning area. The overlaps and conflicts in the arrangement of specific land use and the development time sequence exacerbate the administrative burden and increase the difficulty of forming a concerted effort.

(3) *Incompatible planning conceptions and procedures*
Though based on development plans to make the corresponding spatial arrangements for various types of land use and put forward opinions on the nature of the use of the target land, urban and rural plans and land plans are different in the following aspects. First, land plans are a use-regulated spatial plan focusing on land use control whereas urban and rural plans are a project-motivated spatial plan focusing on the determination of appropriate spatial locations for various urban projects to satisfy the demand for urban functions. Second, land plans aim to limit the excessive occupation of cultivated land whereas urban and rural plans tend to expand urban size and covet more land. Third, urban and rural plans are a bottom-up arrangement for land use that is determined by people and by need whereas land plans are a top-down arrangement for land supply and demand. The total acreage of construction land, and the minimal acreage of land retained for farmland in the land plan shall not be more than and less than their respective control indicators in the land plan compiled by its superior. Therefore, land plans are often incongruous with urban and rural plans.

(4) *Compilation and approval by different planning departments*
The three major types of plans are respectively ratified by three different departments, and the ratification procedures are also different (Figure 11.3). Development plans, urban and rural plans, and land plans are respectively compiled and ratified by development and reform departments, construction departments, and land departments at all levels. Development plans should be submitted to the people's congresses at all levels for ratification. However, for urban and rural plans, hierarchical approval system is applied, that is, the State Council and the local governments down to the county level have the authority to ratify urban and rural plans. Land plans are subject to the land use regulation system, according to which only the

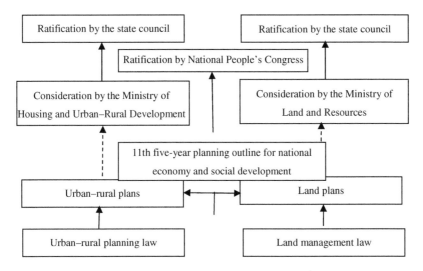

Figure 11.3   Ratification Procedures of Three Major Types of Plans

State Council and provincial people's governments have the authority to examine and approve land plans. As for land plans at the township level, the provincial governments can authorize the governments of provincial-level cities and autonomous prefectures to ratify them. In addition, land plans and urban and rural plans are based on two sets of standards. The 1999 *Land Management Law* is applicable to land plans, the basic data of which are based on the annual land survey by the Ministry of Land and Resources over the years. *Urban and Rural Planning Law* is applicable to urban and rural plans, for which by the Ministry of Housing and Urban–Rural Development holds responsible. The former is to plan the land of the whole administrative region, while the latter only covers the built-up area.

Besides, the compilation years and terms of the three major types of planning are out of phase (Figure 11.4). For instance, Chongqing's 11th Five-Year Plan was started in 2004 and ratified by the Second Chongqing Municipal People's Congress in 2006, and the term for this planning lasted from 2006 to 2010. Its urban–rural planning was approved by the State Council in 2007, the term lasting from 2007 to 2020, which is subdivided into short-term planning (2007–2010) and long-term planning (2010–2020). Its land planning (1997–2010) was approved in 1999 and

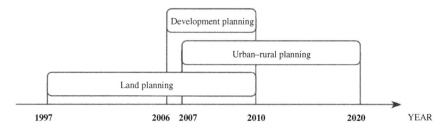

Figure 11.4   Status Quo of Terms of Three Major Types of Planning in Chongqing

revised four times. This shows that it is difficult to ensure the congruities of objectives and indicators in the compilation of various types of planning.

On December 15, 2009, the Beijing Bureau of Land and Resources announced that the General Land Use Planning of Beijing (2006–2020), after five years of revisions, had satisfied the standards of the State Council. This plan is obviously out of phase with Beijing's national economic and social development plan.

11.5.3 The Way Out for the Linkage between Three Major Types of Planning

From the central to the local governments, there is an increasing desire to synthesize the three major types of plans, a wish that is reflected by the planning for major function-oriented zones (MFOZs). However, it is controversial whether it is necessary to integrate them under the current management and administrative modes. From the administrative level, it is desired that the three major types of plans should maintain their relative independence within their respective systems on the one hand and the national plans should reinforce the linkage between them on the other hand in that they are mutually complementary in spatial layout and the national planning cannot escape the constraints of regulations either. At the city–county level, various types of plans often overlap in both planning contents and a relatively small geographic region and thus a problem arises as of "what is the future development of this region."[1] Therefore, plans at the city–county level should be integrated into one and those at

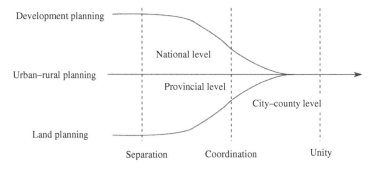

Figure 11.5   Coordination and Unity of Three Major Types of Planning at Administrative Levels

the provincial level reinforce coordination and linkage. The linkage of the plans at all levels is shown in Figure 11.5.

Both the central and local governments are actively exploring how to straighten out the relationship between the three major types of planning. Three suggestions are given below. First, laws and regulations must be issued to define the purview of each type of planning and their relationship. It must be admitted that, across the vast territorial space (9.6 million km² of land territory), the occurrences of overlaps in planning contents and planning procedures within the same relatively small space seem unavoidable. Therefore, it is necessary to conduct research on the division of labor and complementarity among the three major types of planning from the aspects of objectives, tasks, priorities, implementation, and management for the sake of establishing a scientific spatial planning system with a sharing mechanism for convergence and coordination. Second, innovations should be made on the temporal-dimension congruity between them. It is necessary to carry out short-term construction planning of urban–rural planning and short-term land use planning of land planning that are compatible with development planning and meanwhile to make a research on long-term strategic planning that is congruent with long-term (five years and above) urban–rural planning and land planning. Third, the linkage in planning contents is also necessary, and the procedures may be designed in the following chronological order: a pilot scheme for the temporal congruity between annual development planning, annual land

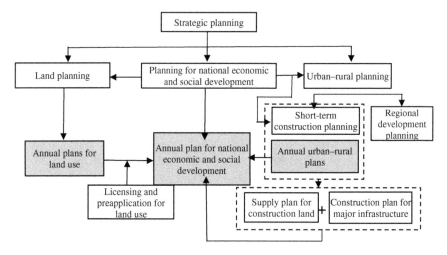

Figure 11.6   Compatibility of Annual Plans Related to Three Major Types of Planning

use planning and annual urban–rural planning (Figure 11.6); enumeration of the detailed information of all major projects in accordance with annual development objective, urban–rural layout and land use scale; the establishment of a coordination mechanism; transform static and rigid planning to dynamic and flexible planning.

Some local authorities attempt to establish a "trans-planning" institution whose responsibility is to internalize the coordination and linkage of the three major types of planning. The practice of Shanghai Pudong New Area is recommendable. As a comprehensive reform experimental area, it set up a Planning Committee Office affiliated to Shanghai Development and Reform Commission that is populated by the same members of the Planning Management Department and whose remit is to orchestrate all planning departments under the jurisdiction of Pudong New Area to handle major planning issues. Nevertheless, its implementation effect still needs to be observed and tested in practice.

Experiences have been also accumulated in coordinating urban–rural planning and land planning in some provinces and municipalities. For instance, Zhejiang Province produced basic land-use maps based on satellite remote sensing images and a thorough land survey to ensure the congruity of basic data for different types of planning. In Wuhan, the capital of Hubei Province, the departments responsible for urban–rural planning and land planning are arranged in the same office building to facilitate exchange of information and paperwork. Shanghai merged the planning departments of urban and rural planning and land planning into the Shanghai Municipal Bureau of Planning and Land Resources.

In Pudong District, Shanghai, an attempt to merge the three major types of planning into one miscarried because it found that the guiding principles and planning objects are quite different. In Chongqing, an experiment to merge the four major types of planning (plus environment protection planning) into one also aborted.

The MFOZ planning and regional planning highlighted in the 11th Five-Year Plan, along with the process of making the three major types of planning compatible, can play a significant role in promoting national economic and social development and rationalizing resource allocation and distribution in space. Meanwhile, from the guiding function of spatial development, MFOZ planning, as the pillar propping the whole planning system, cannot replace any other type of planning. The idea mapping of the across-the-board planning system is shown in Figure 11.7.

(1) MFOZ planning
It is suggested that the MFOZ planning, as the planning of the paramount strategic implications, be directed at, through a scientific division of territorial space, normalizing the exploitation order of land and resources

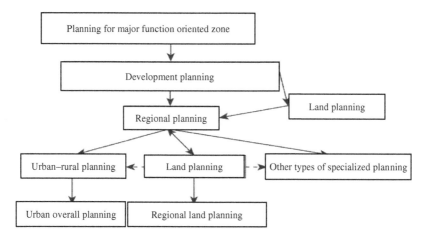

Figure 11.7 Across-the-Board Planning System

and making a permanent, macro and integral arrangement for functional zoning and the utilization pattern of land and resources in the next 50–100 years. It is the basis for other types of planning. Therefore, relevant laws and regulations should be promulgated to ensure its basic and guiding role in the spatial planning system.

Focused as it is on spatial division, the MFOZ planning, an outlined, frame-type planning in its macro sense, is not designed to determine the specific development direction for each plot of land. The determination of the type of each MFOZ and the specific space control at the micro level need to be realized by degrees through urban–rural planning and land planning. Therefore, it is necessary to actualize the linkage between the national MFOZ planning and the provincial city-council MFOZ planning and make urban–rural planning and land planning compatible with MFOZ planning. This requires that the MFOZ planning provides specific instructions for all kinds of development and construction activities such as land use, urban development, infrastructure and environment protection in each type of MFOZ and offers feasible quantitative requirements in spatial measurement.

(2) Development planning

As mentioned earlier, national development planning involves a wide range of activities related to national economy, such as development objectives, priorities, major projects, and policy orientations. The utilization of spatial resources and the adjustment of spatial layout are also important constituents of the development planning. For instance, the 11th Five-Year Plan highlights the spatial allocation of resources. National development planning, especially planning with a term of 15–20 years, is an important link in spatial layout planning.

(3) Regional planning

Since the 11th Five-Year Plan, the central government has worked out several important regional development plans in an attempt to solve the contradiction between regional economic integration and resource allocation in the division of administrative regions. In October 2005, the State Council issued a document *"Several Opinions on the Compilation of National Economic and Social Development Planning"* to guide the compilation of the 11th Five-Year Plan, proposing to establish a planning system that includes overall planning, specialized planning, and regional planning. A regional plan is the concretization of the national development plan in a specific cross-provincial region. A cross-provincial regional plan is the basis for an overall plan and specialized plan at the provincial level. In the future, great importance should be attached to the formulation of the plans for key and optimized development zones determined by the MFOZ planning, the contents of which should focus on land use, population distribution, regional urban system, and infrastructure, and so on.

(4) *Land planning*
Land planning is essentially identical to urban overall planning by nature in that both offer opinions on the use of the target land. Land planning should reflect the target scenario of spatial control specified in the MFOZ planning and coordinate the demand for limited land resources among various departments. Land planning should decide the land-use type for each plot of land. In other words, it should substantiate the target scenario of spatial control into a set of indices, which in turn, serve as the basis for the land use control system.

(5) *Urban–rural planning*
An urban–rural plan, clearly defining its objectives, should make a comprehensive arrangement for the development of each functional zone of a city with the land planning as the guide. The term for such a plan is generally about 20 years.

NOTE

1. Wang, Li, Zenglin Han, and Zeyu Wang. "A Conception of Coordinating Three Major Types of Plans Based on the MFOZ Planning." *Economic Geography*, 2008 (5): 845–848. 王利, 韩增林, 王泽宇. "基于主体功能区规划的 '三规' 协调设想", 经济地理, 2008 (5): 845–848.

Index